D0596984

MY LIFE
EAST AND WEST

WILLIAM S. HART
From the painting by Charles M. Russell
(*See page* 176)

MY LIFE
EAST AND WEST

BY

WILLIAM S. HART

WITH ILLUSTRATIONS

BENJAMIN BLOM  New York/London

First published 1929
Reissued 1968 by Benjamin Blom, Inc.
Bronx, N.Y. 10452

Library of Congress Catalog Card No. 68-20228

Manufactured in the United States of America

CONTENTS

ILLUSTRATIONS

ILLUSTRATIONS

MY LIFE
EAST AND WEST

CHAPTER I
WHITE GOLD

A black night on the Western prairie; a fear-crazed, unbroken colt lunging along a dimly marked trail; a ten-year-old boy, his only garment a nightgown, riding bareback, one hand tangled in the mane of a flying animal, the other clutching the rope of a hackamore; a frightened boy dragged from sleep and sent on a wild midnight ride seeking help to prevent a murder.

A black night pierced dimly and intermittently through a misty fog by street gas-lamps; a heavily loaded ice-wagon, its scale irons clanking dismally against its sides, lumbering over rough cobbled pavements; a man and a dozing boy of fourteen (the first and second hands) on the driver's seat. The man jerks his lines and clucks to his team. An hour's journey brings dawn and the man will be at the back of the wagon weighing ice and the boy climbing New York tenement stairways, with ice upon his back.

I WAS born at Newburgh, New York. My first recollection is of Oswego, Illinois. My father was a miller, and we lived near the flour mill on the Fox River. There were only two houses.

It was springtime. The ice had broken up and was cumbrously and slowly grinding its way down-river. The out-of-banks torrent was still raging, however, and here and there a large slab of ice would be picked up by the very force of the current and dashed hurtling through the air.

3

The sawmill across the river had had no communication with our side since the ice had started to break. The sawyer and his helper needed supplies. My mother filled a clothes-basket with groceries and my father was going to make the trip across in a rowboat, and we all accompanied him to the shore to see him start.

He was to row for a full mile up the river on our side, and then make the dash across nearly half a mile of swirling, leaping flood.

Two foolish children and an iron-hearted, loving father! Nothing else could have done it — we outvoted our sweet, anxious mother and went with our father in the boat.

When we rounded the bend of land, a half-mile up-river, we waved gayly to our mother standing where we had left her, her hand tightly clutching the collar of the shepherd dog, Ring. Ring had begged to come along, but my father was afraid to have him in the boat.

My father reached his proper distance up-river and started across. How the current did drive us down-river! It hit us sideways; it seemed hardly no time at all until we were out — clear of the jutting land — and could see our mother again. And while our father was rowing, with sweeping, powerful strokes, we waved to her.

There was a commotion. Ring thought we were calling him. Our mother was trying desperately, but could not hold him. She hung onto him until she fell; he dragged her to the water's edge; he broke away and plunged into the stream. He was a noble dog and a powerful swimmer. He actually made headway toward us so long as he kept inshore, but when he pointed out into the stream toward our boat, the current fairly threw him toward the mill-dam. It was certain death — a horrible death! But we did not know. We only knew we wanted our playmate and he

THE AUTHOR AT THE AGE OF THREE

was swimming after us in the river. Two children begged their father to get him. The father stopped rowing, and like a bullet the boat shot downstream — the dog was in the boat!

But, Lord God of Hosts! the man's powerful arms could not make the boat gain one inch upstream. No! it was losing! It was losing — going stern first, foot by foot, yard by yard, nearer to destruction. We were slightly nearer our side of the river. My father could see our mother and hear her cries.

The men at the sawmill on the other side of the river were yelling useless, unheard instructions and cursing great oaths. My father rowed. He had lost hope. He knew we were going over, but he was going to die rowing.

The stern of the boat was at the break of water over the dam, and the dead noise of the falling water shut out all sound. Still my father pulled. And then the boat commenced to move sideways — not ahead — but sideways.

I was only a prattling baby boy playing with a shaggy wet dog in a boat; but could I use the brush — what a picture I could paint of a man at the oars in a boat rowing for the lives of his children! The man would not quit — the river had to go on. So the river pushed the rowing man aside. It pushed the boat sideways out of its path.

There was a mill-race at the river-bank. When the boat turned into it, its sides were crushed and broken by the force of the eddying waters. Two children were thrown onto the shore — an exhausted man was lying full length upon the ground, his head in the lap of a woman. The woman wore a white dress, all dotted with black spots.

I remember one night at dusk leaning against a fence and watching the drowned cattle go over the milldam in the freshet. I was playing robber; my fence became a robber's cave. I went to sleep. My dear mother's eyes would fill with tears even after I grew to manhood when she told of what was thought a useless search that lasted until the men's lanterns blended into the morning light.

Then there was a night I was awakened and, sitting up in my trundle bed, saw my father looking intently out of the bedroom window, and heard him say in a low voice:

'Tell me the truth, Rose. What do you see?'

My mother grabbed my father and said, 'No! No! Nicholas! It isn't that! Stay here. Don't go — don't go!'

Then I saw my father gently forcing my mother aside and hurriedly and stealthily disappear through the doorway.

In years later I learned that in passing through the living-room my father picked up a large carving-knife, stepped out into the road, and dropped behind an open buggy as it passed. Beside the man who was driving the stolen mill team sat another man with a rifle across his knees.

It was a full mile to the nearest farmhouse, yet my father remained in his position, one hand on the rear end of the buggy; and, when near the farmhouse, he jumped into the brush and gave the alarm. And, at that time, they hanged men in Illinois for horse-stealing.

And, at that time, too, my father was going blind!

In dressing flour-mill burrs there is used a mill pick, made of the finest tempered steel. While at work, a minute particle of this steel had entered my father's eye. Inflammation grew rampant and spread to the other eye. My father was suspicious that there was a particle of steel in his eye; but all he knew was that a noted Chicago oculist had told him he had granulated eyelids and sore eyes. A short time before this, the owner of the mill had said to my father, 'Nick, you had better quit, your eyesight is going, and you will have an accident and smash all the machinery in the mill.'

'No!' said my father; 'the doctor says it is just a cold. My eyes are getting better every day. Look! See that tall tree over there just to the left of the center of that grove!'

'Yes,' said the owner; and then continued, 'Why, Nick, that isn't so bad. It is all I can do to see that tree myself.'

My father knew the forest was there and he knew there must be one tree that stood above the others. He was fighting for his family.

But that was months before. My father's eyes grew worse and we moved on.

Montgomery, a few miles distant — another flour mill and a lone house, though not so far from the town. My father always had me or my sister walk to the mill with him and always held our hands and would not let us get away from him.

There was a little store on the way where they sold candy. I always stopped in front of the little store. And when I stopped, my father would know where we were and buy me a stick of candy. If he did not buy me a stick of candy, I would stand there and not go on. . . . My father could not find his way alone to the mill.

It is strange! I was just searching my memory for any other unusual happenings to record of my life at Montgomery, and I had a plain, realistic feeling that seemed so natural . . . I am wondering . . . it was that I ask my mother. My mother has been dead for sixteen years.

Aurora, Illinois, was where we lived next. It had been necessary to move on again. We were still on the Fox River, but Aurora, then as now, was far ahead of its neighbor towns in population. We lived about half a mile from the flour mill, right near the C. B. & Q. Railroad tracks and depot.

It was a hard winter. After a few weeks my father's eyesight became so bad that the mill people would not allow him to work any more. We were very poor. We hung up our stockings and Santa Claus brought my elder sister and myself — two pennies and a handful of raisins!

We were satisfied and very happy. But how well I can remember — and now understand — the drawn, pinched expressions of my father and mother! My mother had been crying — her eyes were all red. My father had not been crying, but his eyes were much redder than my mother's.

What peculiar incidents stand out in recollections of early childhood!

The bridge that spanned the ice-jammed Fox River had iron railings. My sister and I, for some reason that could be known only to children, put our tongues on the iron railing. It was a long time ago, but the memory is still fresh, and I warn all little boys and girls never to try it. It took the entire police force of Aurora to get us loose. I was the smaller, so my sister suffered doubly — her lot was a badly lacerated tongue and a spanking, while I escaped the hand-demonstration. But I can almost feel the swollen tongue yet.

My father, when not at work in the mills, had always been at home. But now he was away, gone somewhere. My mother used to tell us to mind her and be good children, because our father was not there to take care of

8

us, and then she would read letters and cry a little. And to show my appreciation of the situation, I would stick pins in my new baby sister to hear her cry, too.

I believe the Bible teaches that God has a special care of children. It must be so — so few fatalities, and all children are children.

I recall a picture that makes me involuntarily move my feet as though to step aside — a little boy, standing in the middle of a railroad track and that track but one of a network of tracks at a freight and passenger terminal of the C. B. & Q. Railroad.

A switch engine — rear end first — ponderously but silently bearing down on the boy, who stands transfixed, his fat little legs receiving from his child's brain no impetus to move.

There is another human being transfixed, also. He is a switchman, standing on a step at the end of the huge monster on wheels that is coming. But the man's brain is working — working and directed by Him who has that special care of children — for the man does not stir, not even a muscle. He looks at the child indifferently. The child is but one of many ordinary objects; but, when close upon him, the man makes a quick, tiger-like sweep of his arm and the boy is gathered up in the man's arms. And the man says, 'Christ!'

One day we all had to stay in the house while our mother washed our clothes. Oh! how happy my mother was! She would hug one of my sisters and kiss her and then run and pick me up and kiss me. Then drop me and run to my other sister and kiss her — until I didn't know what was going to happen. She hugged my baby sister so much she was really rough with her.

When she was washing our clothes, she was laughing or

crying all the time; but when she cried I knew she didn't mean it, because she cried as if she were laughing. Then the next day she washed and scrubbed all of us and combed our hair, and cut pieces of an old apron and tied all my sister's hair back and curled it with the poker.

And then, oh, dear! oh! dear! — and then, we all laughed and we all cried. . . . Our father was home! He had come back to us! He was hugging and kissing us, too; and although his eyes were all wet, they were white, they were not red any more.

In a last desperate effort to save his sight, my father had written to one of the greatest oculists that ever lived, Dr. C. R. Agnew, of the Manhattan Eye and Ear Hospital, of New York City. He told him of his condition and of his belief that there was a foreign body in his eye; and on receipt of this letter, Dr. Agnew had sent my father a railroad ticket to come to New York.

Four times this wonderful oculist operated, and four times he failed to find what he also believed was there — a foreign body.

Then he said, 'Hart, do you know what I am going to do now? I am going to remove those eyes.'

'All right, doctor,' my father replied, 'only leave yourself with a clear conscience.'

Dr. Agnew's conscience is clear. He hunted once more and found the infinitesimally small particle of steel. He performed a miracle! He cut deep into the pupil and did not impair the vision.

The mental gnawing of nearly two years was over — the rest of my father's life was not to be a long, dark night. How well I remember his happiness when in later years he sent his bit toward building a new Manhattan Eye and Ear Hospital!

WE MOVE TO PORTLAND, IOWA

My mother was packing our few belongings. All was excitement — we were going on railway cars to join our father, who had been away again for some time. We left our home — my mother with a baby girl in her arms, and three more youngsters hanging onto her skirts.

Many years after, while playing in Aurora, I visited this spot. The front room of our little home was a cobbler's shop, and the cobbler — a feeble old man — was mending children's shoes. He was named Patterson. He had been one of the world's most famous circus clowns.

I do not remember our railroad journey, but I remember being set off on the prairie — no station, just a pole with an iron arm for a mail-bag. My father was there and I think carried us all to our new home. It was a one-room board house with a false front that had at some time long before been used as a trading store. Across the road was the usual flour mill and our river.

With the exception of a one-room shack used for a school-house, half a mile along the road, I have described the town of Portland, Iowa.

Much of my time was spent with a teamster who hauled flour to Mason City, about fifteen miles away — and also swimming in the river. I must have learned to swim at Portland, but I have no recollection of ever learning to swim anywhere. It is the same with riding — I do not recall learning to ride.

My father was an expert man at his trade and drew a good salary. His work was to get a mill into good working trim and the millstones all dressed in good shape for grinding. Then he would move on. This suited my father exactly. It was just what he wanted, for he was always looking for an ideal mill-site that he could own and with a small amount of capital be able to provide a lasting home for his family.

There are yellow gold pioneers and black gold (oil) pioneers. My father was a white gold (flour) pioneer. He was so known throughout the West. A finder of water-power sites and a builder of flour mills.

Rockford, Iowa, was but a short distance from Portland. So in due time, in another house, near another mill and river, we were duly installed. Rockford was a fair-sized town of a hundred people. When the work was about completed, the owner of the property (or one of his hench-men) and my father had trouble — and with my father, trouble meant a fight.

I was near by at the time, and, while I nearly bawled my eyes out, that did not prevent me from hauling a full-sized, double-bitted axe, that I could scarcely lift, to my father. He was in trouble and I wanted to help. He did not need the axe, however. The vanquished opponent took a thorough licking. . . . But my dad was out of employment — which meant that we once more moved on.

Six months must have passed since Aurora, Illinois (again that strange feeling that I can ask my mother), for it was winter when we left Rockford — a bitter, cold winter. It was during the night and we children were carried by men who wore long blue army overcoats. There were three of them, big stalwart men that had fought under Grant. Fighting men always liked my father.

They made nearly the entire journey to the depot walking backwards in the teeth of a cutting blizzard, each with a child in his arms, while my father protected my mother and the youngest baby.

Minneapolis

Minneapolis, Minnesota, was then and is now the greatest flour-milling city in the world. On our arrival we were housed in two rooms over a saloon, just off Hennepin Avenue and not far from St. Anthony Falls.

The Nicollet House was then the largest hotel west of Chicago. Hennepin Avenue, in front of the Nicollet House, was packed with blanketed horses and sleds of loaded cordwood for sale. The sidewalks, as I remember, were mostly made of boards.

Indians and their squaws walked the streets; the women with baskets of goods upon their backs for sale. In season their principal stock-in-trade was berries. Ox or bull teams were almost as plentiful as horses — and lumberjacks were everywhere. There were only a few trains each day to and from St. Paul, eight miles distant, the engine being a wood-burner.

During my stage career I went to find a little Episcopal stone church (Christ's Church) to which my father had taken me during our Minneapolis days. As I remembered, it was in a well-kept green field on the outskirts of the city. I started from the West Hotel and walked until I was tired. Convinced that I must have missed the little church, I came back to the hotel and inquired.

'It's just two blocks and a half from the front door!' the clerk laughingly said.

I soon found it. It was all hemmed in by skyscrapers; but it was the same little stone church — I could even pick out the pew where my father and I sat.

CHAPTER II

THE UNBROKEN WEST

It was springtime when my father took me on a seventy-five-mile trip to investigate a new mill-site he had heard of. It was on the Wisconsin side of the Mississippi, twelve miles from the river. We walked the last twelve miles of our journey, and, crossing a river, my father had me stop, wash my feet, and put on my shoes so we could make a proper entry into the town of Trimbell.

After I had finished, my father asked a passing stranger where the town was, and he replied:

'This is it, right here. That store across the road is the post office.'

There were three houses in Trimbell. (I had washed my feet in the center of the town.) Two of the houses we had passed on top of the hill before we dropped down to the river; one, on top of the hill, holds dear memories — I will tell of it later.

Our objective point was located about two miles down the river. It was a small three-run-of-burrs' mill and there were two small houses. The owner was a half-breed Indian of about thirty years of age. Playing about the mill was a little Indian girl of twelve, the owner's sister. Standing a short distance away with a blanket about her shoulders was a full-blood Sioux Indian woman, their mother.

Our little family was soon occupying the three-room house by the mill.

The little Indian girl was, so my mother often told me, one of the most beautiful children she ever saw. The little Indian girl liked me and tried to talk Sioux to me, and

SCENE IN 'TUMBLEWEEDS': HAND TALK

her mother enjoyed making hand talk to me. It mystified me so when mother and daughter would talk it. The signs that the old Indian woman used intrigued me; and the Sioux language that the little Indian girl spoke intrigued me also — for I worshiped the little Indian girl.

I used to accompany this aged Indian woman (I cannot call her a squaw. The memory of her kindness to me and mine, her honesty and her straightforward character will not permit me to do so) — I used to accompany her on many trips which were not too far for my childish legs to travel. One of these excursions would be for the purpose of gathering willow bark, which she dried and of it made tobacco.

On one such trip this Indian woman talked to me as though I had been a grown-up boy. As I look back it seems as though she was giving me a message that in later years I could tell. I listened, while the young girl, with her buckskin skirt about her knees, paddled in the stream.

'I can only think and live in the past,' the Indian woman said, as she gazed at me calmly and steadily. 'The white people have taken away all of the Indian's future. The Sioux is the most famous of all Indian nations — a strong and mighty race possessed of a dominant spirit. We are the monarchs of the plains. We once owned all that we could see. What the canoe is to the Indian of the rivers, the horse is to the Sioux. We ride like the wind; we, like the Cheyennes, are a fighting people. Great warriors! We like peace, but we like to fight. If our enemies run away from us and will not fight, we go after them and make them fight. Peace is a great thing — if that peace is a good peace; but if that peace is wrong and does not bring honor on our people, our people will always fight. We will die. Our spirit will kill us. Soon, when you are a big man, maybe, we will be no more. But we will always fight! Our country of beautiful waters (Minnesota) has been taken from us; those of us who remain here must hide our heads; yet every lake and river bears the name of our people — Minnetonka, Minnehaha, etc., etc.

'I remember ——' she paused, smoking slowly. But soon, gazing at her daughter wading in the stream, she continued, as though speaking into space, 'In the summertime of the year 1862, a white trader gave a young Indian — my brother — some fire-water. The white people give pure alcohol to the Indians. It being white in color, the Indians named it fire-water.

'The Indians never had fire-water in their blood until the white man came into the Indian's country and gave it to him, so the white man could take many skins from the Indian in trade, and give the Indian little in return.

'The white man that gave my brother the fire-water quarreled with my brother — they did fight and my brother killed this white man. My brother's blood that had not inherited the use of alcohol from his father could not withstand its poison — it made his brain crazy.

'There had been much trouble between the white people and my people. The Indians wanted to hunt and move their lodges from place to place, as was their custom, as they always had done, as long as the oldest Indian could remember. It was an Indian country — it belonged to the Indians, and they thought surely they had the right to live as they always had lived.

"No!" the white people said. "The Indian must stay in one place and plow and make a farm, as the white man does."

'A war started. The Indians fought like great warriors; they rode their ponies against two forts filled with soldiers.

The Indians and the Whites

[Fort Ridgely and Fort Ambercrombie.] In less than one moon [a month] over five hundred white people were killed. Then the White Father sent a big army of white soldiers [General H. H. Sibley] and they drove Chief Little Crow and all his Indians across the line into Dakota.

'Hundreds of Indians were taken prisoners and tried by the white man's law. The white man's law said that three hundred Indian braves must hang; but the White Father at Washington, he said, "No, not so many — thirty-seven was enough." So they did hang thirty-seven Indian men all at one time. [February 28, 1863.]

'When the winter had gone and the grass came, the White Father sent another big, big army [General Sully]. The soldiers were as many as blades of grass on the ground. So all the Indians that were left had to run away. My father was killed; my brothers and my man they run away, too.'

The pipe was put in the pipe bag and an Indian woman slowly walked the homeward trail leading an Indian girl and a little white boy by the hand.

There was a great deal of bustling around the little three-room house by the mill. The Indian woman was there a great deal — inside or outside I would find her, with her dark blue, beaded, striped blanket wrapped about her. She was not nearly so nice or communicative to me as she had been on our woodland trips. Once or twice she scolded me, and then, one day, to my astonishment, my aged friend was very cross to me and roughly put me out of the house. I made up my mind I would be bad and run away, and I did. But I met a Sioux Indian boy in the woods, hunting. He was about ten years of age and he had a bow and a quiver full of arrows.

Instinctively I spoke to him in Sioux, as I had been taught, and instinctively his hand went over his mouth, which is the sign for astonishment. I promptly forgot my troubles.

My new-found friend lived at Utah, four miles distant. He was almost a full-blood. His father was a half-breed Canadian Frenchman and his mother a full-blood Sioux squaw.

Utah was even smaller than Trimbell; it had but *one* house, and that a little trading store run by my friend's father. I once saw this half-breed and the mill-owner, the Sioux, drink tumblersful of raw alcohol diluted with only enough water to prevent strangulation. I know it made them crazy, for I saw my father overpower, hog-tie, and leave them lying on the floor of the trading store, with the Indian wife standing guard outside.

I crept after my new boy friend through the brush as he hunted partridges, until I must have been a sorry-looking little boy. Finally, he took me to the edge of a clearing and showed me the direction of home. My little shirt was torn, my bare feet were scratched and bleeding, and when I reached home I was all ready and fit to cry a little and have my mother pet me and say she was sorry and give me a big supper.

As for my friend, the Indian woman, I didn't ever want to see her any more; even the Indian girl had faded and her memory was dimmed by my new-found friend who was a mighty hunter.

'The best laid plans of mice and men gang aft agley' applies to little boys as well as 'mice and men' — my mother did not say she was sorry, nor did she pet me and give me a big supper; I did not see my mother.

The Indian woman was not cross any more, but our

home was all upset. My father was laughing and happy. He took me to a little board box with rockers under it — that I had seen him making for some days past — and there was a little baby in it. I had a little baby brother!

I liked my little brother, but that night a tired little boy, with only a little bit of supper, and without being cuddled by his mamma, cried himself to sleep.

I was soon to get a tang of real grief, however. I was soon to see my mother shed bitter tears, and my father have that haggard look that always showed when he was troubled — the little baby brother that I had been standing on my head for, and tickling with a feather to see him laugh, was quiet and still. His little crib had a block of wood under it so it would not rock. It was covered over with a blanket, and an Indian woman sat beside it all night and smoked.

My experience in life has been that whenever in trouble all those who have been brought up to respect religion or religious faith will instinctively search out some little church of their childhood recollection, and under its roof, even in a far, far-off way, feel the soothing presence of a Creator.

It must have been some such feeling that possessed my father, for in a covered wagon drawn by two yoke of steers, he, my sister, and myself — and the little baby brother — went in search of consecrated ground.

After a two-day journey we crossed the Mississippi at Red Wing, Minnesota, and there, on a high hill overlooking the mighty river, our little family gathered alone.

There was no clergyman; my little brother being the first, young or old, to be buried there. My father did not think himself good enough to read the burial service. He quietly spoke each sentence to my sister and she repeated it over the little open grave.

And so, far above the giant Mississippi that was commencing its two-thousand-mile journey to the sea, at the side of a covered wagon, its steers with drooping heads, in a plain little coffin, fashioned by his father's hands, a tiny boy child, that had scarcely commenced to live, was laid in earth's arms to sleep.

All blanket Indians that retain their tribal traits and customs keep their tipis. They may have a comfortable house built of logs, boards, sod, or stone, but near by will stand the tipi of their fathers — the kind in which they were born.

My friend the Indian woman had such a tipi; it was near her house, at the edge of the woods. In searching for her on some errand, my sister and I found her one day in this tipi home. I can remember our astonishment at its size, its roominess, and its complete — though primitive — furnishings. In the center of the room there was a fire on the ground, a thin column of smoke spiraling upwards and out at the top, as though enclosed in a flue. About the room were ordinary living utensils, but of primitive make. Gorgeous soft buffalo robes were lying about.

Our message delivered, our friend sat and smoked while we children looked about. It was my sister who first became interested in the long tails — of whatever they were — we could not make them out. The hair was long and soft, and was fastened to a piece of skin or hide twice as big as a silver dollar; some were black, some were yellow, and one was gray — almost white.

When puzzled, children will look at their elders, from

which source comes the answer to all their childish questions.

We looked at the Indian woman for a long time, and the Indian woman smoked and looked at us for a long time. Finally, her kind brown eyes looking at us steadily, she quietly spoke:

'One black hair and one yellow hair ... killed my father. My brother and me ... took their hair. The marks of our knives is on their heads — their heads are there.'

Where her long-stemmed pipe pointed, upon a green rawhide shield, were two skulls. They seemed to laugh. My sister and I drew close together and clutched each other's hands.

'Ko ke pa schna — ko ke pa schna' (Do not be afraid, do not be afraid), she said. 'They were brave men. We killed them — but they were long hairs. They died as brave men — big men — long hairs.'

The working of a child's mind is strange and oftentimes uncanny in its directness.

'My pa — he is a big man and my pa don't have long hair,' I heard myself saying.

The old Indian woman smoked for a long time in silence.

'Your father is strong man — brave man; before the white soldiers come, your father would have his hair long as an Indian chief. We fight before soldiers come — man against man. Two men — three men — twenty men, against two men — three men — twenty men. Our men all have long hair. So if enemy is the mightiest warrior, he takes our scalp lock. White warriors — they brave men. They fight — one man — two men — twenty men; they have long hair, too. If our braves mightiest warriors, we take their scalp locks. Pretty soon white soldiers come

— they so many — like grains of sand by the river. They fight one man — two men — three men — twenty men, with thousand men. They do not have long hair.'

We were going out at the tipi door. My hand brushed against the scalps and it seemed to feel the softness of one.

'Was the man that had the white hair a brave man?' I asked.

She did not answer.

There was a flour mill building on the Orinoco River in Minnesota. They engaged my father for six months to help install the machinery and dress the burrs. My father would not be separated from his family, so we moved to Orinoco, Minnesota. It was about a five-day trip. Our traveling equipment was three yoke of steers hauling a prairie schooner.

How I envied the driver — a strapping, curly-headed youth of about eighteen, as he curled his long-lashed, bull-whip over his team, while I, whose idol he was, trudged along 'way in the rear ... not with a bull-whip, but with a little switch, urging along a milch cow that moo'd in answer to the name of Nellie. Never mind! the little boy would be a big man some day and drive three yoke of steers with a bull-whip, too.

I was a 'regular hand' at night, though; I slept under the wagon with the bull-whacker and my father, while the girl children had to sleep in the wagon with my mother.

We passed through some little one- and two-house towns; I recall two of them, Hay Creek and Pine Island.

Orinoco was made up of probably a dozen houses, or fifty people, all told. I do not remember anything unusual happening at Orinoco this trip, except that I acquired a dog named Prince, and that we had to say good-bye to Nellie, the cow, when we left for Trimbell again.

My father's work was not finished, but he sent us back ahead of him, as winter was coming on. My father had entered into some sort of partnership in working the mill with the Indian, and as part of his share was to get several hundred acres of land.

The return trip was fast train service compared with the going. I sat on the seat with the driver — a long-whiskered plainsman — and he held the lines over four as spirited horses for road work as I had ever seen.

Our new home was in a widespread tract of timber about three miles from the mill. The house was one large room, and built of heavy logs with high rafters and puncheon floor. Our nearest neighbor was a mile distant through a dense forest . . . not a comforting outlook for a woman of gentle breeding and a flock of young children.

I have an indistinct recollection—for I was not properly awake—of a cougar, or wild-cat, as we called them, tearing off some shakes on the roof, trying to get in the house in search of meat that he could smell. Another happening — at night, also — was when my dog Prince went mad. How my mother got him out of the house without us children being bitten, I do not know, for the poor beast, unquestionably, had rabies. He was running amuck all over the room among sleeping children. The next day my young Indian friend and I tracked him in the snow until even the tireless Sioux boy was worn out, but the dog's long trot had never altered. He must have gone straight into that nowhere space where all who have diseased minds go.

When my father returned, the iron heel of winter was

clamping down. The snow was falling heavily and there were chances of being snowed in. My father acted quickly and, securing the help of our mile-distant neighbor, we moved to one of the three houses of Trimbell. It sat on the hill. There were many buckskin- and homespun-garbed boys of young man age in our neighbor's family — wild youngsters all. One was named Thatcher. My father christened them Thatcher, Lasher, Ripper, and Tearer. They packed our few belongings through the heavy drifts and we settled for the winter in town.

It was a terribly severe winter. The ice on the river was many feet thick. There was no work — therefore no income. My mother sent me to the little store to trade — for flour, tea, and sugar — her most prized household possession, a silver caster or cruet stand. We were very poor, but we never borrowed, and we never begged.

I remember one wickedly cold night when we all waited with 'hungry tummies' and kept ourselves busy rubbing frost off the window-panes so we could watch the blizzard outside; our father was coming, and our mother said he would bring us something good to eat. He did come, and brought a small piece of pork. I never knew where he got it, but he had walked sixteen miles. Mayhap my father had been trading, too.

The woods abounded with maple sap in season; and with pork and corn cakes — as my mother cooked them — and real maple syrup, 'hungry tummies' soon vanished.

There were many long winter nights. My father had a number of paper-covered novels by Charles Dickens. He read them all to us; among them, 'Nicholas Nickleby,' 'Oliver Twist,' 'Barnaby Rudge,' and 'Old Curiosity Shop,' with dear little 'Nell.'

We Move to Prescott, Wisconsin

Spring came; and one night early in May my father got my sister and me out of bed and dispatched us on a three-mile walk for the aged Indian woman — our mother was ill. We hurried going, but coming back our anxiety for our mother's health was forgotten, and when the blanketed figure disappeared in the darkness ahead of us we unconsciously became like wood elves. We danced and played games with the lantern throwing its light on the trees until a new light other than from our lantern commenced to come. It was morning!

Golly! What a surprise when we got home! We had a baby brother! Our friend had brought him under her blanket, and in the darkness we hadn't seen him at all.

The streams were running full-banked again. The mill had started full blast. But all was not well with my mother; this time she did not respond to the primitive Indian treatment. Indian women are almost magical doctors among their own people, or among whites that have generations of tough hard work and open-air breathing behind them. Indian women bear children and go about their usual duties in the space of a few days. It was too much to expect of my mother — a woman of gentle upbringing and refinement; she was failing fast. So the Indian partnership and the swelling stream, with banks running over, called in vain — they were left behind.

We moved to Prescott, where the big St. Croix River flanked in on the invincible Mississippi. My father went to work in the flour mill as an added hand, dressing burrs; for among its two hundred inhabitants Prescott boasted a regular doctor — one that did not work at anything else. My mother was placed under his care.

I recall one night at dusk my youngest little sister was

taken ill. I had never seen any one faint before, and when she slipped down in her high chair, I was gone like a shot over the mountain for the doctor. I *went over* the top all right, but going down on the other side I went *off* the top of a lime kiln that was built into the side of the mountain.

The drop was about twenty-five feet, but I never stopped running. Such is the Providence that guards little children, especially boys.

On my way home I met two boys; one was about my own age, the other, several years older. They were Sioux and they took me to their house. They wanted their father to hear me talk Sioux. Their father was a fine-looking Indian, a full-blood, but he wore the clothes of a white man.

The father and two sons walked home with me and the father talked with my father. The younger boy was my playmate while we lived at Prescott.

One of our favorite sports was to get an assortment of nuts from somewhere, nuts that were aged and had seen their best day. We prided ourselves on which one could eat the most kernels that were the most wormy. I believe we are both still alive, however. A Sioux Indian told me a short time ago that he had played on the same baseball team with both boys and that they live at Hastings, Minnesota, across the river from the same old town of Prescott.

The doctor that devoted ALL OF HIS TIME to medicine could not help my mother. She grew steadily worse. The parting was so sad it is hard to write about even at this day, but my father knew it had to be. There was no work for him in the East, and expert medical attention for my mother was imperative.

So the little band that found so much happiness together

was split; the girl children, the baby boy, and my mother, were put on the train at Hastings, bound for my mother's home, Newburgh, New York, while my father and I stood at the little station and watched the train, containing our all, go out of sight.

We were again at Orinoco. My father was working in the mill all day and often far into the night. So I existed in a sort of boy's heaven; I soon forgot my loneliness for my mother and sisters and was running wild.

Orinoco was noted throughout that section of the country for its fine saddle stock. The report was not exaggerated. I know, for I rode ninety per cent of its horses. It was an unusual day that I did not have an argument with some animal that had a mind of his own, and I never told my father when I got the worst of the argument, either. I was afraid my playful habits might be curtailed.

We boarded at the Len Hanson Hotel; rate for adults, three dollars and a half per week, American plan; and it was good food, too! I do not know how much my board was, probably half price.

About this time I had my first experience of having a tooth extracted. I rode to Rochester with one of the mill wagons, fifteen miles distant, to have the operation performed. I understand Rochester is now famous for that particular specialty. I was a pioneer!

When not having a difference of opinion with some one's obstreperous bronc, my pastime was fishing. The river was full of black bass and pickerel. I would string about fifty pounds of these wonderful fish and sell them to some passing rancher for two bits.

On one of these Izaak Walton explorations I stumbled on

a small Indian village, about four miles downstream. It was in a country dense with plum trees. They were heavily loaded with luscious fruit and reached in every direction as far as the eye could see. I have often wondered if these Indians depended on this fruit for the greater portion of their food.

Sioux Indians do not like fish. They eat it only in the winter when their food supply is low. They then cut a hole through the ice, put a little tent over it, and spear Mr. Fish when he becomes inquisitive.

When Indians had the run of the country which they owned, they always camped on, or established their villages near, the banks of a river; first, for water supply for themselves and their stock, and secondly, for sanitary reasons — they could keep a much cleaner camp. I have often thought that is why our little family came in contact with Indians so frequently. My father always followed the river for mill-sites — the Indians, because it was their birthright and through custom.

There is one band or tribe of the Sioux Nation that always lives near the river and plants corn for its principal sustenance. It is the tribe 'Minneconju,' which means 'plant near river.'

One day (oh! a sad day), a rancher drove in from his place, ten miles from the mill. I fell in love with his wonderful shepherd dog. The rancher proposed to my father that I go back home with him and I could play with the dog all the time and he would give me twenty-five cents a day to do it.

I did. 'Oh! What a fall was there, my countryman!' Play with the dog? From 4 A.M. until 9 P.M. I played with a plow and every farming implement there was on the place; and outside of the night of my arrival, I never saw

28

the dog. He was putting in sixteen hours a day, also, herding sheep.

The nearest I got to playing with the dog was when I first arrived. The wagon was unloaded, three large barrels were thrown into it, and the rancher said, 'Go to the river and fill them barrels.'

I looked about — there was hardly the trace of a trail anywhere.

'Where is the river?' I asked.

'Follow the dog,' he replied, and went into the ranch house.

My boyish intuition in liking the dog was correct, as children's intuitions concerning animals usually are. Children have much in common with all animals. Their embryonic brains seem to harmonize and keep in tune — each with the other.

The dog 'Shep' took the lead and the team followed — I merely held the reins. It was probably a mile to the river. The horses acted peculiarly and fussed when we got there, as if afraid. Shep barked a lot, but I thought him a dumb dog, for, instead of barking at the stubborn team, he directed his canine tirade right at me.

But when my barrels were full, I realized the superiority of horse and dog over boy sense. Answering the lash, my team had gone into the river as far as they could go and hold their feet. I could not drive forward to turn around, and the grade behind was too steep to back out — *I should have backed in!*

Wise horses! Wise dog and dumb boy! But again the Protector of children must have intervened, for when with choked sobs of fright I urged the team forward, they breasted the turbulent water gamely. They swam powerfully, while the faithful dog Shep swam at the head of the off horse and snarlingly turned him upstream. The swift current did the rest; it swung the wagon around, and we made the shore.

(The reader will note that there is still a bit of boy left in me — I put myself in at the successful finish!)

My rancher boss and his wife and brother belonged to some sort of religious sect that was a dissenter from any established church or creed. The wife and brother were sincere — the rancher boss was not. He prayed and watched, but he watched first. For my part, even at my then early age (and ever since), I preferred those of any church or creed that could be religious without becoming professionals and doing a lockstep. The rancher boss was strong for the lockstep.

I liked his brother. He and I slept in the attic together. The ladder to ascend was two uprights with cleats nailed across on the kitchen wall.

The brother was in a pitiable condition. His right leg had been injured in some way on the shin bone and it was an ugly-looking running sore. His incapacity for work soon made me understand why I had been promised twenty-five cents a day by the noble-hearted rancher to play with the dog.

The attic was a bare, miserable attic. We slept on loose straw on the floor. There was no furniture — just a bucket half full of stagnant water for my sick room-mate to wash in. And yet I was more contented here than anywhere on the ranch. Here there was no hypocrisy.

But it was, oh! so sad to see the poor fellow suffer when so full of honest faith; and to hear him pray for relief instead of striving to get surgical attention, when the odor of his wound was almost revolting, even in our attic of many airy openings.

CHAPTER III

A BOY RIDER

THERE was a good-looking, three-year-old colt on the ranch. The boss was breaking him to the saddle and was having a hard time of it. He kept him tied to a hitching rack, saddled and bridled, for a couple of hours almost every evening, as a part of his training.

One night when I had taken care of my work team, I asked him if I might ride the colt. He grinned and replied, quite amicably, 'Why, certainly.'

He must have expected a different result, for when I was unsaddling the colt, after having ridden him for half an hour, without his ever making the slightest attempt to 'turn on,' he walked up and grinned again . . . and somehow his grin made me feel uncomfortable.

A few days after this my room-mate told me the colt had piled the boss and had given him a nasty fall.

I was doing a man's work in the fields, plowing all day — every day. One evening when I had put up my team and was just going in to supper, the boss limped by, leading the colt all ready to go, and said, 'Here, take a ride, boy. Let me see how you handle this colt. He still acts mean with me.'

'Yes, sir,' I said, and started to take up the stirrups.

I noticed that the colt seemed fidgety and sort of wild-eyed, but I thought he would quiet down as soon as I mounted. I thought wrong. Lord! How that pony did buck!

He swapped ends and reached for the sky — not as if he were jumping for plumb deviltry, as most horses do, but as though he were crazy mad. I had no spurs on and I did not kick him, but just rode for all I was worth, and at the first sign of a let-up I slid off and led him back — him fighting his head all the way.

The boss wore a sort of disappointed look, and I did not like his smile as he said, 'You liked to choke that horn plumb to death, didn't you?'

'Yes, sir,' I replied. I had choked the horn, but I was only a small boy . . .

I had just unsaddled and turned the colt in his little corral when, as I started to put the bars up, he ran at me, wheeled, and kicked. I jumped as quickly as I could, but I was not quick enough. He caught me with one hoof solid on that part of my anatomy that is usually used in the seated attitude. The fact that one side of his corral was the straw stable saved me from a bad injury, as I was hurtled full force against it.

I could not get up to my attic, so I lay for two or three days and nights on a pile of straw in the stable, and grew steadily worse. I finally got in a position where I could twist my head enough to see my angry-looking discolored hip. Then I weakened and boy-like cried, and asked to be taken to my father.

The boss did not like this part of the picture at all. He did not go to Orinoco very often, but he had been there often enough to learn that my father was a mighty willing man with his hands. So, whining about the 'hospital I got,' he lost a whole day's work and returned with a squaw. She was old and wrinkled (she must have been a hundred), but she was a wonderful healer of flesh.

For four or five days and four or five nights she kept me lying flat on my stomach — much to my embarrassment — while she poulticed me with herbs that she cooked in a pot on her tripod fire, a few yards away. If she slept, she slept at my side, for she was always there. She called me her 'Indian child with a white skin.'

I recovered, and with a limp went to work again, and in a few days I caught up the colt to saddle him. I was not satisfied and wanted to have it out with him again. The outfit lay just where I had put it — it had not been touched . . . and there was a crushed cockle-burr stuck to the inside of the saddle-blanket.

I apologized to the colt and turned him loose; I hope he understood. Then I went straight to the boss and man-fashion asked for my time. There must have been a look in my boyish eyes that he did not like, for he fawningly gave it to me without comment.

I was sorry to leave my friend with the sore leg, and oh! how it hurt me to make Shep go back when he left his sheep and tried to follow, as with my little bundle on my shoulder I trudged down the road.

I never told my father the particulars of my injury until later years. But the rancher boss never came to Orinoco again to trade, anyhow. I would tell this cockle-burr man's name — but I don't remember it.

I did not know the letters of the alphabet. My father knew full well the value of education and he had never been willingly negligent; we were creatures of circumstance. Where we had lived for any length of time there had been no schools, and where there had been any possibility of my attending, I dodged beautifully.

Orinoco had a school, however, and it would open in the fall, and I was to go. My father taught me my 'letters' so quickly that he seemed encouraged, and said that one winter's schooling would put me up with other boys of my size. But, boy-like, I had no use for school and my father seemed to sense it. So to give me a good work-out and have me come back willing to study, he fixed up a deal on me.

The owner of the mill had an enormous ranch, fourteen miles from town, in the opposite direction from where I had worked before. It was thrashing time and the owner of the mill personally engaged me to go out there and work with the thrashers at fifty cents a day, and I thought, 'What good fairy is looking out for me!' I thought it pointed the way to becoming a cow-puncher and no school.

In those days some thirty or forty men would group together and buy a thrashing machine and go from ranch to ranch thrashing on shares. (I do not remember what toll they received. I know the flour mills received one eighth for grinding the wheat and turning out flour.) Of all the gangs, parties, or crowds of men that ever banded together in the West (not excepting outlaws) I do not believe that for toughness, roughness, real devilishness, pure go-to-hellishness and stop-at-nothingness, there ever was the equal of an outfit of thrashers — bartenders, road agents, faro dealers, three-card men, dive-owners, brakemen off railroads, bull-whackers, cowboys, mule-skinners — the thrashers at this ranch even had a barber from Boston among their number. Such were the types of men that composed a company of thrashers.

My jobs were holding sacks for the thrashed grain and driving the team that dragged the thrashed straw away, and sometimes driving teams that worked in a circle and furnished the power. I lived with the men in tents and felt like a regular man.

It is a pleasant thing for me to look back and think how

34

careful and considerate this outfit of roughnecks were of me. I cannot remember there ever being any bad language used when I was around, and they never would gamble at night in the tent where I slept. All the men in our tent would go somewhere else; also they cared for me without ostentation in other ways.

Some evenings the ranch boys would bring in a 'snorty' one for some ambitious chap to 'top off.' If the animal was a real mean *hombre*, they would never let me mount him, and much to my disgust they made me ride the same horses that the Boston barber HAD TO RIDE. The only satisfaction I had was that I could ride them, while the poor barber was a sorry spectacle. I can see him yet! Golly! what a funny picture he made, with his shirt yanked out of his trousers and flapping in the wind, while his hazers called out, 'Darling, you forgot to put on your overshoes,' and 'Young man, you should never travel without your umbrella,' etc.

The barber was not outclassed in various other ways, though; no one took undue liberties with him — he had a past all right. No one knew his name — he was just 'Boston.'

Gee! what a bitter pill I had to swallow! What an awful humiliation 'fer a big feller like me!' I had to go and sleep in the ranch house on a shake-down, in the room occupied by the foreman of the ranch and his wife. The good woman felt it was wrong for me to be herding with a bunch of men.

A mad foreman, probably exceeding his authority — a blood-mad mutinous mob of men! I don't know how it started. Trouble, trouble, you could feel it in the air, in the covert glances of the men; the way they would gather in groups, their sullen and even hostile attitude toward the resident ranch hands, until the ranch hands, after digging their boot toes in the ground awhile, would join the thrashers' circle.

Every finger of every hand of every man seemed to point toward trouble, while conversation would practically cease when I came around. I could not help hearing at times such talk as:

'Give me a man if he's got hind legs an' front teeth — rather'n a snake in the grass.'

'Don't insult a snake. This feller's crookeder than a rattler with a belly-ache.'

'Well, here's one *hombre* that ain't goin' to roll over an' play dead for no man.'

'Well, boys, the way things is lookin', the sermon will be short an' the preacher will do his talkin' with a shovel.'

The rancher's wife was a comely, rosy-cheeked, almost foreign type of woman — the very antithesis of a sprite or 'goblin damned'; yet it was as the latter she appeared to the scared boy as she pulled him out of his little bed and gasped in a rasping whisper:

'My husband, my husband! They are going to hang my husband! Quick! Quick! This way, quick!'

The boy was but half-awake and awfully frightened. It was night, and night lends terror to juvenile minds; then the moon — the moon cast weird shapes and shadows. The boy was panic-stricken — yet here was the foreman's wife! He knew her ... he knew her, now ... and here, at the side door of the ranch house was tied the dark roan colt from the big pasture that had never been broken or had a saddle on ... he was playing with him only yesterday. No, he wasn't nearly so frightened now!

The foreman's wife was speaking again, and now it was in a low wail:

To Stop a Hanging

'Willie, go to your father, go to your father and tell him they are going to hang my husband.

'Oh, God, give you strength, God give you strength,' she cried, clutching the boy hysterically to her breast, 'the colt was the only one that would come to me, Willie. Oh, dear God, make him let you ride him. You will make him, won't you, God?'

The hackamore rope was in the boy's hand. She gave him a leg up, shook her dress, and cried in a low voice:

'Go, Roanie, go! For God Almighty's sake, go!'

The boy could hear the crack of guns and the sing of bullets the first two hundred yards, but after that there was just the pounding of a horse's feet, and a long, now straight, now winding, ribbon of road. A boy, clad only in a night-shirt, on a bareback horse, was speeding head-long into the night. Staunch, true, wild colt — wondrous animal! The hands that petted you, you are paying back — and God is making you do it!

The bigness of the West makes men quiet; they seldom talk unless they have something to say. The altitude clarifies their brains and gives them nerves of steel.

The majority of the Western men came from the East, the Middle West, or some Southern State. Wild Bill Hickok, Bat Masterson, and Wyatt Earp, celebrated peace officers, came from Illinois; Doc Holliday, a lightning-fast gun-man, from Georgia; Jim Bridger, the greatest of all pathfinders, from Richmond, Virginia; the outlaw Billy the Kid was born on the East Side of New York City, his parents moving West when he was two years old; while the famous cowboy artist Charlie Russell was born in Burlington, New Jersey.

Our Western frontiersmen had to migrate from some-where — the West was too young to have many native

37

sons. But, come he from North, East, South, or Overseas, be his language understandable, or that of a foreign tongue, once a man crossed the Missouri, the West got into his blood. All men were atoms aiding in building an Empire.

Although the night had the coolness of early fall, when I arrived at the mill and found my father, the roan was white with lather and my cotton nightgown was so wet it was sticking to my flesh like a fitted garment. I was hurriedly wrapped in a blanket and laid on a big leather sofa in the office, while a young mill apprentice walked the blanketed colt to cool him out.

But even in this short space of time, a band of WESTERN MEN, with rifles across their saddles, rode off in the night; my father, in his dusty miller clothes, was among them.

Snow was on the ground and I was going to school. It was not nearly so bad as I had anticipated. There were boys almost as backward in their studies as I, and the teacher was a very fine man, one of the kind that liked the outdoors as well as the schoolroom.

I really believe I might have turned out to be a near-the-head-of-the-class pupil, so far as application goes, had I not seen the bear. It was only a little black cub that had probably just been turned loose by his mother, and he was playing in the snow, but to a boy going to school with a book with big letters and a lot of words in it under his arm, how could it be other than a big, savage man-eating bear?

How could the boy help running? And if the river was frozen over, and in taking a short cut across the ice he ran into his friends, the Indians, fishing through the ice, naturally he would stay there with them in their tipis until all danger of the bear following was past.

Oh, dear! Oh, dear! That is the kind of a talk I put up to my wonderful dad when after a couple of weeks of present and not present at school, with the 'nots' far in the lead, I was given a talking to.

But I was just a little bit ashamed of myself, and, besides, there was going to be a Christmas-tree party in the schoolroom, with all the children's parents there, an' presents an' cake an' things, and I was going to sing. My father was writing a little humorous song for me about all the folks in town. I was strong for everything but the singing. Golly! how I hated that! I had a singing voice 'like a girl.' (Lord! how many fights I had with boys for using that very expression!)

So, until after Christmas 'all went as merry as a marriage bell,' as the teacher said in his recitation at the party. Things might have gone finely after the party, but something always happens with a boy that is going to school. This time, it was boots.

I usually wore moccasins in summer and shoe-packs in winter, but my father wanted to make me a fine present, so he measured my foot all over and sent to Minneapolis to a boot-maker that made his boots. And I got a pair of boots ... that ... well! ... that I took to bed with me! Gee! They were beauties! I would not have put my trousers inside of 'em for all the money in the State.

The Indians were my closest friends — so I must show them to the Indians.

Now, as I have before explained, the Indians fish through a hole in the ice, covered by a small tent or tipi to keep the light out. The light was out all right where I went in! I plumped right into a hole, waist deep into the water.

39

I'd have gone deeper and probably with far more serious results if the astonished Indian hadn't grabbed me and pulled me out. In a few seconds I was iced to my middle, for it was zero weather, and, 'Oh! ye immortal Gods!' as the school teacher also recited — the boots! An Indian half-ran and half-hauled me to the back door of the hotel, and I got into the bedroom unseen.

But, oh! the tragedy of those boots — after I had nearly wrecked the room in getting them off. When I looked at them I wept, and when I thought of my father, I nearly died of fear. I do not remember what I did or how I did it — I know I hid out in some way until every one had gone to bed and then put my boots under the big office stove to dry.

I was the first one up in the morning, too, and I don't remember how I did that, either, and ... Oh! ... Oh! ... Oh! (I've run out of quotations from the school teacher's recitations) ... the boots! ... the boots! ... THE BOOTS! ... the 'goddam' boots! They were no bigger than a baby's shoe — they were burned to a crisp!

I saw my father coming. I ran and he ran — all round rooms an' all over everything. ... I ran upstairs into our bedroom and, just in time, I locked the door. My father didn't even stop, he came right through the door as if it hadn't been there at all. I was up in the corner. He was coming at me savagely. Up went my fists and I yelled, 'Don't you hit me.'

The wonderful man in front of me paused — and glared — and then I could see the corners of his mouth quiver and that kind look come into his eyes. He turned quickly, then squared his shoulders, and then walked slowly away. ... And in a month's time there arrived another pair of boots!

Baptism in Ice-Water

The unalloyed truth, probity, and virtue of the simple followers of some religious cults must go unchallenged. Their faith demands it, even though their deeds, at times, place them in a light that tests a normal chain of reasoning.

It was during a late winter month before a chinook had come to thaw the ice that a congregation of Christian people gathered one Sunday around an opening about twenty feet square that had been cut in the ice. Practically the entire town of Orinoco was present, all wearing heavy buffalo overcoats. My father and I were there, also, but on my feet I wore SHOE-PACKS.

The itinerant clergyman was a heavily built, muscular man, about fifty-five years of age. With uncovered head he offered a prayer, and at its conclusion stepped off into the icy water. Immersed nearly to his shoulders, he spoke the ritual of his creed — as though it were a summer day!

There was no play of heroics, no action to seek sympathy; just a zeal, a religious fervor that was carried out in a plain way, just as a cowboy would ride through a stampeded herd and say,

'All in a day's work.'

There must have been a dozen 'candidates' gently lowered down to him — men and women, but he never faltered, he never hurried. His words were the same for each, and if there were a few titters from the onlookers when a shivering, half-frozen culprit would dash for a waiting sleigh, he never heard — he was working for the Lord! A good man he was, one of the pioneers!

My father talked to him that night. He was an Englishman, and came from Liverpool, the same city in which my father was born. He had been a contender for thé middleweight boxing championship of England. Of such brick and mortar was the early West made.

If there is any one event that pulls on a boy harder than another, it is the first swim after the ice has melted and gone down-river. I was no exception, nor was a Sioux chum of mine, who lived at the Indian village. After one or the other of us weakened several times, we at last slipped our clothes off and, shrieking our defiance to nothing at all, dove in. B-rr-r-r! It was cold! We floundered and cuffed each other around in the water so much to keep our blood in circulation that we missed the comedy (later to turn to drama) that was taking place on the shore.

Some ranch hands were riding the trail that led up the river and, seeing two boys splashing around in the water, decided to have a bit of fun. They found our clothes in the bushes and, hurriedly dipping them into the water, tied each separate garment in a knot. As there were just shirt and trousers, it didn't take long. Then our levity-seeking friends hid in the trees, a few yards behind the brush to watch the fun.

It was only a few minutes until 'Young Owl' and myself had had enough, and, with much shivering and squealing, scampered for our clothes.

It might not have happened if I had not laughed, but I did laugh — and it did happen. Young Owl's trousers and shirt were buckskin, and knotted wet buckskin does not lend itself very readily to manipulation ... and I laughed, and Young Owl jumped me. As my father used to box and play with me, I could use my hands, and, having been hurt the first exchange, I was flailing away for all I was worth, to Young Owl's discomfiture. Young Owl's hunting knife was beside his clothes!

KNIFED BY AN INDIAN BOY

The hidden cow-hands jumped for us immediately they saw, but, quick as they were, I was badly cut up, with the Indian boy standing aghast when they grabbed him. A tourniquet was quickly tied on my left arm and my right leg; I was thrown across a horse and in a man's arms raced to town. Fortunately there was an old army major, who had been a 'saw-bones' all through the Civil War, visiting Orinoco and I was quickly sewed up. Golly! I needed it — fourteen stitches went into my arm alone.

I was fishing in a week and Young Owl was baiting my hook for me. The knife marks are still with me.

My father had news that my mother was progressing splendidly under the Eastern doctor's care, and two of my sisters were attending school. So my father again started searching, trying to realize his dream — a mill-site and water-power of his own, which would mean a lasting home for his family.

We were traveling through Central Kansas — Newton, Hays City, Ellsworth, Abilene. I did not care much for these places. To me, to go to bed meant to go to sleep, and I did not sleep so well. There seemed to be, always, a hum of voices, with every once in a while a loud call, and sometimes I would be awakened by a shot and hear a lot of people running, or some one yelling.

One morning, at Abilene, after having been frightened by some sort of unusual disturbance in the night, I could hear my father talking loud, which he seldom did. I went down the stairway that led to the saloon, where I was not allowed to go. My father was talking to a man who was with some other men. I knew that something was the matter, because my father's face was white, and the man he was talking to — his face was white, too. They stood close together, facing each other. The man had a pistol on his hip and I could see his right hand was near the pistol. The man had only three fingers on his right hand. Again my father was talking. Everything seemed quiet and still.

'I don't care if you are Three-Fingered Jack, or who you are. My boy is sleeping in that bed with me and you fellows try and pull any drinking bouts up there again and I'll beat hell out of the whole crowd.'

The man looked hard at my father and nobody moved for what seemed a long time, and then the man saw me where I had walked up behind my father. His face didn't stop being white, but it slowly broke into what looked like a smile, and he said,

'All right, Captain! We won't do it again'; and then, 'Fine boy you got there, Captain.'

And Three-Fingered Texas Jack, followed by his friends, turned and walked away. My father turned also, and I got a scolding when he saw me standing there on forbidden ground.

All of the towns in Central Kansas were shipping points for long-trail Texas cattle herds. Great three-thousand-head herds were also passing, traveling north. My father, on invitation of the foreman, rode with the drag of one of these herds for five days, with me tagging along. This herd was consigned to the Government at Fort Robinson, to be distributed to the Indians.

Most of the riders were real Texans and spoke with the Southern drawl, while some had the tang of the backwoods in their speech, but all were cowmen, all were horsemen; and the cook turned out as fine a plate of pot roast an' horseradish as any traveler ever 'throw'd a lip over.'

A Riding Kid

The cattle moved slowly and were very poor. The fore-man told my father the water on the trail up was far apart and the trail had been traveled so long and so heavily that the grass was all grazed off; that lawless law, 'the survival of the fittest,' that disregards ALL law, had a strangle grip on the cripples and weak doggies that bawled their distress in a pathetic manner.

I made quite a hit with this outfit. My father's horse was cutting up a bit and I traded with him. I had my boots and a pair of six-bit spurs and I gave the 'cut-up' a chance to do his stuff, but after a couple of jumps he decided to behave, which pleased me very much, as the jumps he had taken were high and hard.

Before we turned in that night, one of the men merely suggested to his pardners that 'they had a horse that would jump a little bit.' He was looking at his boot toes when he said it. It was only to try me out, and when I grabbed my breath and said in my best grown-up manner, 'Any time, Mister,' he just grinned and slapped me on the back and said, 'Good kid.'

Cowboys always protect the young, whether animal or human, and when we left, all the riders — except the pointers and wheelers — rode back to say, 'Adios, Mister,' and 'So-long, kid.'

Many years after, I played in Abilene, Kansas. The manager of the show was a man of mature years, a peace-loving 'Shaker,' from Leominster, Massachusetts. He came back-stage and said:

'Well, they're living up to those old days you've been telling me about. Three men just walked past me at the door and when I said, "Tickets," they just looked at me and said they hoped it was a good show.'

'And what did you say?' I queried.

'I looked at that long flight of stairs that went down from the ticket box and remarked that I hoped so, too!' he replied.

I really believe the same building and the same flight of stairs were there in my boyhood days.

CHAPTER IV

THE BACKBONE OF THE SIOUX COUNTRY

My father's object in traveling north was to go up through Dakota Territory, by way of Julesburg, Colorado, or Sidney, Nebraska. He did not know which was the head of the trail, so when we hit the Union Pacific Railroad (I think it was at North Platte) we journeyed west to Julesburg. Here we found that the stages for the Black Hills started from Sidney.

Golly! These towns all seemed upside down! There were crowds of white people, many of them that talked different languages, all carrying rifles and shotguns. There were fathers and mothers with lots of children. Soldiers, Indians, yoked cattle, loose cattle, horses, mules, prairie schooners, teamsters with long-lashed bull-whips, cowboys, dogs, and all kinds of house furniture, stoves, bureaus, bedsteads, chairs, piled everywhere.

Many of the people were cooking and living in the street. There were, also, young women wearing fancy short dresses covered with beads, with a pretty colored shawl over their shoulders and a flower in their hair. I saw one of these young women rocking a little baby and holding a fan that opened and shut over the baby's face, to keep the sun out of its eyes, while its mother was cooking.

My father told me that gold had been discovered in the Black Hills, and that miners from all over the world had gathered here, but that Dakota was an Indian country and belonged to the Indians. So the Government was using the soldiers to drive the white people out and to keep them out, as they were trespassers on Indian land,

and that it was reported that many Indians were going on the war-path, as they were very angry.

My father told me that he was not in search of gold; his object was not the Black Hills, but the many swift-running rivers of this Indian country of which the old Indian woman had told him; that she had sent word to her people that he would come; that he hoped to form a partnership with the Indians and build a little mill and make lots of flour, which was white gold; and that then my mother and sisters and little brother could come and we would all be together again and be very happy.

We journeyed east by the Union Pacific and stage. My father did not tell me his plans until we reached Sioux City. We were still to go up into Dakota. We were to travel as closely as possible up the Missouri River.

I saw two men killed at Sioux City. It was very early morning. My father was going to see about buying our horses. Some men half-rushed and half-stumbled out of a saloon, shooting. My father gripped my shoulder and said, 'Stand still.'

It was a sheriff against two gambler gun-men and the sheriff got them both, although he himself was mortally wounded.

My father had seen in a flash that they were all gun-men, so he told me to stand still, although we were right in a possible line of fire. If near a gun-fight and the weapons are wielded by amateurs, run for your life; if professionals are handling the trigger, *stand still* — they know where they are shooting.

My father did not buy any horses at Sioux City. We traveled by stage to Yankton, Dakota Territory. There my father hired a packer, a French Canadian, who agreed to furnish three saddle-horses and two pack-horses

SIOUX INDIANS ABOUT TO HOLD A WAR DANCE
From an old photograph by D. F. Barry

for our trip into the Indian country. A simple and light outfit was soon gathered together and we rode northwest into the land of the Sioux.

About two days' ride on our journey we passed a small army post. I think it was called Fort Randall. After that we saw no towns, no white people, no log houses, no settlements. We were traveling, as my father said, along the backbone and into the very marrow of the Sioux Indian country.

One morning, on a slight rise of ground, about three miles ahead of us, we saw several horses. My father had a pair of field-glasses and we took a good look at them. Some were standing and some were grazing; nothing else was to be seen. Our course lay right past them, and as we approached we all watched intently to see how close they would allow us to come, as we presumed they were wild horses. We came closer and they paid no attention to us whatever. Then, just as I was no longer able to hold in and was about to yell to startle them, somebody else yelled and startled us.

We could not have been over six hundred yards away, when with loud whoops an Indian rose up from behind the withers of every horse and leaping to the back of his animal was racing toward us. Some had war bridles to guide their mounts, some had nothing at all, but guided with their heels. When within two hundred yards of us, they made a complete circle and then rode straight in. They had seen our strength.

When the leader set up his horse and I gayly started to chatter Sioux, not only the leader's right hand, but the right hand of every Indian in the party, followed immediately by the left, went over their mouths; they were astounded.

49

Our visitors were in full war-paint. I had seen Indians in war-paint before, and I have seen many since, but I have never seen Indians in full war-paint but once in my life, and they were in front of us right there on those Dakota prairies. There was something in their fighting colors and whole demeanor that is indescribable.

They were probably one of the marauding war-parties that had left their reservation and were on the way to attack any incoming white people trying to locate in the Black Hills. There is no question but what they would have stolen our stock and outfit and if we had resisted they would have killed us — they were out for that purpose. Marauding and stealing mean murder the world over, if the occasion arises.

I would like to record here that I was not a bit timid or afraid; it seems that a boy should have been, but I was not. Nor do I believe that, from the very moment those Indians set their horses on their haunches and I started to chatter Sioux, they had the slightest idea of molesting or harming us. Our 'at home' feeling seemed to be as unconscious as it was mutual. I can remember vividly their smiles and their humorous looks, each to the other, at my kid talk.

I am sure my father was apprehensive, and, as for the packer, we would have had no packer had he been able to develop wings and fly. But, to me, these men were Indians, and I played with Indians; they were my friends. Perhaps there is something more behind it all; I do not know. I only know that Indians always liked me; I don't know how they came by this fondness, except that I was fond of them.

No matter what my father's condition of mind may have been, outwardly he was as calm and sunny as that calm, sunny morning. He told them he wanted to see Red Cloud, Spotted Tail, Standing Bear, or any chief, and, while I was incapable of interpreting sufficiently, our friends got enough to convince them of our importance. With a wave for us to go straight ahead, they rode two lightning-fast circles around us, yelling a parting Sioux cry of victory, and dashed away, their bells jingling and their feathers blowing straight back in the breeze.

Again my father explained to me: the Government, under treaty, was supplying the Indians at certain intervals with rations. The Indians were not getting sufficient food to live on. They blamed the agents. Their big hunting country was the valley of the Yellowstone and the Big Horn mountains. If they left the reservations to go hunting without permission, they were declared hostile. In spite of all solemn treaties, white people were coming in and taking what was left of their hunting grounds. The old chiefs were wise men; they knew they were beaten and that they had to stay on the reservations, or be killed by the white soldiers. But the young chiefs could not see this — they were young, and, besides, ALL WERE HUNGRY!

Undeniably, young Indians ran away from the reservations to 'go hunting' and stole horses and cattle wherever they could find them; and, undeniably, the old Indians that stayed at home knew this and shielded them. They knew that the young men had 'gone hunting.'

We worked our way north, never being any great distance from the west bank of the Missouri River. We saw very little game; some elk, some mule-deer in the hills, and some white-tails on the prairie. Once we saw a small herd of antelope, but we did not get near them — the prong-horns got our wind. We saw no buffalo; the Indians said the buffalo had all been killed in that part of the country.

We struck several small Indian villages, or moving camp villages of three and four tipis or lodges each, and finally on White River we struck a village of thirty or forty lodges, which would amount to about one hundred and fifty people. We had no trouble with any of the Indians we met.

We camped a short distance away and visited the Indian village. We found an Indian, Lone Bear, who had received word of our coming, and he told the Indians about us. Of course, it was not necessary to tell any one anything about me — an hour after we arrived, I had forgotten all about mill-sites and such affairs of state and was playing with the Indian children as though I had lived there all my life.

There was a half-breed that acted as interpreter for my father; a little present of tobacco and he was with him constantly. I was not neglecting my father, as my knowledge of Sioux did not go beyond the simple talk of children, and I could have been of no real benefit to him when a mature or weighty subject was under discussion.

It must have been a tremendous disappointment to my father; the most sturdy of the Indians were in an apparent condition of unrest. Winter was approaching, and, instead of their usual tons of dried meat to face it with, they had scarcely enough food to last a week. They displayed the keenest interest in all that my father said concerning the great water-power that could be developed on some of the rivers that emptied into the Missouri, and how a mill could be built and how grain could be planted and grown, and the flour made from it and sent down the Missouri by boat, and how many boatloads of beads and presents would be returned to the Indians and hundreds of cattle sent over the trails to them.

Alas! One lone man knocking at the door of an Empire; and blanket Indians (so-called savages) trying to grope their way out of darkness! 'Planting' meant plows — plows that the agent wanted to give them instead of rifles to hunt with and blankets to keep them warm. 'The time was out of joint!'

The world could ill afford not to have known the lives of people such as these. The opportunity was soon gone. I am glad that I knew them, even though I was a little boy.

Many of these men and women had never seen a white man before. I am quite sure that none of my playmates had ever seen a white boy. While of the same tribe and tongue as the other Indians I had known, these people had never known the chains of civilization. Except that they reasoned and were unafraid, they were like wild animals that roamed the hills and prairies. What clean, healthful lives they lived! A tipi is a poor place to hold secrets — so they had none. They were as God intended human beings should be; there was no lying, cheating, bickering — no strife. They wronged no man or woman either; every custom under which they lived was one of trust and fairness. Their tipis all faced the east, from whence came the sun.

What fun we youngsters were having! We played from the first rays of the morning light right into the late twilight. The boys had many games that I had never seen. One was played with a piece of bone about four inches long, probably a piece of a steer's rib, with two ten-inch feathers in one end of it. With a full-arm underhand throw, we would let that go with all our strength, seemingly aiming to hit the ground twenty feet ahead, but the curve of the rib bone made it rise, and, balanced by the properly trimmed, trailing feathers, it would sail through the air for a long distance.

There was considerable skill required in this game, as

the smallest boy could outthrow me, and I was a husky youngster.

Then we would shoot at a mark and for distance with bow and arrows, and go out to the pony herd and ride horses that needed to be worked; and after a long swim in the cold water we would gather on the bank of the river and tell stories. . . . They would tell of the meat they had killed, the peaks they had climbed to get eagle feathers for their fathers.

I would watch their eyes glow while I told of wires that talked and iron horses on iron tracks running through big camps of many tipis built like the peaks they climbed for eagle feathers, and more people in one camp than there were Sioux on the prairies.

They drew away, awed and puzzled, and looked to the aged squaw that came upon us, and with shaking finger she pointed into the distance and grumbled, disjointedly:

'Mite oihanple canku yu ksan ksan ye yin na i hanke.' (Trail . . . long . . . winding . . . to land of dreams.)

Thin ice was beginning to form near the shores of the river. We would be snowed in for the winter if we did not leave. The night before our departure will live long in my memory!

They gave my father a farewell party in the Council Lodge and I was allowed to sit beside him. I never shall forget the beautiful talk made by Lone Bear. I could not understand it in Sioux and but little better through the interpreter — it was beyond me. It dealt with what was almost a religion symbolically taught — it told of the troubles of the white and the red people; how they were climbing the same mountain on opposite sides, and that one day they would reach the top together, and there be

54

close to the roof of heaven, and that then there would be no more trouble; that the Great Spirit would see and talk to them both — all the time.

It is not for me to attempt to right the wrongs of the Indian. Western men of position — scouts, statesmen, and United States Army officers who knew Indians and fought them — have repeatedly, over their own signatures, fairly shrieked their disapproval of the treatment of the Indian. But I can say this: I respect my Government; I am an American — top-sides, bottom, and through my body from every angle! I am for America to my last breath — but so is an American Indian!

To those who claim superiority of race — the white over the red — physically, mentally, spiritually, or morally, I can only say, 'Arrant drivel.' I am not a psychologist or an historian — I am stating facts.

The camp was astir early. Dogs were barking and all the Indian children were out to see their playmate start on a long trail. With us were the interpreter and two other Indians, making their yearly trip to the pipestone quarry to get a supply of an argillaceous stone, which they baked and carved into pipes.

The quarry was located on the border-line of Minnesota and Dakota, in a direction that was almost an air line, on our way home, and would save us at least two hundred miles of travel over going out as we came in.

There were no words spoken on either side when we left, but it was felt to be a sad parting, and we had been there only a little over six weeks. My playmates were not so stoical when they turned back after tramping with us for a few miles; some of the younger ones cried — and I know my eyes were none too dry.

We were on the trail about three weeks. I don't know

how far we traveled, but it must have been three hundred miles, as we had to wind in and out a great deal — over hills and through valleys. I distinctly remember swimming three rivers: one, the Missouri; and one, the James — I do not remember the name of the other; they all could have been named 'Cold Waters' quite appropriately. Oh, golly! it was cold until we got dried out.

We saw an exemplification of the 'heliograph' this trip; and in all probability the United States Army got their knowledge of this method of communication from the Indians, also.

Quite frequently we passed a small camp, or met Indians on the trail; and quite frequently we communicated with them, before meeting and sometimes after we left them. This was done by the Indians in cloudy weather by smoke signals, making a smudge fire with grass or brush and regulating the signals with a blanket. This is done very easily — short puffs or long puffs of smoke, with various spaces between, are easily made.

But the 'heliograph,' as I will call it, is far more intricate and can be made far more reaching in its results. The sun must be shining; the Indian then takes his looking-glass, which is about three times the size of a silver dollar, and when the sun's rays strike it he moves the glass in such a manner as to shoot flashes of light in any direction and of any length and with any space between that he desires.

The Indians must have a code, for they carry on extensive conversations — I have seen them do it.

The small looking-glass is a powerful factor in any trade with an Indian. He will give almost anything to obtain one. In addition to using them for signaling, they use them as ornaments on their blankets. They also use them to find little isolated hairs on their faces which they pull out. A full-blood Indian never has hair on his face; some Southwestern tribes have patches of beard here and there, but it can be attributed to their Spanish blood. The Sioux, Cheyenne, Crow, Blackfeet, or any plains-tribe of Indians, never have hair on their faces.

At the pipestone quarry we had another parting. The three bucks with ponies stopped here. It is not the custom among Indians to shake hands to greet each other on meeting, or to say good-bye when parting. As it is the white man's custom, they do this merely as an act of courtesy toward the white man. There is no equivalent for 'How do you do?' in Sioux, so the Indian says, 'How, kola!' meaning, 'How do you do, friend!'

Therefore, it added a bit of feeling to our leave-taking when all three of the Indians shook hands warmly with my father and me, and said, 'Me ta kola be, good-bye' — meaning, 'My friends, good-bye.'

They neither looked at nor spoke to the packer; they did not care for him, and Indians never conceal their feelings. Again, I cannot remember how far we traveled before we left the packer.

But I know we landed at Rochester, Minnesota, on the train, and caught one of the mill teams to Orinoco, which we called home.

Nothing occurred during the winter that had any practical bearing on my growing up, except that I continued to grow. I did not see any more bears. The Indian village had moved away. There was nothing between me and school, so I attended.

We had great news at Christmas-time, though; my mother and sisters and little brother were coming home! My mother's health was almost completely restored, and the doctor promised that as soon as the hard part of winter was over she could come West.

There was a chinook in March, and how vividly I remember what a picnic my father and I had! There was no available house in town, so we built one, about two miles above town, on the bank of the Orinoco River. My father did the work and I sort of bossed the job and was general errand boy.

Trees were felled; a log cabin was raised one Sunday with help from the men at the mill, and rough furniture, including the bedsteads, was fashioned from young saplings. All was made ready, and one day early in April my father and I waited for the stage.

The road ran right past the cabin. When we saw the six-horse team coming splashing through the mud, the driver laying on the whip to make time in the heavy going, I seemed to get light-headed, and suddenly I was standing by the smoking horses and my mother was hugging me. She had my little brother in her arms and she was crying, and I could see my dad carrying the two girls into the cabin — he had them both in his arms. The eldest girl had been left with our grandmother in the East, so she could go to school.

My! My! My! What a reunion! The table was soon set, even to wooden spoons that my father had made. The kettle was steaming, the logs were crackling and throwing sparks in the fireplace, candles were lighted! Never was a pioneer cabin more ablaze with all the joy of living and all the affection that could come from human hearts.

My father's former partner, the Sioux, had sent my father word asking him to go in with him on building a mill on a site owned by his uncle. It was to be located at Zumbro Falls, on the Zumbro River. My father thought well of the proposition and I was made ready to carry his answer.

It was a sixty-mile journey. The stage would only carry me about forty miles, and twenty had to be made on foot. The rivers were running high at this season of the year, which made the hiking part not so good. When the stage drove away and left me at the crossing of the trails, I did not feel so good, either. The company of another boy, or even a dog, would have meant a whole lot.

My instructions were to follow the trail for about twelve miles, keeping to the left, when another trail crossed mine; then off to the right, about two miles back from the trail, I would see a ranch house where I could stop overnight. In some way, I walked four miles past the ranch house without seeing it and landed at Zumbro River. It was boiling and running away out of banks, absolutely impossible for any human or any animal to make a crossing, and my destination was four miles beyond its opposite bank. It started to rain — a cold rain — and I lost much valuable time by sitting down and starting to snivel.

But darkness will take the idle fear out of any boy and put real fear into him very quickly, and darkness was not coming on — it was on. It seemed to grow pitch dark in five minutes. Then I did what I should have done an hour before; I started back to search for the ranch house, four miles distant. I once read of General Grant's son running away and following, through a night of mud and terror, the army of which his father was general. I know just how he felt. If I were an artist I could draw how he felt, for I felt it too, on my night of mud and terror.

When the ranch dogs met me with many savage barks, snarls, and growls, I fairly took them in my arms and kissed them. And the dogs *knew!* The rancher and his

59

sons, who came running down the road, said, 'They must have knowed, 'cause old "Slim" at night is mean.'

The table had been cleared, but a place was soon set and I was filled, refilled, and then filled again with hot supper. They spoiled me with food and then told me I was a regular young hero. And, oh, golly! how I did eat that as well as the supper!

Yes! I was a *messenger*, probably the first in that country. I pulled out my credentials, the letter I was carrying, and let them all hold it in their own hands. There were only two things that kept me from having won the Battle of Waterloo; first, I had never heard of it; and second, I fell asleep. A twenty-mile walk through the mud and drizzle, a big supper, and being a hero, had been too much for a small boy. The rancher had carried me up to the attic room, but I awakened while he was undressing me, and, remembering I was a hero, insisted on doing it myself. I thought I saw a trace of a smile on his good face as he disappeared down the stairs.

So to feel secure again in my hero position, I told the other three kids in the bed that if they wanted to dream of a hangin' all they had to do was to put their suspenders over their neck and go to sleep. I did, before the sound of my voice had died away. And oh, horrors! whether it was the mental suggestion in my own kid mind, or too much supper, or the suspenders around my neck, or sleeping four in a bed, I do not know. I only know I disgraced myself. I woke up yowling like a coyote, and there were all my bed-fellows sitting up scared, and the rancher's head appearing above the floor, a candle in his hand, his kindly voice saying, 'Go to sleep, son; you know I think you're *man* enough to make that ford in the mornin'.'

A Dangerous Crossing

Good man! He knew! He knew! *He knew!* what it was to be a boy!

We were at the ford of the river shortly after what should have been sunup, only there was no sun. It was a dark, cloudy morning, and the old Zumbro was still running wild. It was a formidable outlook. The rancher had brought his two hired men and his five sons, the eldest being about sixteen. All were mounted, including myself, so we were just a bit formidable ourselves. At any rate, the rancher was not of the 'quitter' type. He decided to make the attempt.

I do not know whether or not he did it purposely, but he chose his own eldest son to cross with us. I will always believe that, as he was risking the life of another man's son, he risked the life of his own; he seemed to be of that kind of timber.

It took nearly an hour before the place of crossing was selected. We were all placed; the rancher, myself, and the eldest son were upstream, a full quarter of a mile; the next two sons and the two ranch hands being placed at distances about two hundred yards apart, wherever a bank jutted out into the stream; the last one downstream being a ranch hand, with the next best swimming horse to those that we had. This man was two hundred yards below the ford proper. The saddles were removed and all was ready.

The horses had horse sense and fought a bit before taking to the water, but once in the stream they battled like the noble animals they were — and it was a battle. The rancher and his son quit their horses and grabbed their tails, but on account of my lightness, and on account of (what I will always believe) having been given the best horse, it was not necessary for me to do this. My horse fairly lunged through the water.

We were being swept downstream so swiftly that the opposite bank seemed to be going upstream, but the rancher had figured well. Two hundred yards below the regular ford, we made it. We were just opposite the farthest downstream ranch hand on the other side.

Half an hour later, I stood on the bank and watched the father and son go back as we had come — the son riding my horse with his swimming riderless beside them.

The Sioux Indian was glad to see me, and I never was more impressed in my life by any human being than I was by his uncle. He was a full-blood, about fifty years of age, fully six foot six in height, weighing about two hundred pounds, straight as an arrow and not an ounce of fat on his frame. He was the most inspiring figure of a man that I have ever seen, as he stood with his long black hair wafted by the breeze; a worn pair of trousers, a hickory shirt, and Sioux moccasins his only apparel.

A month later our little family was established at Zumbro Falls. It was hard to leave the little Orinoco log cabin — but the frontier was hard. There were four houses in Zumbro Falls. Our house had been a store and had a false front, like the house we lived in at Portland. There was a bridge across the river near our place; it had heavy stone abutments that were bulwarks against the powerful Zumbro and fine guardians for the light wooden structure they supported. We once found my baby brother lying flat on his stomach in the middle of this bridge looking at the baby in the water.

The mill had been built and my father was installing the machinery. It was half a mile up-river on the opposite side. The giant Indian, Running Elk, or, as he was called,

John, with about twenty Indians assisting, was building the milldam. What a glorious picture this Indian made standing on the farthest pier as the stones were being wheeled out and dumped into the last log section! The river that was being checked as it crashed its way through its last escape seemed a background picked by a sculptor. Stripped to the waist, he resembled some bronze Hercules of tradition.

I saw a great deal of this man, as he was in almost constant consultation with my father about the work. I am glad I did; it is good to remember such a man.

There was no school within twenty miles and I was correspondingly happy, but I was at an age when mental or physical occupation is necessary. I was husky and was beginning to be looked at not unkindly by any one needing an extra hand at small wages. I was hired by a rancher to drive plow, at fifty cents per day.

When I reported to 'hitch up,' I found it to be 'yoke up.' My horses were fourteen-hundred-pound steers, and there were four of them. Two yoke of heavy steers pulling a plow through land that was almost virgin soil sure made a whip-lash out of a boy at the plow handles. I did it for a few weeks, and then my father made me give it up. The ranch was close in and I lived at home, and it kept my mother up half the night getting my four o'clock breakfast and starting me off, which she insisted on doing.

Two things stand out in my memory in connection with my 'bull-whacking.' One was the consummate indifference that the whackees developed when they learned that I did not have an arm strong enough to hurt them. Steers, like all cattle, love to lie down, so whenever the spirit moved them, regardless of time, place, or suitability, down they would go, and a tired boy boss could do as he doggone pleased about it. Golly! How I walloped those steers. I worked hard at it. I did it in relays; as soon as I could get my breath, I was my own relief. But they just ignored me. When they had rested, they would get up and work, not before. The steers were right and I was wrong. They did more work under their system of resting when they needed it than they would have done under mine. Our boss knew well every furrow that could be turned in a day's work and he never complained — that was sufficient evidence.

From massive bulls to 'dainty prairie chickens' is a long jump. That is the other thing that is hooked up with my engagement. These birds of the prairie were so many that they would not rise, but just strut to one side as we plowed through their flock. Domestic fowl could not have been more indifferent. I can safely say there were hundreds of thousands of these beautiful birds. They had a peculiar cry. The 'hen' would call, at a soprano pitch, 'Chuck-a-luck! Chuck-a-luck! Chuck-a-luck!' and the cock would answer in deep bass, 'Boom-Boom-Boo! Boom-Boom-Boo!' They are so delicate, so graceful, and so small that they do not take up much room. What a pity that they should go the way of the buffalo!

About this time there seemed to come a tenseness into the life of our little community that bordered on distrust. Two of America's best fighting generals with fully equipped forces had been sent by the War Department to the Big Horn country to destroy Indians that were considered hostile. The news that filtered back to us was most astounding. The acknowledged leader of all Indian-fighting generals had been decisively beaten and forced to retreat while his brother officer, noted for his dare-devil courage, ten days later, when attacking an Indian village, was completely annihilated.

Thermopylæ had its one soldier left that carried the news of its defeat; the Alamo died to a man, as did this other command of brave American soldiers and their picturesque leader.

These disastrous battles took place several hundred miles west of us, but the main body of the Sioux, probably 75,000, with 20,000 of them fighting men, were on the reservation, not over three hundred miles away from us. Also in our immediate country, while outnumbered by whites, there were enough Sioux to cause anxiety in the event of trouble. As late as 1913 there were still 11,338 Indians in Minnesota, outnumbering Montana by seven, which had 11,331.

Instead of going home one night at quitting time, my father remained in the mill. He was smoking, and his face wore that thoughtful look that I had grown to know so well. I saw my father looking at me, and suddenly he seemed to decide on something. He called me to him and said, 'Son, John and some of his Indians are coming in to see me in a little while; do you want to stay?'

'Yes,' I replied quickly.

'Well, you may be able to help John and me some in our talk,' he said, 'but do not talk unless asked to interpret, just listen.'

John and the Indians came and they all smoked — white man's and Indian pipes — and they all smoked for a long time. Then my father talked, and then John talked. I had very little interpreting to do on either side. John spoke English very well. When my father had finished, he had told them of our Dakota trip and of all the hopes that he had had; that those hopes had not yet died, that they were still strong in his breast. He spoke of his admiration and respect for the Indians, their clean living and the simplicity of their lives. And then he told of the beautiful talk made by Lone Bear, that 'one day the reds and the whites would meet on the top of a high mountain, close to the roof of heaven.'

When John talked, he told that Lone Bear was dead; that nearly all of the Indian men that we had met on White River were dead; the whole village had moved to the Big Horn country; that they were a hunting party with their women and children with them, and were in camp when attacked by the soldiers.

'John, how do you know this?' my father said.

The Indian replied, 'We knew it one sleep after each fight!'

'But,' said my father, 'there were no men posted to signal; the country is rough and with many mountains. How could you get information so soon?'

John placed his hand upon my head, but he looked at my father, and then replied, slowly and impressively: 'I will tell you. The Indians have a way of talking through the air — that is known only to a few of the older chiefs. No one is admitted to this inner circle until there is a vacancy caused by death. We knew everything two moons ago. We knew our warriors were crying loud in victory, but we also knew our women sang the death song of the Sioux and the Cheyenne. That is why our hearts have all been sad.'

My father's voice was low. 'John,' he asked, 'is the old chief that can read words through the air near your people here?'

'I am the old chief,' the Indian replied.

Our meeting ended. John took my father's hand in his

66

A TYPICAL SCENE OF THE WEST OF MY BOYHOOD

Big Foot's band at grass dance on the Cheyenne River, August 9, 1890

and looked into his eyes. If an Indian looks straight at you when talking, it is good; if he looks past you, it is not so good.

I do not know, but perhaps the lives of a stout-hearted white man and a little white boy had been a bit helpful as arbiters of destinies.

CHAPTER V

TWO FUGITIVES AND A CIRCUS

A LADY lived a few hundred yards from us who had some chickens. She used to give me pennies if I could find the nests of the recreant hens that were holding out on her. The hunting ground in which I found the most game was a strawstack at the rear of the barn. If any one had been in that locality one July morning, he would have seen a boy wearing a 'fright wig' on the Western prairie. In my search for nests, I had seen the straw wiggle.

It was not a mistake. I *saw* it wiggle. The sly old hen was just underneath . . . I must be cautious or I should scare her and make her break the eggs, and then there would be no pennies. Slowly, stealthily, my hand moved down underneath the straw, but it was no feathered bird I grasped; it was something hard, and it pulled and wriggled. And the harder it pulled, the harder I pulled, when back I went on my haunches with an empty boot in my hand, only to scramble to my feet and see a man's stockinged foot and head and shoulders sticking out of the straw. And oh! horrors! Up came another face alongside of the first one. I stayed not upon the order of my going, but 'I went.'

In less time than nothing a breathless boy was gasping to his father in a mill — and in a not much longer time a man and boy were both back at the strawstack. Two men stood with sheepish grins on their faces, and all my father said was, 'It's all right. Sam, this is my boy.' And then he said something about night that I could not hear and pointed to where our house was.

A Hold-Up

The one big room of our house had a curtain through the middle. My father and mother and the other children slept at the rear of the curtain, while I had a makeshift bed in front that was bundled up in the daytime.

As a dream! I can remember waking in the night and being half-asleep, and hearing my father talk to two men, and hearing him say: 'Sam, you see that boy lying asleep there! Well, I wouldn't take a chance of going to the pen and being shut up away from that boy for the rest of my life for all the money on earth.'

Perhaps I dreamed this — I do not know. I only knew that among the men caught in a hold-up in the north a short time afterwards there was one that wore a suit of clothes that had belonged to my father. Years afterward my mother told me that my father had given the man his best suit of clothes and ten dollars stage fare to leave the country. Sam had once worked alongside of my father in a mill.

I know what a big circus is — one with three rings and lions and tigers and elephants and beautiful ladies on swings, way up in the air — all at the same time. I was at one (the largest in the world) three years ago. I had with me six children with tin horns, flags, and peanuts in one hand and a bunch of taffy candy in the other, with much of the latter smeared all over their faces.

I have enjoyed such circus joys, whenever the opportunity presented itself, all my life, but there never was in this wide, wide world but one circus, one 'Greatest Show On Earth,' and that gave its world-renowned performance at Zumbro Falls, Minnesota . . . in a flour mill!

'The Greatest Show On Earth' arrived in two schooner wagons. The owner and his wife and their necessities of life occupied the first wagon, and the whole circus, encompassed in the person of the driver, was in the second wagon, together with cannon balls, trapezes, hoops of fire, and such things that it is necessary to have in 'The World's Greatest Show.'

Before the wagon train of 'gilded cages' in the form of two canvas-covered Studebakers had come fairly to a stop, I was engaged as manager, from provider of hay for two tired teams to securing the 'lot' for 'The World's Greatest Show,' and the necessary properties that all first-class shows need in their local showing.

Then, as now, politics must have been practiced in the show business, for, in spite of the 'grand' sites that I reported as available for the location, the fat man that rode in the first wagon and owned the show selected a 'lot' which I had overlooked — the interior of the flour mill — which I, as *manager*, promptly secured.

Of course, my duties also included advertising. The fat owner, from his office in the flour mill, dealt out flaring bills, which he took out of a black trunk marked with white letters on its side, 'The World's Greatest Show' — 'Advance Car.'

Inside of two days I had ridden a rancher's best saddle-horse almost to death, but every ranch barn within thirty miles, any direction, had been plastered with pictures of lions and tigers and elephants — all with their mouths wide open as if they could not help announcing the merits of 'The World-Famed Show.'

The only performance of this mastodontic achievement of entertainment was to take place during the evening at the flour mill, with no advance in prices — *and* — at four o'clock in the afternoon on that day, would be given *free* the greatest outdoor exhibition ever seen in the world;

a daring feat attempted by only one man on earth, who received, at Minneapolis and Chicago, five hundred dollars for each and every time he so risked his life.

At 4 P.M. on the eventful day, Mons (I forget his name, but it was the driver) would walk across the Zumbro River on a slack wire, far above the heads of the throng that would congregate, etc., etc., etc., etc.

Everybody in that part of the country came to the show. I am quite sure; counting men, women, and children, there were forty people present.

While waiting at the bridge for the big act, some of the ranch hands that had ridden in got to making their horses jump a bit. That was the cue for calls from the crowd of 'Ride him, cowboy!' — 'Knock on him, Dave!' — 'Oh! you Jimmy!' And in a very few minutes there were horses bucking all over the place. I was on one, too! I had on my beaded cap that the Indian woman had made for me, which gave me a 'circus' appearance, and, golly! wasn't I proud, for my horse jumped splendidly. My dear mother was nearly frightened to death, so my father told me to quit, and I did. Among some things that were always held dear by my mother and that were placed in safe keeping after her death, there is a boy's beaded cap.

From the attempted spirit of levity in which I have tried to describe the pitiably small, meager wagon show, it would probably follow that the show would be awful. But that is the result of my inability to express myself properly. The show was not 'awful' — it was distinctly good. I say it in all seriousness. I shall never forget it. The owner told my father before leaving that the acrobat was one of the greatest in his line, but his enemy was drink.

There was a rimrock bank on one side of the river near

the bridge. A wire was staked on top of this high bank and run to the top of the bridge in the middle of the river. The distance was considerable, and the wire slack. When our driver friend was in the middle of it in his red tights and wearing my beaded cap, which he had taken from my head, much to my delight, he rocked and swayed like an enormous swing. It was a great feat!

At the show that night there first appeared the fat man. He played the violin beautifully, also the banjo, cornet, and tambourine. His wife, dressed as a colored mammy, sang little Southern darky songs, and then in white face she sang 'The Last Rose of Summer' and 'Ben Bolt.' She had a well-modulated, sweet, wholesome voice.

The driver! The *driver* was a paragon! He turned one and two somersaults, backward and forward, and then turned them continuously until he made a complete circle of the stage. He did innumerable stunts, including the giant swing on the horizontal bar. He twisted his body into almost unbelievable shapes, and, to top it all, doubled himself up and worked his body through a small steel ring. Each performer appeared three times during the show, and it really was an excellent performance.

We were sorry to see the two wagons pull away. My father would take no theater percentage, so for my managerial ability the driver presented me with his small steel hoop that he worked his body through. I am quite sure that under ordinary circumstances I should have kept it for many years, but after a fond but cussing father had filed until the sweat ran off his chin to release his doubled-up, yelling offspring from its grip, I lost interest.

CHAPTER VI

THE EAST

My dear mother was ill. A doctor had been brought from Lake City, many miles away, and he told my father that she needed expert surgical attention that was beyond his ability, as he was a doctor of medicine, and that it was imperative to take my mother to some big surgeon at once or her life would be in grave danger.

No money was coming in; the mill was not yet completed and ready for grinding wheat; so my father turned over his share and interest in the mill to the Indian. Once more the dream of a Western home was dimmed.

On the little station platform at Rochester, our little family was waiting to go East. A giant of the rails was coming to separate us. This time I was to accompany my mother and sisters. They needed me. My father was turning his face to the Northwest. He must earn money to support his family, and then he hoped once more to go to the country that he and I had covered together, ever seeking the permanent little Western home.

My hand was clasped in my father's. I looked out over the prairie. A vibration filled the air. The giant of the rails was coming.

'Pa, aren't we ever coming back?' I asked.

'I don't know, Willie,' my father replied. 'Only God knows that.'

And we never did go back to see that Western sun set in silence. It was the end.

The six or seven months that I lived in the city of my birth were not kind to me. It took what money my father could send to pay for medicine and medical attention for my mother. We lived at Crow Hill on Washington Street, opposite a graveyard. We had two rooms in a little frame house. My eldest sister went to work in a soap factory. I sold newspapers.

There was a place called the long dock, where coal cars were emptied. Boys used to jump into these moving cars and pick up stray pieces of coal as the train was pulling away. It was called 'picking coal.' I was one of these boys. Except in very cold weather, I could get enough coal for our needs.

There was a place where several of us barefooted newsboys used to congregate to keep warm. It was a bakery, corner of First and Colden Streets. We stood on the iron grating. I can remember vividly the precise location of every stand of cakes and cookies and exactly how they looked through the frost-covered window-pane.

A clergyman stopped one day and wanted to give me a pair of shoes. I would not take them, so he had me agree to keep the snow shoveled off the sidewalk in front of his church and rectory until Christmas-time. I agreed to that and took the shoes. I used the clergyman's shovel and earned quite a bit shoveling off other people's sidewalks in the same neighborhood.

We moved to a cheaper rent; it was out on Western Avenue, near a little brick chapel that was connected with the church where I kept the sidewalks clean.

Somehow I got two rabbits — I kept them in our hallway. I walked a long way out in the country to get something for the rabbits to eat. A farmer gave me some turnips, and then employed me for two weeks, at fifty cents a day, cutting the tops off turnips. He called it 'topping' turnips. I worked in a barn as early and late as I could see.

My mother asked me to go to the little brick church to Sunday School. I went to please her, but got into a peck of trouble — they heard my voice. It ended in my having to go to the big church, where I shoveled snow, and sing on Christmas Day. I was the soloist, and an adult, paid choir accompanied me. The minister gave my mother *five dollars* for my services.

A big, well-dressed, well-fed boy laughed at me, and said that I had a 'voice like a girl,' and I whipped him. A few days afterward, when I was shoveling snow, he hit me on the head with the spoke of a wagon wheel. I was unconscious for some time.

I got along finely with most Eastern boys, only they did not understand me or my ways. I could only play Indian games, and I always talked about Indians. So they named me 'Indian.' I did not mind — Indians to me were great people, good, kind people, and wonderful fighters.

But one day some of the boys yelled loudly and made funny noises by putting their hands over their mouths and taking them away without ever stopping yelling. We all had a fight, and, while I did not get hurt worse than any of the other boys, it hurt my heart, oh, so much! I went home and cried all the time for two or three days. I seemed to feel that I had been responsible for bringing my Indian boy friends into ridicule. I could not understand how or why it could be so — I only knew it was so — and I blamed myself.

Never, never, never again did I speak of the West or of Indians — no one understood them, nor understood me when I spoke of them — the West I knew and revered could not be understood. So never after did I volunteer any information of my past Western life. This gave rise

75

to a peculiar situation, one that has had a unique bearing and influence on my life. It will explain to many boys and young men who knew me in early youth why they never heard of my Western upbringing.

My father came East; he had been for some months in the heart of the Indian country. He had again been unable to secure a water-site and a home for his family. He told us sad things! The War Department had ordered the soldiers to follow and fight the Indians, all winter. This meant cruel, horrible suffering, both for the white soldier and the red Indian. It was awful in its hardship and devastation. It made all thinking people stand almost dumb and wonder if God had indeed turned away from his children. Old people, women, and children were being attacked in their tipis and shot down in the snow and brush as they tried to run away.

My father took me to school, but I could not get in, as we did not have the money to buy the books to start with.

We moved again — this time to Cart Alley, a little blind street about one block long that ran off Academy Hill. On one side were stables where stores kept their horses and wagons, and on the other side were small frame houses. We lived on the top floor of one of these houses. The basement was occupied by a deaf and dumb cobbler. I could not understand his finger talk, but he could understand many of my hand talk signs. I used to like to visit with him. He had a young wife, and his son ran away with her.

My father had a few weeks' work breaking stones for the city with a sledgehammer. The clergyman got the work for him — his pay was sixty cents a day.

Then, my father said good-bye to us all and started for the northern part of the State, where there were some flour mills. He took three dollars to pay his fare to Troy.

In the Suburbs of New York

I walked across the Hudson River with him on the ice. My father met a man on the ice that he knew and talked to him and I saw him hand the man something. At Fishkill Landing my father did not want me to wait for the train to come — he sent me home. . . . That night a meat-market man came and left us a shoulder of bacon that cost three dollars — it had been paid for. I never knew how my father got to Troy.

Some millers at Troy told my father of a mill at West Farms that was putting in a new set of mill burrs and needed a stone dresser. So after working at Troy as an extra hand long enough to get railroad fare, my father went to West Farms, New York City, and secured the work. And on one of the first barges that went down the Hudson River when the ice broke up was our little family.

We were in the suburbs of the foremost city of the world — we were prosperous and very happy. I swam in the Bronx River in the summer and skated on it in winter. My father sent me to a private school in Morrisania, and when the West Farms public school opened I attended that. After school hours my father had me at the mill with him and started to teach me to dress millstones. When we went West again and I grew up, I was to become a miller and help in running our own mill.

On Sundays I attended Grace Church with the family, and also attended Sunday School. Here my Nemesis was once more on my trail; when the Sunday-School teacher quietly urged me to 'please try and sing just a little bit,' I was undone. There was no concealing those hateful tones if I made even a gurgle. Every head was at once turned trying to locate that soprano-alto, or 'whatever-the-hell-it-was' voice. And at Christmas-time, there I was

77

again, doing my stunt with the professional choir of adults accompanying me.

The boys started the old snickering stuff, but they only *started!* All my past wrongs came to the surface with a hundredfold force, and, backed by doubled-up fists and a well-fed body, my belligerent attitude commanded not only the laying off of direct insults, but just a little bit of nebulous respect, such as, 'Gee! He sings nicer'n my *sister,* an' she sings in a the-a-ter in Harlem.' This was such a concession, in view of past experiences, that I was glad to allow the matter to rest with his *ipse dixit.*

There was a miller who worked with my father who had been a professional performer in a circus. He could lie on his back and keep a barrel spinning in the air by kicking it. Whether this man was responsible for the offer or not, I do not know. I only know that a representative of Barnum's Circus came to my father and wanted to take me on the road with the circus to sing. My father just smiled and said, 'No!' My father *knew!*

About this time something happened that hurts me to record. It is so large in my memory that, did I live to be as old as Job or Jacob, I could never forget.

Our little home Christmas tree had nice presents for all us children, and a big orange for every child. I ate my orange, stole another, and ate that also. . . . The smallest child, my baby brother, was the one that did not get any orange. . . . I can see his manly little face, brave in disappointment, now as I write — through eyes that are filled with tears.

My father met with an accident; his hand was caught in some machinery (a conveyor) in the mill. It was pulling his whole arm in and would have torn him apart. He braced himself and pulled his crushed arm free. The back of his hand from the wrist down was torn off. He was home for some weeks.

Our little baby boy was with him almost constantly. I can remember well his 'Who cut oo han', Pa?'

And then God touched this wonderful little boy with His hand, and he went away. . . .

How strange are the minds of children! I can remember going skating just the same after we had placed my little brother in his cold grave; I can remember, also, many nights when my mother would awaken me and tell me to go find my father. I always found him with his mangled arm at the same place — my little brother's grave — his great heart was breaking!

Years afterward (it was winter, too), when I was leading man with Madame Modjeska, I rode in an undertaker's wagon to West Farms, and a former playmate and I disinterred the little boy and took him to Greenwood Cemetery and placed him beside his father, who loved his little Western 'Trimbell boy' so much!

My mother's health was very bad and there were several doctors called in consultation. This, coupled with my father's accident and my little brother's death, made it necessary that I go to work. I secured work as errand boy with a butcher.

The doctors took my mother to the Women's Hospital, in New York, where an operation was performed. My mother was there for many weeks. I left my butcher's boy place and got work as helper on an express wagon. It made daily trips to the city, and I wanted to be able to see my mother. The wagon passed the hospital twice every day. Her room was on the top floor, and when she was getting better she used to wave to me. Once every week I was allowed to go in and see her.

Honesty was always taken for granted in our family to such an extent that I scarcely knew what dishonesty was. It seems wrong to say it, but honesty carried to extremes places those who are so rigidly taught it at a disadvantage when dealing with those who have not been held so closely to the line.

I remember once carrying a heavy trunk up three flights of stairs. The lady gave me two bright new dimes for myself. When I came back to the wagon, I gave them to the boss and he took them. And that night at One Hundred and Twenty-Seventh Street and Third Avenue he left me out on the wagon in zero weather while he ate a warm meal in a quick-lunch place. He said we had had a hard day! It was perfectly legitimate, *but that's all!*

The boss was the owner and therefore could do as he pleased, and as soon as he discovered that I could handle horses he would take an occasional day off and I did the work alone. On one such day a rear axle broke and my load was scattered all over Pearl Street, 'way downtown. I stored the merchandise in a bootblack's cellar, put the wheel in the wagon-body, rigged up a four-by-six timber under the broken axle, and made the fifteen-mile trip home . . . and I was just a boy. I could not do it now!

My next work was as 'second hand' on a Bronx River ice-wagon. I worked twelve hours a day, 3 A.M. to 3 P.M., for fifty cents. I cleaned and fed my team while the wagon was being loaded, and we started for Harlem and York-ville at about four o'clock each morning. I know we were serving ice shortly after daylight.

The 'first hand' on this ice-wagon was a full-grown man with a family. His boy had told him of my singing and that Barnum's Circus wanted to hire me. He could not understand why I would rather stagger around under a hunk of ice than go with a circus and make lots of money. He told me they might pay me twenty dollars a week. That was more money than could be counted!

I thought about it all night. Twenty dollars a week! It would mean everything for my mother, and the next morning when cleaning the horses I had made up my mind. I would tell my father that very night that I wanted to go with the circus and sing. And, to reassure myself of my new resolution and to seal the bargain, I opened my throat wide and threw back my head for the clarion tones of 'Shout the glad tidings, exultingly sing! Jerusalem triumphs, Messiah is King!'

My God! The discordant, frog-like sounds that came forth frightened the horses — my voice had changed . . . I could not sing a note . . . *and I was glad!*

My mother came home to us, pale and deprived of physical strength, but full of courage. Our little band was once more united.

The mill was sold — changed hands. The new owners brought in their own crew, which put my father out of employment. It would have been inhuman to start West with my mother at this time — and there was the school question, also, the little girls were going to school.

So my father took the big leap — we moved to the big city, little dreaming that our Western hopes were never to be realized, that the 'big city' was to be our home for many, many years.

The Everett House, at Seventeenth Street and Fourth Avenue, and the Clarendon Hotel, one block above, were under the same management. The former was my home for the next two years. I was the messenger boy for both hotels. My duties were to make two trips daily to the general post office for mail, and do such other errands as were required between the hours of 7 A.M. and 7 P.M. My salary was seven dollars and twenty cents a month. Carrying messages for guests when not performing my usual duties raised this amount considerably. The telephone had not yet been extensively installed.

They were lucrative days for the messenger boys. I quite frequently did errands for the hotel clerks and bartenders, and in return they gave me passes for theaters. When I had no pass, I would go anyhow and sit in the highest gallery for fifteen or twenty cents. With one exception it was my sole dissipation. The other exception being ice cream. The bakers used to bribe me to smuggle in pails of beer to them; and I ate quarts and quarts of lemon, vanilla, strawberry, or any old flavor. On my fifteenth birthday I weighed one hundred and fifty-three pounds.

The elder Salvini, Madame Gerster, Annie Louise Cary, Signor Brignoli, Fanny Davenport, and many other theatrical celebrities were guests at the Everett House. I once carried a huge bouquet for Clara Morris to Sarah Bernhardt on her opening at Booth's Theater. The Madame pinched my cheeks and said, 'How red they are.'

On the plains the foreman of a wagon train, when going into camp, always pointed the tongue of his lead wagon toward the North Star. If it was cloudy the next morning or if he broke camp before sunup, he had his direction. My father's 'North Star,' to which he always pointed in cloudy weather or sunshine, was a river of rippling water that had power behind it. The scorchings of fate only burnished his desire and made him stick the stronger to this direction. He never wavered.

CHAPTER VII
ATHLETICS AND ROUGH CORNERS

Our family had lived in East Seventy-Third Street, but found the rent too expensive and moved to Diamond Street, Greenpoint. My father was running a little flour mill at The Glades, Hall County, Georgia. He wrote me to send him illustrations from papers and some pictorial advertising cards. There was a white family that lived near the mill, with many children who had never seen pictures or drawings of any kind. He also wrote of a man negro that put his hand on the 'white-heat' sheet-iron stove, in the mill, when stooping down to see where the fire came from.

As the months passed, I found another outlet for my youthful energy. There was considerable excitement about running and walking races that were being held in Madison Square Garden. As I was walking constantly, I developed, and when sidewalk pedestrians could no longer give me competition, I used to spend many evenings around the hotel racing with horse cars. There was one place that lent itself admirably as a substitute race-track — Eighteenth Street, from Third Avenue to Broadway. The drivers of the one-horse cars got used to me and would race. Going over that smooth pavement at night gave me a false idea of speed, and made me think I was a wonder.

I entered a race at Madison Square Garden — the winter games of the Manhattan Athletic Club. Some one told me to eat raw onions, that they were good for my wind. So! full of onions and with a sad-looking athletic suit of old drawers, a discarded shirt, my feet encased in battered old street shoes, I was ushered into a dressing-room full of up-to-the-minute athletes. There were snickers; but they soon stopped, for, while my heart was sad, I was only nine blocks from home and I was a husky kid.

Oh! what a difference between cutting through the dark street at night with a big-hearted driver as opponent and trying to work up speed under the glare of hundreds of lights, in the midst of a yelling audience. IGNOMINIOUSLY DEFEATED! would not describe it. It seemed as though I was walking backwards, while dozens of lithe, white-clad figures flittered past. The only saving grace was that it was an eight-lap track, and I was passed so often that I was sometimes in the lead. In the dressing-room the boy that won came over and patted me on the back and smiled. He was a bright, well-bred college boy. I like to think of those things.

My father had gone from Georgia to Kansas City and had worked there, and was home again. He moved our little family from Greenpoint to One Hundred and Fifty-Second Street and Third Avenue. The girls were being kept in school. Another baby came. The little fellow weighed seventeen pounds at birth. He was normal in every way, but the heroic measures used by the doctors in his delivery caused his death in a few hours.

My father went West again, this time to Yankton, Dakota, and put a mill in running shape. They urged him to stay, but the welfare of my mother and the children's schooling demanded that we remain in the East for a time at least, so he came home. He would not be separated from his family. It was cold weather when he came home, and he brought a hind quarter of venison and a saddle-sack packed full of butter. There must have been a hundred pounds.

I had broken into the athletic game and was getting to be considered pretty good. I took my father to the American Institute Rink to see the games of the Williamsburg Athletic Club. I won the two-mile walk. My dad didn't say anything, but afterwards I learned we would have walked home had I lost. There were some twenty contestants in the race. But odds made no difference to him. HE WAS BETTING ON HIS BOY. I did not take him any more.

Some athletes working for the H. W. Collender Billiard Table Manufacturing Company got a position for me as sort of an apprentice where I could advance. It was a bad change. I left the home of two years where every one was kind to me and where I made a great deal of money for a boy. And my new apprenticeship consisted of pumping water by hand several hours a day from the cellar to a tank on the roof. I stuck it out for several months, but the pump would not wear out, and I did.

I then worked as errand boy for Charles E. Ward, a Broadway tailor. My employer was a sporting man. He had a strong liking for pugilists and professional athletes. One day a great boxer, Mike Donovan, the instructor for the New York Athletic Club, was in the store, and Mr. Ward was expressing his opinion that boxing and all athletics were soon coming into their own. As proof he showed Mr. Donovan a daily paper describing a big athletic meet at Madison Square Garden the night previous, with the cut of a struggling finish and a small inset of the winner.

'See here, Mike,' said Mr. Ward, 'eight thousand present. The wealthy people are taking it up. The best families of Fifth Avenue all have their boys fighting for athletic supremacy.'

I was passing on my way out of the store with a box to deliver. Mr. Ward saw me and looking at the inset picture said, jokingly, 'By golly! That picture looks like this boy!'

Mr. Donovan glanced at me, held the look for a few seconds, and said, 'That is the boy, Mr. Ward; I saw the race.'

'Well, I'm damned!' said Mr. Ward.

We were down to case cards. My father was making his big try to remain in the East. We were a growing family of children. It was essential that we have larger living quarters. The existing rents were beyond our means.

My father answered an advertisement for an engineer. He was not an engineer, but through his extensive knowledge of machinery he had no difficulty in going before the City Board and obtaining a license. The work was at an apartment house, in West Fifty-Sixth Street. His salary was sixty dollars a month and the basement for his family to live in. It was our home for three years. It stands there still, and I love every brick and stone in it.

Two of my sisters attended Fifty-Fourth Street School. The school was considered one of the best, and the neighborhood very high-class. The elder of the two school children was canny and outwitted the girls that walked home with her; but the younger was soon discovered, and when sufficient time had elapsed for the little playmates to tell their mothers that a little girl they walked home with lived in a basement, the little girl that lived in a basement walked home alone.

It hurt! It must have hurt! All little girls love their playmates and love attention. But perhaps it was just

86

as well — perhaps it held off other hurts; for this little girl could not attend the school receptions nor class graduation exercises. She had only one dress and she wore that to school every day; she wore it when she was given her prize by the teacher during school hours. I can remember her having but one new dress, that being the one in which she graduated at Normal College. She was handed a first prize there, too! This little girl's name was Mary. She abides with me still.

I never had but two ambitions. One, to go to West Point; the other, to go on the stage. The desire to become a United States Army officer was probably born of my Western life. Soldiers and forts were a part of the West. The stage idea just came, always remained, and will be with me when the final curtain is rung down.

I talked to my father. He liked the army idea, but explained to me how woefully lacking I was in education, and how improbable it was that with the most strenuous work I could learn enough to pass an examination to enter West Point in a short space of time.

As to the stage — yes! I had a chance! Being a good 'jawsmith' ran in the family. But there again, he explained, I was handicapped; I was a boy only a short time removed from the prairies; a white Indian boy with many of the Indian characteristics. I was not uncouth; I was gentle in manner; but I was strange, and all the rough corners would have to be rubbed off and smoothed down by education and cultured surroundings before I could ever hope to become an actor. He would always hope and plan for a mill with himself and me in it, but I was his son and what I wanted he wanted, and he would help me to get it with every possible effort.

He advised that I take fencing and dancing lessons and go to Europe. He explained that England was an older country than ours; that it would be well for me to travel and see the result of ages of proficiency in all arts — to rub shoulders with knowledge and stability.

He said: 'America is the flower of the human kingdom, the smile of the Sea. But America is new; you are of the new era; just as you are, you represent the new. You are fitted for the country you were born in; but to become an actor you must have a thorough knowledge of and be thoroughly schooled in the old — those countries that are rich with the spoils of time.'

My job as errand boy with the tailor sort of went up in smoke, and the useful salary tagged along with it. The Manhattan Athletic Club had taken me in. I was a member of the famous Cherry Diamond Track Team, which was composed of Lon Myers, Harry Fredricks, Arthur Waldron, and Jack White. I won about twenty races that summer and fall, including track meetings held at Chicago, Philadelphia, and Montreal, being second in the American and Canadian championships.

I was seventeen years old. This fact was brought home to me quite forcibly while we were on tour. The Montreal natives made quite a fuss over 'the kid,' and tossed me in a blanket until I nearly hit the Windsor Hotel ceiling, but when the team was trailed around town during the evening, I was trailed off to bed. It was my just due, however, for I was as much behind the team in ability as I was in years. Lon Myers was a world-famous runner, and the others were only a notch below him.

The medals and cups I won for athletics were quite pleasing to look at — as long as I had them, but I never

THE MANHATTAN ATHLETIC CLUB HAD TAKEN ME IN

had them long. I think the interest I paid on them, at 'three per cent for the first six months and two per cent thereafter,' would have purchased them all many times over. I finally tore up the tickets, some ten years later, and let them go.

I secured four months' work that in no way interfered with my athletic activities. I saw a negro on horseback, all tangled up with a bunch of lead horses. I helped to straighten him out and took half his stock and followed him to his destination. It was a Riding Academy on Fifty-Sixth Street.

Oh! Shades of darky harmony!! How that colored boy could play the mouth-organ. I tried to find him in later years. Vaudeville would have been his for life!

The boss at the stables engaged me to exercise horses in the park. My hours were 3 A.M. to 9 A.M., for which I received one dollar per day, seven days a week. Golly! I was sorry when I lost the job!

There had been many complaints about horses that were sent out. 'They shied' — 'They danced' — 'They jumped sideways' — 'They did skittish things.' But I knew no-thing of these reports when I went to work nor when I was questioned occasionally about this or that horse. Had I known, I surely would have been sorely tempted (in con-sideration of my seven per week) to say: 'He did jump a bit.' But, not knowing, I spoke the truth and said: 'They never do a thing with me. Tell whoever rides 'em to let up on their mouths; tell 'em to ride in the saddle and not on the bit.' I don't know whether the boss ever told them or not, but he told me I was through, and thanked me — I had talked myself out of a seven-dollar-a-week pension.

I never dressed in any studio outside of California but once. That was in the Famous Players' New York Studio.

They told me it was on Fifty-Sixth Street. It was the same Riding Academy. The stage was the tanbark ring, and I dressed in what had been one of the box stalls that housed the horses I exercised in the long ago.

That winter I worked as errand boy for another custom tailor store, in Fifth Avenue.

In January a little baby girl, to whom I was later to be father as well as brother, was born.

The old Manhattan Athletic Club Track at Fifty-Sixth and Eighth Avenue was flooded that year and turned into a skating rank. Being a member, although I never paid dues, I was allowed to skate for nothing, and I did.

An amusing incident occurred that I knew of, but was not a party to — again on account of my youth. The 'Track Gang' headed by Lon Myers and Harry Fredricks, played pool and billiards with accompanying refreshments nightly for over a month at a billiard hall across the street, as guests of the proprietor. The proprietor was selling out! The place was doing such a land-rush business that the purchaser must have had something wrong with his head. However, he bought, and, so far as I can remember, prospered; but how he must have marveled at the dropping off of his Athletic Club trade!

One night in 1918 I walked up to visit the location of the old track and was astonished to find it looking the same. It was being used as an open-air picture theater; the picture being shown that evening was one of my own.

I walked east to pass the old home where I had lived, and when I reached it I stood and uncovered my head. Two ladies, who must have recognized me, had been walking along behind.

'Too warm for you, eh, Bill?' said one, as they passed.

'It isn't much like the West, is it, Bill?' said the other!

I Win Two Cups in England

I made some stumbling, halting answer. How little they knew what those basement steps meant to me!

When spring came, my father talked to me. Athletics were getting me nowhere — I ought to make my plunge and try for a stage training — go to Europe; he had no money, he knew I had no money ... but lack of money had never stopped his going anywhere. Why should it stop his son?

I worked my way to England on the steamship Egypt. When I landed, through work, lack of food, and seasickness, I was trained down. I was in excellent condition.

The championships of England were to be held. I entered. It was a seven-mile race. The first mile was awfully fast — far too fast, considering the distance still to go. It was well under seven minutes. I was leading, and had killed off the best competitors. I considered I had the race won — but I was disqualified. There was a big hullabaloo about it, and another race was arranged a week later with the same contestants. I won it — in unusually fast time. Then, two weeks after that, they had another big, special race, at a distance of two miles. I won that, also! I just had to win those cups — I needed the money. I redeemed them later.

There was quite some talk about the whole thing. I remember 'The Spirit of the Times,' the foremost American sporting periodical of those days, published excerpts from all the articles written in both the prominent English and American newspapers, under the caption: 'We Have at Last Had a Real Anglo-American Contest Without Any Peremptory Fuss or Feathers.'

During the period of my training days and those that followed, I had a room in a tiny little cottage near the

Lillie Bridge Athletic Grounds. The mother of the family cooked any food I brought in. I paid half a crown a week for my room and the cooking, which is about sixty-two cents. I did not bring in much food, however. Raisins were my principal sustainer. I bought them at a grocer's and ate my meals as I toured London on foot.

Of all the locations that I can remember, I liked best the quaint, old places, such as Bethnal Green, with their ancient ale houses, red-faced landlords, and Bill Sikes characters — dogs and all!

With my mind on the 'rough corners,' I visited the Tower, the art galleries, and all places I could enter free. I saw Henry Irving and Ellen Terry in 'The Lyons Mail' and 'The Bells' — five times. If I could have gotten in for a penny, I would have been there every night, but my usual top gallery bench cost me sixpence, which is twelve cents! ... I could get many raisins for sixpence — and my tummy was astonishingly healthy!

Like my father, I liked to wander; but like him, also, I could not remain too long away from home. So I forgot my 'rough corners' and on the good ship Helvetia, sailing from Liverpool, I started for home — in the same manner.

My mother fed me up for two days, while she scoured and pressed my coat and trousers. I must have looked a bit like a brown-skinned thoroughbred. When the track gang saw me, they nearly ate me up — they danced around me in the old shack of a clubhouse like a bunch of Sioux warriors! I was eighteen years of age.

A few years ago I was injured. The studio doctor thought my knee was broken. I was rushed to an X-Ray specialist in my make-up, and he for once found no bones broken, but he told me that there was a piece of bone broken off and buried in a muscle that had evidently been there for many, many years. I have wondered since if that bone could have been broken off at about the time of that English race, when I was disqualified. I was certainly walking fairly, but it may have caused a temporary unconscious movement of those knee muscles that misled the judges . . . I do not know.

I secured an excellent position. Usually I could not get the good positions on account of my being short on education, but the principal element sought for in this case was honesty — and they took a chance. I was cashier at Caswell & Hazzard's Drug Store, from August until the following May. I received nine dollars per week and was off duty every other evening.

I attended a dancing school all winter, and I believe it did me much good. My two eldest sisters attended also.

I had some trouble with a clerk in the store and, as he was a druggist, and I was not, the manager of the store gave me a beautiful letter of recommendation.

I entered a civil service examination for a clerkship in the general post office, and, to my intense astonishment, I passed. When I saw my record, I shivered — I had stolen my way in. The minimum was 70 per cent and my mark was 70 and 21/100 per cent. However, I passed, and my appointment was assured. So while waiting I turned to athletics.

The latter part of May, on the new Manhattan Athletic Club Track, at Eighty-Sixth Street and Eighth Avenue — walking against time — I did eleven miles in one hour, thirty-five minutes, and six seconds. This record remained on the books for over thirty years. I saw in a daily paper where it was beaten a year ago. Lon Myers and Harry

Fredricks ran with me alternately and coached me the last four miles. I was then nineteen.

During the summer I was notified to report for work at the post office. I was appointed as a junior clerk at forty dollars per month and was assigned to the Third Division, the Department of General Distribution. I remained there over three years.

All clerks worked on different watches or 'tours.' My hours were from twelve o'clock noon to nine o'clock at night.

On going home one night and reaching our street, I saw two men fighting. It was what a lover of the game would call a 'bird of a scrap.' I halted forty yards away and watched it in the flashes of light from the street lamp. One man seemed bigger, much younger, and more agile. But the other man kept boring in, and every time he landed on the larger man's body there was a businesslike thud. A few more exchanges and one of these wallops sent the big fellow down, but the other stood and waited for him to get up, when, zowie! down he would go again. About three of those and he had enough. The next time he stayed down, and to make it good measure he rolled over on his face.

I then walked up and spoke ... Good Lord! The man looking at me was my father. 'Can ... I ... do anything ... Dad?' I stuttered. My father returned my look, took a long breath, and saying, 'Don't be a damned fool!' walked into the house!

The next day I learned that the man who rolled over on his face was a 'gentleman boarder' who lived next door and spent his leisure evening hours on the stoop and ogling the girls as they passed. My sisters going down the basement steps were his special mark. Finally they told my father. He waited until they had gone to bed and the street was deserted. The man who rolled on his face moved that night and never came back. The landlady said she couldn't understand it, as he was paid two weeks in advance.

There was an Episcopal Church on Fifty-Seventh Street. The rear of the church came within a few feet of the rear of our building. Christmas Eve, when I went home, I asked where everybody was. My mother was alone. She told me that one of my sisters had a dress and had gone to the Christmas-tree festivities in the church, and that the rest were on the back stairs trying to see her through the window.

I found my father with the two-year-old, round-eyed baby girl on his lap, and my little sister Mary seated on the stairs beside him. They had no presents and they were looking at their Christmas tree ... through two windows, from a back stairway.

Competitive examinations were started in the post office and I dug in. These examinations consisted of post-office work only. Each clerk that wanted to enter was assigned to a certain 'table.' It was studying the distribution and the time of departure of mails. The letters were all cased in different boxes. When full, the letters were taken out, tied up, and labeled to whatever railway post office they were meant for. The large cities were picked out and cased by the regular clerks that did not work on a 'table'; New York State was one table, Pennsylvania was another, the New England States another.

I was assigned to the hardest one of all, the West Table. It had Ohio, Indiana, Illinois, Tennessee, Texas, and Virginia. It also had the Territories, but they were intact and required no study. Any clerk who worked on the West Table was supposed to know the distribution of some ten thousand post offices, for, while the usual number of cards submitted was about four thousand, the clerk being examined did not know which offices would be selected.

The method of examination was standing at a case and correctly casing the cards placed there by the examiner. Speed was counted as an important factor also.

I do not know who instituted this form of examination for advancement, but I hope it has been discontinued. It was a rank injustice to the older clerks, first-class men, war veterans, heads of families; men with ten, fifteen, and twenty years of service behind them were reduced. In some cases their salaries were cut in half and their hours of labor changed to the most undesirable hours of the office. They were all good clerks, thoroughly efficient, and would accomplish just as much work in a day as the youngsters that replaced them.

I jumped from a forty-dollar a month junior clerkship to the 'Head of the Table' at one hundred dollars on the first examination. I held it through a second, and resigned holding the same position. My examination was a post-office record. I cased three thousand three hundred and eighty-three cards in one hour and twenty minutes and made only a few errors. I answered nearly three hundred dispatches and made no errors. When I resigned, I was offered a chief clerkship and the postmaster wrote me a personal letter of commendation!

Fine for the youngsters! But terrible for the older men. On our West Table after an examination one man lost his reason; one resigned and committed suicide a few months afterward.

The mental resolution to 'dig in' was made with my heart in my hand, but the realization of my hopes brought different results — results that I hate to record. Out of my one hundred dollars a month salary I gave my mother twenty dollars for my board and washing and everything else that a mother can do and kept eighty dollars for myself. My mother should have had the eighty and myself the twenty.

For nearly a year a twenty-year-old boy imagined he was a young man about town and hung around such dives as the Haymarket and Tom Gould's. Together with my hundred a month I had won the crack working hours also — 8 a.m. to 5 p.m. I had all of my evenings to myself.

It was a very narrow trail that I traveled; it was tortuous and ran along the edge of a cliff that shunted off into a mighty deep chasm. If my head had ever been light from the cup that cheers, I probably would have lost my footing — but I did not drink or smoke.

A youth who had been a boyhood companion in West Farms, and was then clerk in the postmaster's private office — a fine intelligent youngster — was my companion a great deal of the time. He became enamored of a 'lady of the evening,' and reported 'ill' too often to suit the wise postmaster. One morning when he did not come to work the postmaster personally called up to inquire about him. The lady on the other end of the wire said, 'What in hell do you mean calling us up at this hour? Why don't you call before we go to bed?'

It was 9 a.m. A dismissal from the service followed. The 'lady of the evening' did not dismiss him; he remained — it was sad!

I saw in a newspaper a few years ago that the one-time king of night life in the tenderloin, Tom Gould, was a night watchman at some new buildings under construction, uptown somewhere.

In the days I speak of, Tom Gould was a big, powerful middle-aged man, with a huge mustache and wearing headlight diamonds. If he just nodded to any one in passing, they were in the charmed circle. In appearance and bearing he was exactly what the Easterner pictures the Western gambler to have been, but never was.

I have tried to remember any printable outstanding incidents of this short period of my life, but the one that seems most prominent is favorable to the resorts. I do not recall any robberies, hold-ups, or loss of property of any description. The habitués would leave expensive garments, handbags, and even purses lying about while dancing — I never heard of any loss. Perhaps it was too easy to get the money by usual methods — I do not know. I only know the fruit of my eighty a month was but a fraction of a drop in the bucket; I was tolerated . . . that's all.

One night during my rambles I met some chorus girls; they belonged to an English company playing at the Casino. As I did not shine as a night-life Romeo, I invited these young ladies to attend the Horse Show at Madison Square Garden. They did. My afternoon of imparting what I did not know about high-stepping, many-gaited animals set me back something awful. Had they been cowponies, I could have made good, but the greater my lack of knowledge, the more money I chucked out in an endeavor to cover it up. All I owned was reposing in 'Simpson's' on the Bowery, and I owed money to every clerk in the department that I was on speaking terms with. That was my first and last dip in 'high society' for many years.

One of my sisters had secured employment in a dressmaking establishment; another had finished a course of instruction at Cooper Institute, where she learned telegraph operating, and had gone to work at the main office of a railroad company.

We had moved to Sixty-Second Street, near Ninth

Avenue, and my father was engineer in an office building downtown.

So, even with my backsliding from my duty, my mother, by attending to all household work, washing, ironing, mending, and darning for the whole family, was keeping up a New York apartment.

Like all wrongdoers who hate to face an issue squarely, I decided to run away. I censured myself by day, but rambled again at night; I knew I could not go on.

I visited the ships below Brooklyn Bridge on the East River. The captain of one sailing ship that was going out in a few days said he would take me — I could work my way. The next few nights, to keep my courage up to the sticking point, I rambled all the harder; and when the night came that I was to sneak out of my home with my bundle, I did it. My foot was on the top step of the stairs when I heard my father's voice — he was in his nightgown.

'Where are you going, Will?'

'To Australia ——!'

'How?'

'In the sailing ship Arrow!'

'When does she sail?'

'At six o'clock!'

'What's her port and length of passage?'

'Sydney! She usually makes it in five months!'

'All right! Good-bye, my boy. I'll meet you there.'

I went back to bed.

One of my sisters married. My mother had to work harder and scheme more on meals to make up for the loss of money that had been contributed toward the upkeep of the apartment.

It was a chilly morning, before daylight. I came home and could not find my front-door key. I waited in the vestibule for some one to come along and open the door. My father came out. He had to be at his engine and boilers downtown at six o'clock.

He looked at me kindly, and said: 'Will! There is so little time in life — none of it should be frittered away.' And passed on to his toil!

I did not ramble any more.

I went to my father and told him I was sorry. He made no comment. He just indicated that he understood, and placed his hand upon my shoulder. He advised me to save all the money I earned for six months, quit the post office, go to Europe, and make my bid for a stage career.

He told me that, as the family was now small, my mother and he had agreed that he should get another position where he would be allowed his rent; that this would relieve me of contributing to the household expense and give me a chance to make my effort.

With my father to decide on a thing was to do it. We were soon installed in Grand Street. The salary was seventy dollars a month and a large, airy, second-floor apartment included.

In four months I was on my way to England on the steamship Wisconsin, this time as a cabin passenger. The ship was small, the voyage frightfully rough. I contracted a violent cold. On reaching Queenstown, we learned of the terrible New York blizzard.

My first day in London I visited a dramatic instructor and paid five pounds in advance for a course of lessons in acting. I then visited a doctor, and, being an American, he filled me up to the throat with quinine; I temporarily lost my hearing.

At the Lyceum Theater I saw Mary Anderson and Forbes-Robertson in 'A Winter's Tale.' I say 'saw' them advisedly — I could not hear them; I was practically stone deaf.

Although my quarters were better than on my previous trip, the routine was the same. I had to do my own marketing and bring in my bit of food for the landlady to prepare my meals. I was lonely. I was homesick. I threw my limited wardrobe into a bag, caught a train for Liverpool, and walked onto the deck of the steamship Wisconsin just before she loosened off her mooring lines for her return trip — I was going HOME!

On my arrival, my father smiled. I believe he recognized in my actions a similarity to strange things that he in his youth had done.

Had I been gifted with second sight and acted in compliance with some fixed law, I could not have made a better move than by my seemingly crazy action of running away from London. I was soon studying with F. F. Mackey, a fine actor, a fine teacher, and, in a game where there are many charlatans, an honest man. I am grateful that I fell into his hands.

In the several months that followed, when not studying I exercised at Wood's Gymnasium, and about three days each week at daylight I would walk to the ferry at Bowling Green, and for a ten-cent fare journey to the end of the railroad line, Arrochar, on the ocean side of Staten Island. There was nothing there but the station — no habitation whatever. I could swim, do deep breathing, talk Shakespearian lines to the waves, or race against an imaginary foe on the beach — there was no one to interfere.

One day a dead man washed in on the tide while I was swimming. I remained with the body for hours before any one came. The man had been shot through the head. I never knew what became of the case.

No one ever bothered me or mine, but there was no denying that the corner of Grand and Mott Streets was a mighty tough neighborhood. Directly across the street was a green-goods game lair. I saw it worked at least once every day; the arrival with the victim; their happy businesslike entrance; then, after a lapse of usually ten minutes, the hurried exit of the decoy, followed by the hatless, disheveled victim, he in turn followed by the confederate that showed him the way to the police station; the clean-up confederate who then came out and in a few moments changed the signs and outward appearance of the place; the return of the victim with an officer — the place is locked, the victim is not positive of the location; the officer makes careful entries in his notebook. Next!

The most notorious of all the Bowery saloons and dancehalls were but a few blocks away from our neighborhood. The streets were filled with men who were ready for anything. I shouldered through them many times ... when the slightest resentment at their strange glances would have precipitated a scrap. I used to flatter myself when safely away from them that my protection was my cleancut build. But, I'm not so sure ...

Indians will not harm a crazy person; these New York toughs and jail-birds were as primitive in many ways as Indians. The room where I studied had two windows, and with me murdering Duncan and stabbing my friend Cæsar, with the usual redundancy of gesture that accompanies the full-voiced, student amateur, which action must have been plainly visible to the occupants of the surrounding tenements, it makes me wonder whether my outward physical being was my protection or not. And I'm NOT so sure!

CHAPTER VIII

THE YOUNG ACTOR

AFTER answering many advertisements that were intended to catch the unwary, and being immune on account of being penniless, I landed an engagement. Again I was fortunate, most fortunate! Daniel E. Bandmann was the star . . . and a better master to break in young actors never lived. He was on his ranch in Montana and did not join us for some months, but his leading lady, Louise Beaudet, rehearsed us just the same. All it cost was one-fifty per day rent for the hall!

We went on tour once before Mr. Bandmann joined us (a Thanksgiving Day — 'turkey date'), and although the round-trip fare by boat was one dollar, and although we gave two performances, and although no salaries were paid . . . we were so good, we lost money. The plays were 'Romeo and Juliet' for the matinée, and 'Dr. Jekyll and Mr. Hyde' at night.

My initial bow to any audience was as Friar Lawrence, and, by a strange coincidence, it occurred in the city of my birth, Newburgh, New York.

When the star arrived, all our plays were put aside and we opened in January in Tom Taylor's 'Dead or Alive,' retitled 'Austerlitz,' at the People's Theater in the Bowery. On tour we journeyed as far west as St. Louis and Milwaukee.

My salary was twelve dollars a week. It was the bare necessity of life, as I had to eat and sleep somewhere. At intervals of four or five weeks, Mr. Bandmann would call me into his dressing-room and, in the presence of his lead-

ing lady and his manager, compliment me on my studious-
ness and my work, and then, in his most gracious Svengali-
like manner, raise my salary — two or three dollars a
week. He repeated the performance regularly; it increased
to fifteen, eighteen, twenty-two, thirty — at the end of
the season I was getting a salary of thirty-five dollars a
week. But I never *got* but the twelve with which I started.

Our company was a cast of beginners. Some bluffed a
bit (laudably) and claimed experience, but they were
beginners like myself. One had been with Irving, but he
dressed wigs for the gentleman. He was an actor with us,
but on one occasion, owing to some of our troupe quitting,
Bandmann engaged an actor of experience. This actor
had been a minstrel man for many years. He wore a long
tan coat and a high hat. He was to get forty dollars a
week, but, as he never got it, he quit at St. Louis and
attached the show.

We had a few old side wings and a drop that we carried,
and these were at the depot. Our last glimpse, as the
train moved away, of our brother actor, he was sitting on
the few strips of wood and old torn canvas, wearing his
high hat, his tan coat fluttering in the breeze. His name
was Otis Turner. He was one of the pioneer movie
directors.

All actors become stranded with some show at some
stage of their career. My baptism came my first season.
Our tour was temporarily halted and we were taken into
Chicago for a short vacation and to rehearse a new play.
Mr. Bandmann was called on business to his Montana
ranch.

Miss Beaudet rehearsed us conscientiously and we in
turn rehearsed in the same manner for two weeks; but

after that period of time all of our waking moments were needed to rustle food. We stalled our landlords the first week, but the second attempt was as frigid as the weather, and it was March in Chicago.

We were out in the cold, and that did not mean figuratively either. I met one of my actor comrades several days later. We were both overcoatless. His shoes were thickly caked with clay, and his clothing was all smeared up. 'He was keeping books at a brick yard.' The damned liar! He was *carrying* bricks.

'*I was cashier at a restaurant!*' I was a damned liar, too! I was peeling potatoes at the back-alley door.

The most privacy I could find for a waking and walking night was along the Lake Front, its great disadvantage being the cold. There was shelter, however, under the old Illinois Central depot sheds.

One 'pleasant' night when cold was turning a drizzling rain to ice as it fell, I stuck close to the sheltering sheds. There were other unfortunates like myself that were doing likewise. The seating space was not great. Two males that had chosen me to sit between them sported an odor that even the bleak winds of Lake Michigan would not waft onward — I could not stand it. I arose suddenly and moved away. I was halted by a figure clothed in glistening rubber from head to feet. The figure jammed his wet gloved hand down my spine and shoved me before him, until we reached the bench from which I had started.

The figure jabbed the two ragged unfortunates until they realized their surroundings and asked them had they lost anything. They didn't have to look — they had nothing to lose. They said, 'No!' I was jabbed with the club and told to move on.

'Mister,' I said, 'do you ever say your prayers?'

The dropping of the rain on the shed was the only sound.

'Mister, before you go to bed to-night you say your prayers and thank God, for if I had a gun I'd kill you.'

There was still no sound but the dropping of rain on the shed — I walked away. Two weeks later I was home.

Louise Beaudet is now working in pictures in California.

Daniel E. Bandmann was a German Jew; he had played starring engagements in London with Henry Irving as his leading support. Many of the foremost actors of the English speaking stage owe much to Bandmann. He was bulky and almost ugly to look at, but his personality was most magnetic, and his knowledge of the art of reproducing human emotions was remarkable. He was a very old man when I was with him.

Among the many applications that I mailed seeking an engagement was one addressed to the manager of Booth and Barrett. I trembled as one palsied when a letter came instructing me to call at a certain hour to see Mr. Lawrence Barrett at the Players Club. I was engaged at twenty dollars per week for the season opening in September.

I was in such a dazed condition, through actually talking to Lawrence Barrett, that I can remember very little of that interview, but one incident was so outstanding it seemed to break through everything. It seemed then and still seems so odd! Mr. Barrett asked me the nationality of my parents. I told him my father was English and my mother was born in the North of Ireland, her parents coming to America when she was three years old. He then asked my religion. I told him 'Episcopalian,' to which he replied:

'The reason I ask, I am a Roman Catholic and Irish on both sides.'

In any subsequent happenings or affairs of the company I never heard the subject of nationality or religion mentioned again.

My father was restless. He wanted to try once more for the running stream and the mill. The husband of one of my sisters, a young railroad man, had gone West on my father's advice and was located in Washington Territory. So once more our family, filled with high hopes, moved westward. I was rehearsing in Chicago when they passed through, among them the round-eyed girl child of six, looking in wonderment at the beds that came down out of the wall.

There had been only a few rehearsals held in New York. Booth and Modjeska were to head one company, and Mr. Barrett the other; Mr. Barrett being proprietor of both companies. Mr. Barrett was first to produce a new play, 'Ganelon.' I was hoping I would be selected for the Booth-Modjeska Company, as their repertoire was to be larger on account of having two stars. But there were several of us youngsters that Mr. Barrett had picked out for 'Ganelon,' and there we remained.

Both companies left New York together. I saw Mr. Booth at the ferry — the only time I was ever close to him. He looked at me and smiled. I think he knew through his nephew, Sidney Booth (one of our gang), that some of us wanted to go with him.

'Ganelon' was a tragedy. It ran true to form the opening night, and in so doing proved that Lawrence Barrett was a great man as well as a great actor!

The action of the play was laid in the Middle Ages. Ganelon was a traitor; he had betrayed his people; the only possible end was death. He was to fall in battle during the last act — run through by the spear of a huge Saracen chieftain. The Saracen chief, after the big climax of the third act, did not go on again until he killed Ganelon at the end of the fifth act — the close of the play.

The actor who played this rôle went to his dressing-room after the third act and washed up, and, instead of being in his brown-stained skin when he heard Mr. Barrett's peculiar, savage, yet plaintive, cry of 'Musetto! Musetto!' he was milk-white from the waist up, with every particle of make-up removed.

He dashed upstairs to the stage. Richard Barker, the stage director, was frantically waving a colored flag which he used to direct supers. The 'white' Saracen chieftain grabbed this flag, rushed on the stage, and struck Mr. Barrett over the head with it, instead of stabbing him with the death-dealing spear.

When the curtain fell, Mr. Barrett walked silently to his dressing-room, entered, and closed the door. He did not discharge the actor ... and, so far as I know, he never mentioned the subject.

It took a big man to do this. He had just divided his company and separated from Mr. Booth. He had spent fifty thousand dollars and a whole year's preparation on a production, so he could star alone. Yes, it required a big man — and Lawrence Barrett was a big man!

'Ganelon' was a real success. It went over big in all cities. But Mr. Barrett was a sick man; he had large growths on his neck, which must have caused him great suffering. During the Baltimore engagement there was a consultation of doctors, and Mr. Barrett was told he must submit to an operation.

He evidently thought it was the finish, for while he posted the notice that we would close in three weeks, at the end of the Washington engagement, the notice also stated that he would play repertoire the last two weeks.

Even in those days of changing bills and quick study, such a task was unheard of. Here was a special cast for a new play, instructed to costume, study, rehearse, and give a performance of at least twelve plays on two weeks' notice — and it meant furnish your own wardrobe, too! The old actors in the company who had been with Mr. Barrett for years touched their foreheads with the index finger significantly.

But on the stage, as in other walks of life, it seems that nothing is impossible. The performances were given, and they were highly creditable, too!

I believe Mr. Barrett's sole object was to play his old rôles before he gave up. He had been virtually supporting Mr. Booth for several years. He was going on an operating table, which probably meant the end; he wanted to play once more 'Hamlet,' 'Shylock,' 'Richelieu,' and such rôles as had been denied him, and which he played so well.

How well I remember his 'What page man in the last court grammar made "you" a plural?'

His 'Angels and ministers of grace defend us'; or, 'But I'll not eat with you, drink with you, nor pray with you.'

His voice sometimes was a peculiar whine. But, oh, the moving quality! It seemed as though a breaking heart was in it!

The important rôles were so many that the leading actors could not possibly study them, so many of us young

109

actors fell heir to a rôle far beyond our station. I was in every bill.

Oh, how I had to hustle for wardrobe! To this day I do not know how I did it. There was a lady in the company, the stage manager's wife; she sewed night and day for me . . . or I never should have made the grade.

There was one awfully funny evening — I blush when I think of it. The bill was 'Julius Cæsar.' I played Trebonius. I thought my wardrobe was complete — a borrowed pair of high-heeled sandals, and a few yards of muslin hastily converted into a toga. In the dressing-room I was informed I must be in full Roman armor when with Cassius and Brutus on the plains of Philippi . . . I didn't have the semblance of an armor.

We carried a great many fine singers in 'Ganelon.' These singers were used in big scenes as supernumeraries. They resented this very much, and, while they would go on, it ended right there — they were like automatons. Now, the mob in 'Julius Cæsar' is as important to Mark Antony as the immortal 'The evil that men do lives after them. The good is oft interred with their bones.'

John A. Lane, an excellent actor, was Antony and he knew what his finish would be with a frost-bitten mob to work with. On my frantic search for an armor, a hand suddenly clutched me — Mr. Lane would loan me an armor if I would throw on an old shirt and go on in the mob scene and stir up the jellyfish. I was saved!

All through Antony's speech I harried that mob as a terrier would a rat, and Mr. Lane was so full of gratitude he almost fell downstairs to dig into the bottom of his trunk for the extra armor. . . . Oh! Oh!! Oh!!! It had been made for Mr. Lane twenty years before and he was a thin man at that moment! That armor didn't meet in the back on me within eight inches, and, as I was admittedly six inches taller than Mr. Lane, the bottom of the skirt or lambrequin came but little below my waist.

They were holding the curtain for me! They were calling! Up I rushed . . . it was a dark scene. Would it had remained so!

As the sun rose on the camp of Brutus and Cassius on those historic plains, no such Roman was ever seen as I. With the high-heeled sandals I looked eight feet tall — and the funny dinky little red armor. No shield — no sword — no warrior's red cloak! Omigod! I had forgotten the helmet — yes, I had a helmet — it was a super's and was four sizes too small.

Mr. Barrett always objected to having tall men come near him on the stage, as he was short of stature; but he didn't wait *for me* to come near him — he came to me and he came fast!

'Get off the stage! Get off the stage!' he snarled.

And I obeyed as fast as I could *sideways* — I wouldn't have turned my back to that audience if I had been fired on the spot. The next day at rehearsal, Mr. Barrett looked at me, smiled grimly, and *turned his back!* He was always surcharged with dignity — was Lawrence Barrett; but don't tell me he didn't have a sense of humor.

A short time afterwards I was living in a little attic room in Fourth Avenue, New York City, into which three other penniless actors also crowded to sleep. I received a letter from Mr. Barrett, written at Boston the night before his operation, wishing me success and telling me if he survived he hoped to have me with him the next season.

So far as I ever learned, it was the only letter he wrote. I was one of the least important members of the company. . . . He was a strange man.

The personal representative of Mr. Barrett recommended me to Margaret Mather, a star, with whom he had become associated in a like capacity. A telegram came to the little attic room for me to report at once in Buffalo, to play utility rôles in the eight plays of Miss Mather's repertoire — 'salary thirty a week,' and adding, 'Bring wardrobe.'

Buffalo was four hundred and fifty-eight miles away. I didn't have a fraction of four hundred and fifty-eight cents, nor a stitch of wardrobe. The weather was so cold that an overcoat was an actual necessity, if only as a safeguard against being arrested and put in a home for the friendless. I could not pawn my overcoat, but the coat and vest underneath went.

On a deposit of two dollars I persuaded a costumer to allow me to rent a shabby, threadbare Elizabethan shape — he had no shoes. I purchased a pair of slippers of some sort of material for fifty cents and hammered them full of flat-topped brass tacks . . . and on a second-class ticket was off for Buffalo.

I opened the night of my arrival, my first part being Tybalt, in 'Romeo and Juliet.' Tybalt is not so long in lines, but he is a very important part, and has three changes of costume. Oh, dear! I was a spectacle at first! How terrible I must have become in the eyes of the star, when, instead of appearing in a different costume, I constantly bobbed up in my same old attire!

The man who had recommended me was sent for and duly chastised. I was a goner sure had it not been for a wonderful old actor, J. B. Studley! He took a hand and volunteered to dress me out of his wardrobe — of which he had abundance.

After we left Buffalo, we played a week of one-night

stands. As it was necessary to have at least one short rehearsal each day — on my account — everybody in the company was in ill-humor, the star included.

I was always wearing an overcoat — it attracted attention and comment: giggles from women and 'damn' from traveling men. The members of the company were all complaining. My principal hurdle was meals. I would wait until just before the dining-room closed and then rush in, seat myself hurriedly, and bolt my food — to emphasize the necessity of haste. I dare not take off my overcoat — I dare not even open it.

About the fourth day, as I was making a rush from the dining-room, rushing out to go nowhere, dear J. B. Studley grabbed me.

'Say, laddie,' said he, 'you're a damn promising young actor, but are you a nut, or are you just fooling? What in hell are you wearing that overcoat to meals for?'

I just opened the coat — and he just motioned for me to follow him. . . . Five minutes later I was wearing a coat and vest of J. B. Studley's.

Years afterward, shortly before he crossed the 'big divide,' J. B. Studley needed help — I am so glad that I was near.

My father and all the family, including my married sister and her husband, returned from the West that spring, when Miss Mather's season had closed. The plunge to the Yakima country had failed — the effort was made just about twenty years ahead of time. Land on the Columbia River around Pasco — that is now so valuable — could be bought in those days for, as my father aptly put it, 'fifteen cents an acre, or two acres for two bits' — with no buyers. The Northern Pacific was carrying trainloads of people, but they kept right on going. No one would stop—at what is now one of the richest of countries.

That winter my father, unarmed and unafraid, had taken a rifle away from a so-called bad man. It is a thirty-eight, fifty-five Marlin. It came into my possession three years ago.

My father obtained another position, with 'rent included,' in Brooklyn. This time we again went below-stairs. Our family still consisted of my parents and the two youngest girl children; I lived there, also. All that summer I studied and slept in a vacant apartment.

My next season's work was with Robert Downing. My salary was forty-five dollars a week and I furnished all wardrobe. I shared leading rôles with an excellent actor, Edwin Holt. Dustin Farnum was in this company and his father was the manager. The best part that came to me out of the repertoire of seven or eight plays was Appius Claudius in 'Virginius.'

I had been an inveterate reader of everything I could find in the libraries concerning stage history. Prominent among the theories advanced by writers was the never-settled subject: 'Do actors feel the rôles they portray?' ... I had made quite an impression as Appius Claudius. I liked the part and the part seemed to like me. Appius Claudius seemed to present an excellent opportunity to settle this 'feeling' business. I became ambitious; I determined to find out which was correct—to feel or not to feel.

The opening night of our engagement at the Grand Opera House, Philadelphia, was the time and place where I went into executive session all by myself.

That part of the story of 'Virginius' which concerns this

test of mine was where the young, lascivious patrician, Appius Claudius, selects the daughter of Virginius as his legitimate prey; and where Virginius, to save his daughter's honor, seizes a butcher knife from a market-place block and kills her.

My object was (in my search for proof) to feel beyond consciousness in this situation. I must have done so. When the curtain descended to desultory hand-claps, instead of the usual thunderous applause, my wig was twisted over one ear, my patrician wreath was underfoot, my chair of state was upside down, showing the store chalk marks on the bottom, the daughter of Virginius was backing away in a half-frightened *ingénue* manner; and Virginius, the star, who happened to be his stage daughter's husband, was posed in an 'I dare you' manner, butcher knife in hand — glaring! While out of the haze somewhere I faintly heard the stage manager's voice saying, 'What in hell is the matter with you?'

Ever after, I was content to leave the subject to greater minds than mine.

It made no difference how long or successful the season, it was beyond the terminal of possibility for the average salaried actor to return home with over a few dollars in his pocket. He paid his own railroad fare to the point called for rehearsals; he rehearsed several weeks without salary; his hotel bills, sleeping-car berth (if he had any), and all expenses, except railroad fare during the season, were paid by him. The average outlay for wardrobe with a repertoire company, including wigs, footwear, and costumes, would be around five hundred dollars. This, coupled with half-salary weeks before Christmas and Easter, makes it easy to figure the profit!

There was quite a prominent club formed at this time for athletically inclined actors. The dues were very moderate. At the close of the season I spent many hours of thought before putting up my very near-the-last ten dollars to join. I believed it would help me to know actors and managers and so aid me in getting employment. Also the club was going to hold a set of games, and at the bottom of my heart I had fond hopes of being able to shine among my brother actors — to say nothing of the rather inward blushing hope of being able to show off before my sister actresses.

Everything worked out as planned; the events were all posted on the clubhouse bulletin board, and every race had numerous entries. There were two races, the one-hundred-yard and quarter-mile run that were open to all amateurs. And as the day of our games was the Saturday preceding the amateur championships, all the crack athletes of the country entered these two events. . . . They, also, were not averse to competing before Broadway's leading actresses.

To make the actor races look businesslike and to regulate a few of the boys that were trying to get a little the best of the club member handicappers, the club races were turned over to the official handicapper who was to handicap the two open races. That was my finish.

'Why not give Hart the prize now?' he said. 'I can't handicap him out of it. If it was an *open* race, I would put him at scratch.'

That settled it; it was made an open race and I was put at scratch — with two champion athletes.

Oh, golly! Instead of doing a nice parade and getting a prize for it, and maybe being admired a bit by the ladies, I had either to withdraw or go out there and take a licking — I hadn't been on a track for six years!

THE FIVE A'S

Suddenly I got a brilliant idea. The race was one mile, the handicap limit seventy seconds. It would be quite an honor for me to stand there with the two other scratch men, while athletes of championship caliber were receiving starts of from ten seconds to over a minute.

Yes! I could stand so the crowded grandstand would see the big 5 A's (Actors' Amateur Athletic Association of America) on my shirt — and they would all wonder who I was. An actor in an open race, starting at scratch! Then I would walk the first quarter as though it was the last step I would ever have a chance to take in my life . . . then jump off quickly, stoop down, and tie my shoe. Yes, I could do it! And I would do it!

The races were held on the Manhattan Athletic Club track. There were a great many of our old athletes there — Lon Myers and Harry Fredricks were there. First, to see the actors work out; and second, they had formed a partnership and were well-known bookmakers at all race tracks. I told them the truth — just what I intended to do. Then they did what they pleased!

They told one of the scratch men, Lang, that I had been training for months — Lang had been a former competitor of mine. I had always given him a twenty- or thirty-second handicap and beaten him. He forgot that he had improved wonderfully; he put on his street clothes and watched the race from the grandstand. He won the championship a few days later.

Lon and Harry tried the same talk on the other scratch man, but he did not scare; he did not know me — I meant nothing to him.

The race was called, and I went to my mark. When that actor crowd got a glance at those twenty-four-sheet 5 A's on my chest and saw those handicap men leave the mark, they fairly groaned in embarrassment at what was going to happen to me. I suffered keenly at my contemplated trickery. Golly! If I could only sink into the earth!

How well I remember hearing a star comedian's stentorian tones: 'Well, can you beat that! Who is he? Did anybody ever hear of him? Oh, transfiguration of souls — where are the police? Oh! Somebody please do something — this is terrible!'

Golly! My knees were weakening. The assistant starter touched my arm, 'Get on your mark.' We were off!

I could always walk fast for a quarter of a mile, and I put all I had into it. At the first quarter I was leading my scratch man competitor about ten yards, when just as I was about to jump off the track, *he did it!* Only he did not stoop to tie his shoe. The poison that Lon Myers injected had worked. A roar of cheers went up from the grandstand. I was almost giddy with exhaustion and happiness. I could now finish seventh, tenth, or last, with honor. There is no disgrace in a scratch man being beaten ... all I had to do was to keep moving to be a hero!

Alas! This was not to be. The memories of the old days were aroused, and now that Myers and Fredricks saw that I really had a chance, they forgot all about their profession as bookmakers and writers of one of the biggest betting sheets at Sheepshead Bay and Saratoga — they were once more the leaders of the old track gang of the M.A.C., and out there on the track striving to win was what a few years before had been their red-cheeked 'kid.'

Out on the field they dashed, Myers chasing ahead at each turn and spraying water in my face, while Harry ran alongside of me, just inside of the cinder path, with the same old jog-trot that had made me break a record on this same track.

I Win the Race

I won, and in fast time, too! — 6.53. The grandstand was a howling, yelling, shouting mob! While I, with some one's coat over my shoulders, was being led by Lon and Harry to the dressing-room. They were once more the gamblers.

'Doggone it!' said Myers. 'What a clean-up we could have made if we could have doped this out.'

The trophy for the race was a heavy hunting-case gold watch. It is the only prize I have left. I've earned it, though; I've paid interest on it over half of the years I have owned it.

We buried Lon Myers in 1899. Harry Fredricks hit the long trail just a few months before I am writing this. When informed by the nurse at Roosevelt Hospital in New York of the doctor's orders that he could see no one, he replied, 'All right, but if Bill Hart comes, be sure and let him in.' I was in California. Harry lived only three days. His last resting-place is scarcely a hundred yards from my parents' home in Greenwood.

I studied hard all summer. I was engaged at forty dollars a week as leading man with McLean and Prescott. I had the best line of parts I had so far been cast for, ranging from the meticulous Bassanios and Romeos to the fiery Antony and Phasarius, and including the arch villain Iago — arch villain he was to me, cunning, sly, and roguish, backed by vindictive hatred.

I could never agree with the academicians, pantologists, or the searchers of truth, who claim that in Iago Shakespeare created a villain without cause, one motivated by villainy for the pure love of villainy; a character without mercy or justification for his hellish deeds. Even Tommaso Salvini, acknowledged to be the greatest Othello of all time, held these views, and emphatically stated them in his writings.

Is it possible that even this master of all Othellos was unknowingly actuated by that green-eyed 'monster' that Iago warned him of? Is it possible that he was jealous of Iago? I am inclined to believe he was, for I cannot conceive of an actor of his ability holding his views.

Iago, when alone, talking to his conscience, says:

> 'I hate the Moor;
> And it is thought abroad that 'twixt my sheets
> He has done my office. I know not if 't be true;
> But I, for mere suspicion in that kind,
> Will do as if for surety.'

Then, when he comes upon Emilia in Othello's room, he forgets all about the handkerchief he has set her on to steal — he is first the jealous husband.

Iago: How now! What do you here alone?
Emilia: Do not you chide; I have a thing for you.
Iago: A thing for me? It is a common thing —
Emilia: Ha!
Iago: To have a foolish wife.

In the last act when Emilia denounces him, he does not call her a traitress, he calls her 'villainous whore' and kills her.

Iago had several causes for hating the Moor and one of them was the strong suspicion that his dusky chief had used his wife.

We were called for rehearsals at Lexington, Kentucky. Getting my wardrobe together had taken every penny I could gather and plunged me deeply in debt. My brother-in-law being a railroad man, after oodles of red tape, procured me an employee's half-fare rate! I was so pleased

120

with having the ticket that, crossing Brooklyn Bridge, on my way home, I took it out of my pocket to read it over again. I was seated at an open window. A sudden gust of wind ... and my ticket was sailing out over the East River.

No words that I am capable of using can describe my feelings. I could not leave the train until we reached the Brooklyn side, but, in the face of the hopelessness of it all, I took the next train back, made my way to the end of a dock, stripped and swam out in the river. I knew I was crazy, but I didn't seem to mind it! I swam about the location where I imagined that ticket would have hit the water.

There was a dock watchman, with two police officers, waiting where my clothes were. I didn't care what happened to me — I told my story sullenly and doggedly. They did not laugh, they did not arrest me — they said they were sorry!

The McLean-Prescott Company was a first-class barnstorming troupe, but we made a little money, and if there was a one-night stand on the map smaller than Demopolis, Alabama, or Waycross, Georgia, that we didn't hit, I have never heard of it. About the middle of the season Mr. McLean's father died, and he came into some money. I played his rôles while he went to New York on a business trip.

At that time the Union Square Theater was a first-class house, but business was fast moving uptown. Mr. Mc-Lean rented the theater for three weeks at twenty-five hundred dollars per week. The joyous wire came to our company manager telling the good news, and adding that its manager, J. M. Hill, was delighted.

McLean was a good loser. I never knew what our losses were, but it is a certainty that the seventy-five hundred dollars rental that delighted J. M. Hill never was seen again.

The many excellent parts I had gave me quite a boost. The New York critics liked me, and this was responsible for my getting a real leading man's position the following season — with Madame Rhea.

How grateful I am that this engagement came at this time. My father had not been well, but he stuck to his post. It was only when I was able to put my shoulder to the wheel that he yielded to our pleas to take a rest. We took a house at 63 Jefferson Avenue, and we were very happy.

I was engaged at seventy-five dollars per week, but they liked my work, and shortly after the opening of the season I was raised to one hundred.

At the close of the first season, the spring of 1893, my father's health was not good, and, as I had been re-engaged for the next season, I persuaded him to go to England and visit the home of his boyhood and young manhood. We agreed that I should go to Paris and visit all the theaters and then join him in Liverpool.

I saw many interesting performances during my short stay in Paris. I visited many art galleries and tramped through the surrounding country. I did not like the tone of my father's letters, so I cut short my stay and went to Liverpool.

How strange it seemed! An alien city with everything strange about me — to have my father of the prairies who had guided my way from the cradle to manhood still directing my steps.

We went to an eminent Liverpool doctor — to the same doctor that had attended my father's only brother after an accident that caused his death. He patted my father on the shoulder and told him to go home to his family. . . . It was the first great shock of my life.

I had some wonderful rôles with Madame Rhea — Benedict, Armand Duval, Claude Melnotte, Julian Gray, Pygmalion, Napoleon, and many others. She was a delightful woman; never a great actress, but of remarkable training and experience. She had been for ten years the leading lady of the Court Theater at St. Petersburg, Russia, and was a highly trained diplomatist. Washington was her strongest city. We played there twice during each season.

The Madame gave little parties almost every night after the theater. It was a treat and an education for me to sit in a corner and listen to the witticisms, quips, and serious discussions of those bright minds. I liked General Wade Hampton, the great Southern cavalry officer, best of all. I used to walk home with him at night. He was an old man with a cork leg. He wasn't much on walking, but, oh! Man! Man! Put him on a horse, golly! He did sit an animal pretty! He had a few horses in Washington. He liked my riding, too.

There was a conversation one evening that I wish I could remember more clearly, as it was typical of General Wade Hampton, the man! Some prominent character of the Civil War was under discussion. The General was silent. The argument, or whatever it was, kept right on going — for a long time. Still the General remained silent. Finally, he was appealed to directly and asked to express an opinion, if he had one.

'Oh, yes!' he said, 'I have one; it is this: I never liked the damned scoundrel; when he came into Columbia and burned my house . . . he shot my dog.'

123

In the spring of 1895 I was engaged by Madame Modjeska as leading man for what was to be her farewell tour. My salary was still one hundred dollars per week, but, although it would cost me considerable for wardrobe, the parts I would play made the engagement highly desirable and a big step forward. I was to play Macbeth, Benedict, Lord Leicester; Angelo, in 'Measure for Measure'; the Duke of Malmsbury, in a new play by Clyde Fitch; Armand Duval, and other fine rôles. How glad I am that my father knew of it and thought my future assured!

His health had been failing constantly. His trouble was enlargement of the spleen, and at times he suffered very much. At fifty-nine years of age he had been as fine a specimen of manhood as ever walked; at sixty-one, he had lost fifty pounds in weight and was but a shadow of his former self. His courage was the same. He ever remained undaunted.

My sister Mary was with him constantly, and my youngest sister Lotta, eleven years of age, was his baby child. Her daddy knew he was going away soon; that he would see her little brothers and sisters, and he talked much of them to Lotta, and asked her what she wanted him to say to them for her.

All too soon the time came for my father to leave his little girl. He sat beside his bed and talked to me; he told me how sorry he was that he had not been able to make his plans go through. He spoke of the West and the many easy opportunities he had had to acquire land and property, and of his regret at leaving me practically penniless, with my mother and sisters to care for. He said that for the benefit of his family he was sometimes afraid that he had been too damned honest.

Had he the same life to live over again, he would have

been just the same — honesty and manhood were all he knew. He went on his long journey June 20, 1895. I am glad I had such a father.

Madame Modjeska opened her season at the Garrick Theater, for an engagement of three weeks, followed by one week at the Montauk Theater, Brooklyn. Then we went on tour. In the middle of the season, Madame's health failed, and the season closed. It was wonderful to have been associated with this great actress in such rôles as Macbeth — it was a great honor. Madame liked me very much; she told me I was the best Armand Duval she had ever played with. This pleased me greatly, as I was fond of the part.

My vacation was short. I played a week in support of Robert Mantell, at Newark, New Jersey, doing Iago and the heavy part in Monbars. Mantell was an excellent actor; but business was bad — I did not receive any salary.

I then joined a prominent woman star — as leading man, at my then fairly well-established salary of one hundred dollars per week. The lady had just separated from a wealthy husband, and was starring in Shakespearian repertoire. Had this lady lived in Hollywood at the present time, Hollywood would be the Hollywood of its reputation — instead of the Plymouth, Massachusetts, or Plymouth, Vermont, village that it really is.

The lady was not a soiled dove, by any means — she was just a party fiend that never seemed to sleep. Long after the usual bedtime, two actors that did not drink — Bill Farnum and myself — could be found bowling or playing pool until ejected; then roaming the streets of strange one-night stands, cutting foolish pranks in the early morn-

ing hours that should have landed us in jail. It was anything, anywhere, except go home; we dare not go back to
the hotel; we were afraid. Were we caught, it would be a
case of acting as messenger boys to get more champagne
or dodge an empty bottle.

One cold night, or, rather, one cold morning, we waited
until we thought everything was quiet and the coast was
all clear. But when near our room we were gathered in by
an excited figure in semi-negligée — a man had been trying
to force his way into her room. The mistress and maid
both pointed out the room the man had disappeared in —
and then the mistress swooned.

My position as leading man cast me for the rôle of hero.
The good Lord must have been on my side that night. I
was angry at myself and the falseness of the whole business
and I took it out on the door. I walloped with busted
knuckles until the door busted inward. . . . The window
was open and the man had gone.

It makes me shiver when I think of what would have
happened to my mid-section if that fellow had ever started
to throw lead through that door. When the man had
gone and could not be killed, the maid revived the mistress
and we learned the story of what really had happened.

They were having a usual party; the man, hearing many
voices and much gayety, had knocked on the door and
asked if he could join in the celebration. I shivered some
more. The man would have had no trouble in being
acquitted after the fact.

There soon followed another particularly hectic party at
Youngstown, Ohio. Bill and I flatly refused to become
involved and were told that we would get ours at Pittsburgh. Why Pittsburgh? thought we, and then thought
no more about it. The lady was our employer and could

discharge any or all of us at any time — and we knew that outside of her party proclivities she had many excellent qualities. Also we believed her — on account of her sporting nature — to be a square shooter.

Square shooter or not, she was a scrapper. Whether she ever intended us to 'get ours' to a finish or not at Pittsburgh, we never knew; but a finish it was, and Bill and I did not come out of it ingloriously. We finished the season happily. We had fought it out on our own lines and won!

A few years later, I waited from early morning until late at night at the Little Church Around the Corner in New York, where they were to bring this lady's body for burial services. The plans were changed . . . they took her remains to a Western city.

She was a healthy, young woman . . . it was the parties!

We still had our Jefferson Avenue home, but we were awfully short of money. There was a young actress living at Asbury Park who was going to play a line of Shakespearian rôles. She engaged me to come down three days each week and coach her. My pay was only five dollars each lesson, but it paid the expenses for a splendid boat trip for my sister Mary and little Lotta. They used to wait for me in a cool shady grove, and when my work was finished I would join them for the return sail home.

In September I played the hero rôle in a melodrama, 'The Great Northwest,' which opened after four weeks' rehearsals for a run at the American Theater. The run was three weeks, without salary. It was a well-known cast, too, containing many actors of excellent standing.

At the dress rehearsal the property man cut out the fire effect in a prairie-fire scene which was the big climax of the play. He happened to be related to one of the owners of the show and kept carefully to himself the secret that there was no more money in the treasury and that he could not buy any fire. We had the prairie and all other accessories ... but no fire!

The action of the play called for me to jump on a horse, dash off over the prairie, pick up a lady, and carry her back to the cheering ranch hands that filled the stage — watching the rescue with breathless suspense. The rehearsal was all right — minus the fire.

'Where is the fire?' I modestly asked.

Willie Seymour, the well-known stage director (also unconsciously without salary), haughtily informed me that my business was to play a part, not stage the production. I remember mumbling something about 'It's all right for me, but how about the horse?' But I didn't mumble it very loud. Mr. Seymour was not only competent to stage a production, but he was a man of position in the profession.

Doc Martin, the most prominent horse trainer and dealer in New York who was renting the animal to the company, grinned at me and said, 'This mare is all right. She works over at the Metropolitan in Grand Opera.'

I was not scared of any horseman. I didn't mumble to him. We spoke the same language. I came back with 'A horse may get broke to heavenly singin' — but at the same time object to having hell fire burnin' under its belly!'

The opening night the fire was on hand, a packed audience was in front, and my mother and sisters seated right in the first row. The play was going finely. When the big fire scene came, I leaped on the big mare (she was a beautiful animal) and dashed off through the fire, just cutting the corner of it. I might just as well have gone through the middle of it so far as the damage done was concerned. The mare had felt fire, and whether it was in a tin pan, masked behind some prop weeds or not, meant nothing to her — she had been burnt and she knew it.

The crowds yelled louder, the fire burned fiercer, the audience was at fever pitch waiting for that mad dash back through the flames. Back-stage the lady was thrown up into my arms and we braced ourselves for the dash through the scorching flames in sight of the audience. The mare would go everywhere but forward. The poor beast was willing; she would have tried to climb the side walls of the theater, but she would not face that fire. Doc Martin was furious; he was jumping around like an insane man. This time I talked horse language to him that did not need to be interpreted — it did not improve his humor.

Suddenly I felt the mare quiver and squat, and I knew it was coming. She seemed to leap eight feet high! She almost cleared the flames, landed in the center of the stage mob, and kept right on going — head on to the audience.

I threw the lady into the crowd and lay back on the reins with every ounce of strength in my being. Slowly the mare came up — she was half over the orchestra. Her hind hoofs were not twelve inches back of the footlights. I could see the transfixed faces of the audience — the looks of fear and anxiety of my mother and sisters. They were right under me. The mare hung in the air — then slowly, then like a shot, straight over backwards.

There is a time for all riders to quit, but I had to pull until the last eighth of a second. There was no time for me to fall clear — I had to take it. My leg was all bunged up. They cut my boot off, carried me upstairs, and put me in the theater owner's bed. The doctor had me working the next night. The poor mare died at five o'clock in the morning.

At the closing of 'The Great Northwest,' I was fortunate in getting another engagement almost immediately, another juvenile part with William A. Brady's production of 'Under the Polar Star,' which was staged by David Belasco. It had a fine cast, and, as its title indicates, was a play of the Arctic.

The most interesting thing to me in this engagement was eight massive dogs that Peary had brought back from near the North Pole; they were in charge of Matt Henson, who later was the only man with Peary when he reached the pole. Henson drove the dogs in the big ice scene in the play and was with them constantly. On account of the associations of my boyhood, I am very familiar with the characteristics and manners of an aborigine, and I was carried away with the counterfeit presentment that this colored man gave of the Eskimo.

While I know nothing of Eskimos, counterfeit in this instance seems just an idiom of speech. Matt Henson, when he had his furs on, seemed *to be* an Eskimo. He certainly had all the ear-marks and one could never question but what he was an Eskimo Indian. The silence, the stoicism, the occasional little gleam of humor in the eye — it was all there. He was a living embodiment. He told me that sixteen years of his life had been spent among these Far North people. He was always the same, he never changed. He was not acting.

On account of pneumonia among them, the dogs had to be destroyed. They are now in their last home, the Smithsonian Institution at Washington. Matt Henson left us when the dogs left. A fine fellow, Matt Henson. He has proved his metal.

CHAPTER IX

A STARRING SUCCESS WITHOUT CAPITAL

I FELT that I could star. I had seen many thousands of dollars spent in an endeavor to make stars. Some succeeded, others failed, but all had backing. I had no money, nor could I control any money, and yet I felt I could succeed. John Whitely, who had been manager for both McLean and Prescott and Madame Rhea, when I was a member of their companies, thought as I did.

We scraped up two hundred and fifty dollars each for printing, and Mr. Whitely started to book a tour for the following season.

I was afraid my household expenses might be in jeopardy, so I tried to keep them as low as possible; at the same time endeavor to make a permanent home for my mother and sisters. Asheville, North Carolina, seemed to me the best place I had ever struck in my travels for a small-salaried man to live, that was anywhere near New York. So we moved to Asheville in the spring of 1897. We shipped bedding ahead of us by express, carried cooking utensils in our trunks, and we slept in our new home the first night of our arrival. It was a little four-room cottage on Orange Street. We paid fifteen dollars a month rent.

Among the plays that I had selected for my starring tour was 'The Man in the Iron Mask.' It was one of the published fifteen-cent acting editions written from the story of Alexandre Dumas. The play appealed to me, only I thought it too gloomy; so I worked awfully hard and carpentered together a new and original third act, which I took from the Dumas novels, introducing Louis XIV and

131

his court. This not only lightened up the play, but gave me a dual rôle; also, the rather dramatic twist of one brother sentencing another, inasmuch as I played both parts — to wear the Iron Mask.

The play was always liked wherever we played it. We usually used it for our opening bill. I had always been what, among actors, is known as a 'hard study.' It took me much longer than the average person to memorize a part. For some seasons past, my sister Mary had been of great help to me in holding the book and prompting me; sometimes six, eight, and ten hours a day.

As a professional I could get tickets for most theaters in New York, and I always took my sister Mary with me. So in helping me study and in seeing so many plays, together with her fine native ability, she became an excellent critic, and was a great help to me, both in my acting and in any writing or dramatic work that I tried to do. This condition remains unchanged up to the present time.

There was a barn belonging to our little home. We found an old woolly-headed darky (Uncle Aaron) in it. He did the little chores about the place for his rent . . . and we felt quite like landed proprietors.

Little Lotta and I used to start out at five o'clock in the morning and walk several miles over the mountain to Chun's Cove to get water from a natural spring for our mother. We were all happy. It was a happy summer. How it hurt me to leave! In passing through the town on my way to the train, I saw a sign, 'Arbuckle's coffee, seven pounds for one dollar.' I gave the grocer a dollar and told him to deliver the coffee. It is strange what simple little things we remember and what a grip they have on our hearts.

We opened at Travers City, Michigan, and our tour

THE MAN IN THE IRON MASK

took us all through the middle and southwest; 'The Man in the Iron Mask,' 'The Bells,' and a one-act comedy, 'Delicate Ground,' constituting a double bill, and with 'The Lady of Lyons,' 'The New Magdalen,' and 'Camille' for matinées, made up our repertoire. We made a scant living — that was all. But we could not get discouraged, as everywhere we played they liked us very much and were enthusiastic about a return engagement, which, of course, on account of being booked ahead, could not take place until the following season.

We opened the Turner Opera House at Muskogee, Indian Territory. It was just a small place with board sidewalks and dirt streets. Two transgressors of the law, covered by one sheet, were hauled into town in a box wagon while we were there. It seemed quite like my boyhood days.

The only profit we had to show, after playing some weeks in the State of Kansas, was a dog. They gave me a fine blooded hound at Coffeyville, and I had great sport running big Kansas jack-rabbits with him. As we journeyed East the dog's vocation was gone — there were no more jack-rabbits.

At Peoria, Illinois, we stopped at the best hotel, The National. We were not paying salaries, but paid all hotel bills — we had to do so to get out of town. The hotel management would not allow the dog in the rooms, so at night he was tied in the porter's check-room. During the night he must have dreamed of once more chasing over the prairies, for he chewed the whole end off a leather trunk, and made a rat's nest out of a man's fur overcoat: total damage, two hundred dollars. We settled for one hundred — shipped the dog back to Kansas. The leading lady left her small diamond ring with the hotel proprietor and we entrained for Mattoon, Illinois. It was Christmas Day.

Mr. Whitely was a splendid man, but he didn't have a particle of bulldog in him. He lacked the 'hang-on' instinct. He finally came to me and told me he was through and proposed that we take the company into Chicago and disband.

I put it up to the company. I told them that we were a real success everywhere we played; that excellent reports had continually gone to New York about us; that we were booked as far east as Youngstown, Ohio; that I would use every means in my power and sign any kind of contract to get booked in New York City, and if we failed we would fail before competent judges, and die game. They were all with me. They said they'd stick, and, if we could not make railroad fares, they'd walk to the next towns.

Mr. Whitely left, and, before we reached Youngstown, I had a contract to play the People's Theater on the Bowery for one week in 'The Man in the Iron Mask.' The People's was at that time a neighborhood theater, but it played all first-class attractions — Joe Jefferson, Mrs. Langtry, et al. I had played there the season before in 'Under the Polar Star.'

We lay off a week before opening our engagement. Seven men, including myself, lived in one back-parlor room in a boarding-house on Fifteenth Street. Our combined bill was forty-two dollars a week, room and board.

'The Man in the Iron Mask' was a real hit; it drew all the first critics, and the big New York managers either came themselves or sent their representatives to see the performance.

The two hardest hurdles to get over in the big city were Alan Dale and Acton Davies. Alan Dale, of the 'New York Journal,' wrote:

134

A Real Hit

William S. Hart, the new young 'star' who has just crept into New York via the Bowery, need not feel in the least afraid of metropolitan criticism. . . .

This young star was something of a surprise to me. I saw him a long time ago, I now remember, in the 'support' of Modjeska, in a Shakespearian rôle. His artistic temperament was quite apparent. But he has improved, developed, and sprouted quite unusual power. In 'The Man in the Iron Mask' — still quite an interesting 'romantic' drama — Mr. Hart richly deserves all the encouragement that my feeble pen can give him. It isn't every actor that can appear as twins successfully. It isn't every actor that you would care to see doubled. As a general thing half of the average Bowery actor is quite enough for the unaccustomed stomach.

Mr. Hart has everything in his favor. He is young, spectacularly picturesque, and fervid. He is brainy, instead of beefy, and the quieter moments of his work as Louis XIV and Gaston D'Orville were admirable examples of repression and art. The rôles were surpassingly well differentiated — the somber king and the enthusiastic twin brother stood conspicuously forth in separate lights.

. . . I don't want to swell Mr. Hart's head or mar his career at its start, but I venture to say that here is a young actor who is cut out for a romantic star. He is a sort of masculine Julia Marlowe, and he will ultimately reach Broadway with triumph, as Miss Marlowe has done. And then there will be a cry of 'I've discovered him' from at least a dozen earnest pens. Mr. Hart is already discovered, and all that he has to do now is to place wet compresses on his forehead and hope for the best.

Acton Davies, of 'The Evening Sun,' the other hurdle-maker, headed his criticism in large type:

MR. HART MAKES A HIT AS THE MAN IN THE IRON MASK

As a star, Mr. Hart, who is playing this week at The People's, promises to become a much greater success than he was as a leading man. The last time that Mr. Hart appeared here was at the Garrick as a leading man to Mme. Modjeska during her last, or rather her latest, farewell engagement. At that time he played many parts, but none of them nearly so well as the dual rôle in which he is now starring in 'The Man in the Iron Mask.' Evidently this young actor has been working hard in the interim, for from every point of view he has made great progress. There is undoubtedly a place for Mr. Hart in the line of romantic drama.

My heart was full of gratitude. I had urged the actors to stick. They had believed in me and done so. Had we closed before we reached New York, all the sacrifices we had made, all the hardships we had undergone, would have been useless. We would have left no more trail than a ship sailing over the open sea. But, above all, I was most gratified at our success for the ease it gave my conscience. I had taken away the small, sure competence that I owed my mother and sisters — in working for a salary — and placed them in almost actual want. Had I been a failure, artistically as well as financially, and thereby proved that I was all wrong, the knowledge of what I had done would have been a heavy burden to bear.

Frank Dietz, a well-known manager, came to see me and we quickly made a deal for him to finance a short spring tour. He did not assume any part of the back indebtedness of the company. On account of the New York success, there was no trouble about getting time. Mr. Dietz booked six weeks, by wire, in two days; the unfortunate part being that we had to make big jumps to get to theaters that had the open time. We jumped to Rochester, then back to Brooklyn, then far up into New York State again; yet in spite of the heavy railroad expense we made money. Mr. Dietz made a good profit and I cleaned up all back salaries due the loyal boys and girls that had stuck to me.

A Golden Opportunity

It was pathetic, and yet laughable, when the money first came in. I doled it out according to immediate wants. One had to have a pair of pants; another, shoes; another, a new hat; another, a pipe; another, a suitcase. I asked no questions of the girls — I gave them all I could and let them do the rest. I closed my starring season of eight months with two dollars and sixty cents.

When I was in France I had met a playwright, Adrian Barbusse. He wrote a play for Madame Rhea, 'The Queen of Sheba,' which she used in her repertoire while I was with her. Mr. Barbusse spoke English. He and I became quite well acquainted. Several times he had me recite (in English) at literary gatherings. I brought two plays to America for him; one was produced by Stuart Robson. Mr. Barbusse felt grateful for the part I had taken in the matter, and wrote me that he would watch the play market in France and England and, if he saw or learned of any play that would be suitable to me, he would let me know immediately. He was very enthusiastic about my chances of becoming a star.

When our little company reached New York and said good-bye to each other, I received a letter from Mr. Barbusse saying that he had waited nearly four years to find a sure-fire play for me . . . and at last it had arrived; that a play had just opened the night before in Paris that was a colossal success; that he had information it had been printed as a book in play form and shipped to New York. He advised me to go to Brentano's in New York immediately, buy a copy, and through some twist of the copyright law — or the lack of it — I could lawfully produce the play without royalty. Here was my golden opportunity!

I made the best of time to Brentano's. The foreign

shipment case had just arrived, but was not yet opened. They asked if I would call the next day, or could they send the book to my address? I replied, as nonchalantly as I could, that I was only in town for the day, and, as I had no appointment for an hour, I would rather wait and search for some books I wanted. Could they oblige me? In one hour I purchased two copies of the prized book at seventy-five cents each. I sauntered out.

But once around a corner I made a dash that nearly knocked people off the sidewalk — and never slowed down until I arrived at the B. J. Falk Building. Mr. Falk was very friendly to me. He also thought I had a chance to become a real star. I explained hurriedly what I had, and how I came by it. Mr. Falk could read French, and, in addition to that, he called on the telephone a friend of his who was a French scholar. Thirty minutes after my arrival, they were in the private office behind locked doors, reading.

The result was cyclonic! They both raved over the book. Mr. Falk consulted his attorneys over a private wire. 'Yes, if the book had been bought in play form, we could play it without royalty!'

I was to get on the first steamer that sailed, go to Paris, and see the performance, while Mr. Falk immediately started work on the production. The name of the play and every move we made was to be kept a buried secret. Joy just would not be confined! We laughed little short, half-hysterical laughs — our blood was stimulated — we all had flushed faces.

Mr. Falk would put up fifty thousand dollars to finance the play — *but* ... just one little 'but.' On account of some particularly French situations in the play, and on account of the whole action fairly reeking in French atmosphere, would it be accepted in America? He, Mr. Falk, believed it would be — beyond question. But he wanted one expert opinion. He wanted some first-class American playwright, who was a French scholar, who could do the translation and what adapting that might be required; he would accept as final the decision of such a man, but he must be one whom we could trust unreservedly. Did I know of such a man?

The cloud that had momentarily shut out the light became non-existent. Did I know of such a man? I surely did! A man who was one of the first to predict a future for me; a man who, in addition to being admittedly one of the first high-class authors of America, was a French scholar of distinction; a man of irreproachable character and honesty — Mr. William Young.

I had worked in a play of Mr. Young's, 'Ganelon,' with Lawrence Barrett.

We waited three days. Mr. Young had read the play carefully, twice. It was his opinion that it would never be understood in America; all of the student atmosphere that was so essential to its success would be entirely lost on an American audience; the big balcony scene, where the leading man made love by proxy, and himself remained in the shadows, would get laughs, where in France it would bring heart throbs and tears; and finally, the American public was too practical ever to stand for a man with a huge nose being a hero, and making love to a beautiful girl.

The play was 'Cyrano de Bergerac' — the author, the then unknown Edmund Rostand.

Mr. Falk, excellent, keen-minded man that he was, quit cold. Three months later, Augustin Daly produced 'Cyrano de Bergerac,' starring Ada Rehan in the woman lead at his theater — WITHOUT ROYALTY. Richard Mansfield followed a few weeks later with his production at the Garden Theater — it was a man's play.

Two years later, Mr. Young told General Lew Wallace in my presence, 'General, I feel that I robbed this young man of the greatest opportunity any young actor ever had in his life. I made a terrible mistake in judgment and he suffered by it!!!'

Mr. Falk loaned me two hundred dollars. I went over to Brooklyn and got our old family dog that had been in a friend's back yard, bought a cut-rate ticket from a scalper, and started for Asheville. My family had written me that they had moved, but they did not enlarge upon the cause and I had not inquired enough. I found them on the outskirts of the town in a partly abandoned, old brick Southern house of pre-Civil War days. They were living in two rooms, with a woodpile in the corner — the spring where they got their water, a hundred yards from the house. They had concealed the fact from me, but they were in actual want of proper food and clothing. I then and there resolved I would never again try to become a star at such an expense.

Old Uncle Aaron was still in the offing; and an old Southern mammy, Aunt Clara, who lived in one of the cabins on the place, was a constant visitor. She would sit beside the woodpile in the evenings and smoke, while her little pickaninny played at her feet. These old former slave darkies had been a great help and comfort to my mother and sisters. They always held a warm place in my heart.

The baby of the family, my sister Lotta, was growing to be a bouncing girl — she was beautiful. Among her playmates was a little boy whose mother had a cow, and the mother sold the milk of the cow and the little boy delivered it — fresh from the cow, just milked, and it had cream on it *half an inch thick*, and 'couldn't we buy milk from the little boy's mother?' We did!

We found a little frame house, rent seven dollars a month, at the edge of a grove of trees. What a beautiful, peaceful place it was! It seems as though I can hear the wind sighing through the pine trees yet. It is not the East calling . . . it is the South; but it pulls just as strong as 'Come ye back to Mandalay.'

I interested some of the younger set of Asheville and put on 'The New Magdalen,' with home talent. It was so successful that I staged 'Camille,' also. It was 'occupying my time.' The real reason was, I was getting about thirty very welcome dollars for my bit, out of each performance, and each dollar was needed for food. The plays were put on at the Opera House and were more than creditable performances. The lady who played Camille, Mrs. Frank Darby, two young men, Francis Gudger and Phil Cocke, also a young Miss Gudger, stand out in my memory as giving performances that were far and away above the average, judged by a professional standard.

George Tyler, of the then just beginning firm, The Liebler Company, wrote me and asked if I would like to play John Storm in support of Viola Allen in 'The Christian,' which he was to produce.

I had written to every manager I could think of that I thought might star me, but I did not receive the slightest encouragement — in many cases, receiving no reply at all. So Mr. Tyler's offer came as a windfall. I was to be in New York at a certain date to make final arrangements and start rehearsals.

The little house among the pines was too isolated a place

to leave my family when I was not home. I moved them to a two-family house in town. Again the leave-taking was hard.

On my arrival in New York I invested five dollars and eighty cents in a blue serge suit — I saw the advertisement in a paper going North on the train. The next morning, all washed up, shoes shined, and wearing the 'five-eighty,' I visited Mr. Tyler.

The Liebler Company, at that time, as I remember it, was not rolling in luxury; on the contrary, I think they had desk-room in a printing office on the second floor of one of the two-story buildings on the west side of Thirty-Seventh Street and Broadway. The building still stands. I saw it recently on one of the night walking trips I usually take when I am in New York. Like the boys of Dotheboys Hall, I like to go back to old locations, whether I have been wounded there or not.

Mr. Tyler explained to me that his firm was just getting started; that they had taken Viola Allen away from the Frohmans; that Miss Allen had met Dan Frohman in Europe, and, as he was very desirous of having his leading man, Edward J. Morgan, play the part of John Storm, Miss Allen had gladly consented to it and had asked him (Mr. Tyler) to please arrange it that way.

There was nothing to be said ... I did not get the part; and with a heavy heart thumping under my 'five-eighty' I bowed myself out with as much of a pleasant smile as I could twist my face into!

My shoes had been tapered at the heels, but I finished them in making daily calls at the agencies and managers' offices where they would permit of actors calling. There was not the remotest sign of work — no possibility of it.

'The Christian' was to open at Albany. I wanted to

see the performance. I met my brother-in-law, who was then auditor of the Long Island Railroad, and he got me a pass to Albany and return. It read 'for two.' It was a corking performance. Miss Allen was splendid; Morgan ran off with the honors. Just as I figured, John Storm was the star rôle, and Morgan played the part beautifully.

Sam Rork, A. M. Palmer's manager for years, was there, taking care of the publicity for the opening. He was going back to New York that night — so was I. With as much dignity as I could assume, I invited Mr. Rork to return with me, as I had transportation for two. Sam Rork doesn't know yet that he rode back to New York that night on an employee's pass, after first buying supper for an actor who hadn't had any and didn't have any money to buy any.

CHAPTER X

JULIA ARTHUR AND BEN HUR

JULIA ARTHUR, an established legitimate star, was about to open her season when her leading man, an Australian actor, committed suicide. I was engaged in his place. It was an ordeal. The company had been rehearsing for several weeks in repertoire. I think I was engaged on Thursday. We left Friday night for Detroit, had a dress rehearsal Sunday night, and opened Monday in 'A Lady of Quality' in which I played Sir John Oxen.

How I got through I don't know, but I did. After the performance Miss Arthur thanked me and complimented me on my work. I went to the telegraph office and wired home that I would soon send some money. My salary was, as usual, one hundred a week, but it was all mine. For the first time in my career, outside of 'Ganelon,' I did not have to furnish wardrobe. Miss Arthur furnished everything — costumes, wigs, shoes, *et al*.

A few weeks later at Buffalo, Mr. Tyler called me up and offered me the part of John Storm. Mr. Frohman had taken Morgan out of the cast to put him in another new play. I did not go! We went into New York for a long engagement.

Our long run at Wallack's Theater was memorable and unique. Miss Arthur had married the wealthy B. P. Cheney of Boston, a man through and through. Miss Arthur's idea was to put on a repertoire of first-class productions on Broadway. It had never been done before. I doubt if it has ever been done since. It must have cost whole carloads of money.

IT WAS A FAR CRY FROM THE WESTERN PRAIRIES TO ROMEO

'A Lady of Quality,' after a run, was followed by 'As You Like it,' 'Ingomar,' 'Pygmalion and Galatea,' and 'Mercedes.' We were scheduled to do 'Romeo and Juliet,' only Miss Arthur became ill, which caused us to close — temporarily. We did 'Romeo and Juliet' at Chicago. Each of these productions was made as though intended for a season's run. The scenery and costumes were magnificent. I was told that 'Romeo and Juliet' alone cost a fabulous amount of money. The costumes I wore as Romeo were marvelous — I had five changes. The material did not seem to be like ordinary costume goods at all; everything was thick, heavy silk, beautiful cloth and fine brocades. It seems to me that the costumes alone would have played the parts.

I had played Macbeths, Iagos, and Ingomars and almost a hundred wonderful rôles, but it was such a far cry from the Western prairies to Romeo that somehow I wished my father could have been there and witnessed a performance — and then have read what the critics said in their reviews. It would have pleased him so much to know that those 'rough corners' had been smoothed down ... a little.

Amy Leslie said: 'William S. Hart played Romeo from a purely romantic standpoint of youth and fiery impetuosity. He did not grow old in the night of agonies thrust upon him, but was a boy through it all, quite to the very end. His Romeo is not matured by tragic sufferings. Some moments of Mr. Hart's Romeo were most real and all of it was sympathetic and graceful.'

I had so many changes and they had to be made in such a short space of time that for one of the few times in my stage career I engaged a dresser. He was a conscientious chap and was always following me on the stage with something I might need. We had rehearsed nearly all night the night before, and I was all in. Up to the parting scene I hadn't a moment of rest — I was either on the stage or rushing through changes. After the parting scene, Romeo has a long wait — he does not go on until the apothecary scene at the first of the last act. Before rushing out of the dressing-room for the parting scene, I told the boy to get me a bottle of beer, that when I returned I would have time to quench my thirst.

But, as I have stated, my dresser was always just one jump ahead on service. The back-stage view of the parting scene is — Juliet leaning out of the window, about four feet above the stage, and Romeo on a ladder that goes down into a trap through the stage — to get the effect from the audience angle of Romeo climbing up a ladder to a second-story window. In the play, Romeo draws back when the nurse comes on, and goes up the ladder again when Juliet calls.

When I dropped down from the window there was 'the faithful' and with him the bottle of beer. He knew nothing of my return cue — he only saw me panting and exhausted. Off went the cap on the beer bottle — it was shoved into my hand. I was only human ... down my throat it gurgled.

'Art thou gone so, my lord, my love?'

The lines were spoken, and there was Juliet — gazing at her heart-broken lover *guzzling a bottle of beer!*

How we finished the scene I do not know. I only know that I expected surely to be discharged. A production that cost a fortune — the opening night — the star's big scene! For any sane man to do such a thing was beyond all reason. The damned bottle was still foaming and still clutched in my right hand. I spoke my last line as we passionately kissed — 'Dry sorrow drinks our blood. Adieu! Adieu!' God! It was terrible — but it was funny!

I changed to my last-act costume and after the curtain fell went to Miss Arthur's dressing-room to apologize and to be discharged. I knocked ... the door was opened. There she stood in all her glorious beauty, her dark eyes dancing, her husband beside her. She looked at me — but she spoke to him, 'And, Ben, you don't know the worst of it — the selfish beast! It was a QUART bottle!!'

JULIA ARTHUR! A glorious actress, and a glorious woman!

In the spring I was engaged by Klaw and Erlanger for the production of 'Ben Hur.' It was a long wait. We did not open until November 29th, but it was an excellent part, 'Messala.' We rehearsed six terrifically trying weeks. It was an enormous production, and I have been told that Klaw and Erlanger had every dollar they possessed in it.

General Lew Wallace, the author; William Young, who wrote the stage version; Mr. Klaw, Mr. Erlanger, Mr. Brooks, the proprietors; Ben Teal, the stage director, and half a dozen assistants, were always on hand. We had a small audience at every rehearsal. There were many changes made in the cast.

At one of the final rehearsals Charles Frohman was with us all night. As he was turning up his coat-collar to leave, he said to the Big Bosses, 'Boys, I'm afraid you're up against it — the American public will never stand for Christ and a horse-race in the same show.'

I was guilty of creating quite some disturbance myself, for which I have always been sorry. Ed Morgan and I were having an actor's jangle about his putting his hand on me and turning me around. I had convinced him that he was wrong, but Ben Teal caught some of it and asked what was the discussion. Morgan wouldn't place me in the position of usurping a director's authority. He refused to talk . . . so of course I had to be just as magnanimous and say, 'I did it . . . etc., etc.'

Teal lost his head and gave me the devil. I went back at him something shameful and walked out of the theater, straight across to the Vendome Hotel, wrote out my resignation, took it up to Mr. Erlanger's office, and shoved it under the door.

In the morning, before nine o'clock, Thomas — Mr. Erlanger's colored man — was at my little flat with a note. Mr. Erlanger wanted to see me at once. I went! And in the presence of a whole office full of generals and bosses, golly! what a hauling over the coals I got! I had no comeback — I was guilty and I knew it! An actor, like a fighter, must learn 'to take 'em.' I had not been game! But finally the Big Boss got to piling it on too hard, and left me an opening.

'You can't quit — you owe me five hundred,' he fired at me.

'Mr. Erlanger,' I replied, 'that five hundred isn't worrying you a damn bit — you know I'll pay it back if I have to work on the front end of a trolley car to do it. What's worrying you is — you haven't got a Messala.'

He sort of grinned a little and said, 'I guess you're right about that. You get over there to rehearsals.'

Ben Teal forgave me, too! He was a regular director.

I have always felt quite proud that, after the first performance, I was sent for and complimented by the author, General Lew Wallace. His exact words were: 'Young man, I want to thank you for giving me the Messala that I drew in my book.'

148

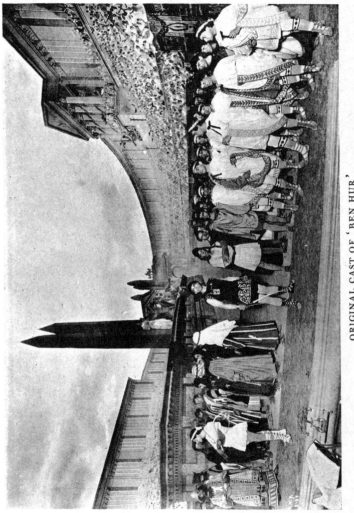

ORIGINAL CAST OF 'BEN HUR'

Edward Morgan (left) and William S. Hart

The Chariot Horses

So far as I know I was the only member of the cast so honored.

In the third act of 'Ben Hur' I drove a team of horses on the stage among eighty-five dancing girls. A minor character in the story was in the chariot with me, and when I jumped out to play a scene with Ben Hur, he steadied and held the team. The opening night Doc Martin, the owner of the horses, shaved off his mustache and doubled for this young Roman, so if the horses got to cutting up he could handle them.

While I was playing the scene with Ben Hur, the horses did 'cut up.' I could see Doc was in real trouble, so I vaulted into the chariot and spoke my last lines from there. Doc simply said, 'Take 'em,' and, as I started to work on the horses, he hung on to the side of the chariot. He could have driven those horses up an elevated railway pillar out in the street, but Doc was long on stage fright. His stage career was over — his mustache started to grow again right then.

'Ben Hur' was a tremendous hit. We were all sure of a full season's work and we were very happy. I, in particular, got all swelled up. The Eden Musée made a wax figure of me as Messala — I posed for the artist several times. When the figure was dressed in duplicate, it was uncanny in its realism. We closed in May. I was re-engaged for the following season.

The second season of 'Ben Hur' had an almost entirely new cast. As I remember, I was the only male member left of the principals in his original rôle. Mabel Bert, Mary Shaw, and Adeline Adler were the only ladies of the original cast.

At the stage door one night I found a friend of mine,

149

Frank O'Donnell, from Asheville. Frank was the proprietor of one of the leading liquor emporiums of the town. Through never having seen Frank drink, I had gained the impression that he was a teetotaler. I was wrong — there was nothing of the never-take-a-drink about that red-head right then. He was happy. He was in New York seeing the sights, and he didn't care who knew it.

I gathered a couple of actor friends of mine and we all started to have some refreshments and a bite of supper. O'Donnell had seen the performance that night and, as he had always been a booster of mine, I expected a whale of a compliment for my performance of Messala, for the benefit of my actor friends. In spite of a little mild fishing — no compliment came. But, of course, it was his mood of conviviality — it was hard to break through.

I couldn't turn back in the face of the enemy — I fished harder. Still no result! That Irishman had one of those actors by the lapel and was giving him the only true story ever told of Robert Emmet and the days of ninety-eight. I had unmasked my guns in the face of the enemy. I had to fire. I clutched him by the arm and gently pulled him around.

'Frank,' said I, after I had gained his attention and made the proper pause, 'you saw the performance to-night. What did you think of me as Messala?'

He shook his red Irish locks a minute. . . . At last he had it — it was coming. 'Fine! Fine! Fine!' he joyously cried; 'the horses were great.'

I had no fear of any harm befalling Frank O'Donnell on his personally conducted tour of the big city. He was a powerful man, physically, and his rollicking good nature would disarm all intention to affront any one. But I was worried about his protracted stay — he had a business that needed his attention. He had a large family of young-sters. He should go home, but, by golly, he wouldn't! Nothing I could say would move him.

Again, one night, he was waiting at the stage door, pale and SOBER. He clutched my wrist as we walked along. When at the corner under a street light, he stopped and looked at me earnestly.

'So you're here, an' you're all right,' he said.

'What's wrong, Frank — what is it?' I inquired.

'I was takin' a walk downtown, and I followed some people into a show. I was strollin' round, an' all at once you were right there in front of me, just as you are in the theater . . . you had the whip in your hand . . . an' . . . an' . . . you looked dead. I stood there an' crossed meself.'

I did not laugh. I said quietly, 'That's all right, Frank, that is a wax figure — you were in the Eden Musée.'

We walked to his lodging-place in silence and he shook my hand. 'Take a good night's sleep, Frank,' I said.

'Take nothin',' he replied; 'wait here for me a minute till I get me bag. You're goin' to the midnight train with me, an' I'm goin' home!'

I remember only one of the names of Ben Hur's four bay horses — he was called 'Monk.' My four were 'Tom' and 'Jerry,' two snow-whites, and 'Rosie' and 'Topsy,' two coal blacks.

The race was handled off stage by certain levers that worked smoothly running treadmills. Ben Hur and Mes-sala would alternate in the lead until about the center of the stage was reached, when Ben Hur would slowly draw ahead and Messala's chariot collapse. Every night and every matinée for one year and a half Rosie, Topsy, Tom, and Jerry had seen this happen — over four hundred times. They had done their best to win, and over four hundred times they had been beaten. No matter how they strived or struggled, the result was always the same — just when victory seemed within their grasp the four bays would draw away.

But their spirits remained unbroken. They knew they COULD win.

Nine tenths of the population of Bucksport, Maine, were Bill Farnum's relatives. Bill (who was then playing Ben Hur) invited the entire population of the town of his birth to see him play the part at the Colonial Theater, Boston. They came. No one was left at home but the watchman ... half of the front row was occupied by those grizzled old sons of the sea. Bill had told me they were out front. We both worked hard and took a keen delight in stealing an occasional look at their pleased, beaming faces.

It happened! It was no one's fault; one cannot blame inanimate things, and no one outside of that Gargantuan mass of wheels and steel cables could possibly be blamed. But it happened. . . .

The race was on. The whirring of the treadmills, the machine-like cracking of our whips, the pounding of the horses' rubber-shod hoofs. The applause and an occasional shriek out there in the darkness! All was there! The eight dumb animals were again running low, their necks stretched, their manes flying, their nostrils flaming. Now the four bays — now the four blacks and whites — were in the lead. The noise was deafening — the applause was thunderous — we were at the center of the stage — we held there ... WE HELD THERE. Neither chariot was gaining an inch. Shadowy figures were dashing here and there in the wings — everything was blurred.

Slowly, inch by inch, foot by foot, the blacks and whites were forging ahead. The poor beasts knew it! They knew it! They stretched out — their bellies were touching the treadmills — they quickened their action to lightning strides. I crawled out on the chariot tongue — I put my hands on their backs — I begged them, I implored them, I urged them, I cried to them — like one bereft of reason. ... They ran like creatures possessed — their veins stood out like ropes — they were out in front — they were gaining! They strained every muscle to the breaking point — they lunged ahead in a death-like dash! And — they won! THEY WON!

And to my dying day I will feel that they won in spite of all machinery, in spite of all inanimate or human things. After we left the center of the stage where the machinery went wrong, those noble beasts won on their merits. The whites know it — the blacks know it — and I know it.

Poor Bill was broken-hearted. But I don't think those simple, honest folks of Bucksport, Maine, minded it in the least. They were like kids at a circus — and, besides, they loved their Bill for himself.

CHAPTER XI
'OUT, OUT, BRIEF CANDLE'

'BEN HUR' closed in Brooklyn at the Columbia Theater. I went home to Asheville for one of the happiest summers I have ever known. We were not very much ahead financially, but our wants were few.

My family now lived in a comfortable house. There was a barn near where old Aaron's woolly head could be seen on guard under a pine-knot torch that cut a hole in the darkest night. Darkies are champion chicken-stealers, but no night-hawking cowboy or sheep-herder and his dog ever guarded their herds and flocks better than that old darky guarded our chickens. We *never* lost one.

We would go to church at Biltmore. How it pleased little Lotta to have Mr. George Vanderbilt receive her five-cent-piece offering on the plate which he passed! And how it must have pleased and what satisfaction it must have given to Mr. Vanderbilt to see such an innocent, glad young face in that little ivy-covered church, with its fine scholarly pastor, and to know that it was his means and his work that made it all possible!

It must have pleased God, too, for God was watching that little girl for his own.

There was a little scene that took place at the back porch of our home nearly every morning. Old Aaron would approach as though going past on his way to work.

'Good-morning, Uncle Aaron!'

'Mawnin' — mawnin', Miss Lotta!'

'Think it will rain to-day, Aaron?'

'No, I reckon not, Miss Lotta. I reckon the sun'll shine all day to-day!'

'Did you have your breakfast yet this morning, Aaron?'

'Not yit, Miss Lotta, not yit — not this mawnin'.'

'Would you like some breakfast, Aaron?'

'Well, Miss Lotta, seein' I'm a little early fo' to cut Miss Webb's lawn, I reckon I could drink a cup of coffee!'

And soon, for the fourth time in as many days, a heaping plate of bacon and eggs would be on this old colored man's lap, with a steaming bowl of coffee by his side, prepared by the hands of a little white girl ANGEL who loved him — as she loved everything on earth in which there was good.

One day some playmates, little girls younger than she, were going home and they said they might not be able to come again for some time. She told them they had better come, as she was going away . . . and that she liked them . . . and wanted to play with them . . . but while she had a good mother and a good sister and a good brother that she loved and would hate so much to leave . . . she knew that she was to go away on a long journey and maybe never see anybody that she loved any more.

The time came for me to go. It seemed so hard again to break the chain, so hard for me to leave. Dear little Lotta smiled through her tears until she could not stand it any longer. She broke down and cried bitterly. I called up from the station and she answered the telephone — her glorious young voice was choked with sobs. It hurt me terribly.

I was playing John Storm in 'The Christian' at Providence, Rhode Island. It was a matinée. After the second act, a messenger boy was standing in the wings, waiting — he handed me a telegram. It was from the doctor. It said my little sister was dying of typhoid fever. I caught a train at seven o'clock. I reached Asheville in thirty hours.

When my darling little sister saw me, she broke through her delirium and greeted me, but the fever pulled her right back. Five days she had been ill, and five days her temperature had been one hundred and five. I begged — I pleaded with God to leave her with us, not to take her away. During the watches of the night I cried out to Him until it seemed my heart would break, while the little girl talked her childish stories beside me.

But God would not hear me. Three days and three nights He left her with us, and then He took her away. And although I went to all the places among the trees and rocks and brooks where we had been and found blackberries, and loudly called her name, I knew that she had gone; and I am quite sure that then, as now, it was for me the end. . . . My world could never be again the same — a part of my life passed from me.

We laid her in the room she had so delighted in decorating for her joyous children's parties. I slept by her side, and an old colored man sat in the corner and kept watch; the wild pet animals moved about the grounds softly. A mother and daughter sobbed in a sleep of exhaustion upstairs.

Through the stillness of the night came the weird, quaint songs of negroes as they sat before their cabin doors singing.

We all left Asheville together. Mrs. Webb, who lived across the street, loved our Lotta. Her husband, Senator Charles Webb, accompanied us as far as Salisbury, North Carolina, where we changed cars. On the station platform some college boys came romping past; they stopped, became quiet, and said they were sorry. That night in the baggage car I fell asleep. When I awakened, I was covered with empty mail sacks, and a blanket had been spread over an angel that was riding to join her kind.

We placed our little girl in her last resting-place with her father and little brother — and there she rests. But her spirit is with God, where she knew — yet did not know — that she was going.

I placed my mother and sister in a boarding-house on Classon Avenue, Brooklyn, and rejoined my company.

In February, 1902, we played in Great Falls, Montana. Together with several members of the company I met Charlie Russell, the cowboy artist. My heart was sad. I had little to say. After the performance Charlie was heard to remark: 'The feller who doesn't talk none in the daytime is the star of the show at night.'

Charlie and I became fast friends and ever remained so. I am glad that I was one of those who induced him to come to New York and meet all the artists. It was the opening up of his splendid career.

We closed our tour at Vancouver the latter part of March — it had been a short season. And when just my railroad ticket was handed to me and no sleeper accommodations for the long return trip, I put on a blue flannel shirt, bought some crackers and cheese, rode in the smoker, and roughed it going home. What money I had I needed badly.

The most fortunate and the most unusual happened. I stepped right into another engagement — a racing play, 'The Suburban.' We opened at McVicker's Theater, Chicago, about the first of May and ran well into the summer. After a vacation we opened again and played on tour all season, closing with a ten-week engagement at the New York Academy of Music.

The season of 1903 opened auspiciously, but it just *opened* that way, that's all; it and the year following proved to be disastrous financial years. I commenced rehearsing in July and opened in August as Patrick Henry in 'Hearts Courageous,' with Orrin Johnson as the star. It was a beautiful production and fairly successful. For seven or eight weeks we were on the road, including Philadelphia and Chicago.

I was credited with having scored quite heavily as Patrick Henry, which pleased me very much, as I loved the part. Just before we came into New York, Al Levering, the manager, came to me and asked me to cut out the faint touch of Irish brogue that I was using as Henry — to play him absolutely straight. Levering may not have known, but this would have been correct, as Henry was Scotch descent — not Irish!

However, the change would have materially weakened the part of Patrick Henry, which was just what Levering was aiming at. Henry was too strong for the star rôle which was played by Orrin Johnson, and Levering thought this was hurting the play. He was not seeking to hurt me personally. I did not intend to budge in the matter, but I had no chance to fight for what I considered my rights.

Orrin Johnson came to me and asked me if Levering had spoken to me about the matter. I said, 'Yes.'

'Don't you do it,' he replied; 'tell them to go to blazes.'

He was the owner of the show. A regular actor, Orrin Johnson, AND I'm glad to say there are lots of regular actors in our country!

I had been palling on the road with Frank Stammers

and Tom Ince. We usually roomed together. Johnson always referred to us as 'The Three Musketeers.'

Tom was tremendously interested in hearing about the West and he importuned me so much, and he and Frank lent such appreciative ears, that I thawed out of my long silence. Frank was a fine musician. He played a 'cello exquisitely; his own instrument was in New York, but he would hire one in different cities and play soft, beautiful music, as I told tales of my boyhood and my Indian friends.

We all got by nicely in New York. I came through with flying colors, but our business was bad. It was inevitable that we should close; we were to play up through New England to let us down easy.

The company purchased a handsome loving cup to be presented to the star the closing night. There was never a more laudable project. Johnson had been kind, considerate, and generous in all things. He was an excellent actor and a fine man. The play failed, he did not make it fail, it was not his fault; and yet there were three anarchists who refused to go in on the cup — three renegades who did not know why they were renegades — Hart, Ince, and Stammers.

After the closing performance, when the presentation was made, these three malcontents sat at the top of the stairs and contemplated their own greatness, their soreness on all things in general, and this 'damfool' cup presentation in particular which was going on down below.

The next morning, at the train, Orrin Johnson came to the three of us with his happy smile and taking us by the arms walked us around behind the station. He said: 'You three, wonderful, fine-natured fellows! God bless all three of you! I know who did all this and I know who remained in the background out of pure modesty.' His eyes filled with tears, he gripped our arms and walked away.

We all had about forty dollars each. We found the treasurer of the cup committee. The usual subscription had been five dollars — we gave ten dollars each!

Twelve years ago Orrin Johnson was starring in two pictures, when Tom Ince was manager and I was a star. I asked Tom to let me tell Orrin. He said if I did he'd jump in the ocean. Perhaps he was right — I might have jumped in with him. I know I would have done so . . . if it had seemed to hurt Orrin.

Tom, Frank, and I all lived together at the Old Barrington Hotel, at Broadway and Forty-Fourth Street. Tom and Frank occupied the larger room with a double bed, and I had a small communicating room with a cot. Total cost for the three, $9.50 per week.

Golly! We became mighty hard up. There was a bakery on Eighth Avenue that sold little deep tin pans full of baked beans for ten cents. We used to buy stale bread — three loaves for a nickel. These, with a tin of beans, would last us two or three days. After one hiatus, when even the bread and beans did not materialize, Frank's mother, who knew nothing but of her son's prosperity, sent from Boston a fruit cake. It was delicious, but oh, so rich! We ate the whole cake at one sitting. Its richness on empty stomachs made Frank and me feel squeamish . . . but it finished Tom. He was really ill. We used home remedies of hot cloths on his stomach, but it took a couple of days to pull him out of it. I don't yet know whether hot cloths were good or bad for the ailment.

Frank hung on to his 'cello. He could pawn that for enough to keep us in room and eats for some time. But music had become a part of our life. I do not know whether fasting makes the mind's eye more fertile or not; I only know that those soft cadences of the 'cello made even our hunger seem sweet, when, supperless, we would feed on it. At night Tom would cover our one electric bulb with red paper off the writing-pad, and in the half-light Frank would play and Tom would listen.

While the 'cello breathed its harmony, I would tell of the American Indian; I would tell them of the deer, the elk, and the berry-eating bears; the prairies, the hills, the woods, and the birds that are always flying; of the storms, the thunder and lightning and the thick driving clouds; of the winter's biting blasts, and of the great snowflakes as large as a hand that came down soft and quiet to protect and keep warm all helpless things.

I would tell them of a country where there are no spies or newsmongers — only kind-hearted, friendly things; those that would fight to the death in battle, but in peace would shrink from inflicting pain. I would tell them of the land where none are strangled for free speech, where none are stoned for adultery of mind or body, because there is no adultery of mind or body; of the land where all men lie down and rest, and, when they wake, thank the Great Spirit for a better sleep.

I often think how the little triumvirate of those lean but happy days followed their bent and destiny. Tom's inclination every waking moment was all for management; he became one of the first rank. Frank was a born musician; he became a fine musical comedy and comic opera director, staging most all of the Morosco light operas ... while I drifted back from whence I came.

The time came when our $9.50 a week conservatory of music and home-made Chautauqua could be held no longer; the 'cello had to go for back rent, and there were no more dimes or nickels for beans or bread. So we took a last look at our 'council tent of the prairies' and separated on the corner. It was the middle of a cold winter in a bad year. Shows were coming in instead of going out. . . .

Through my brother-in-law's influence I secured a position with one of the largest detective agencies. It paid ninety dollars a month. It paid the rent and kept down that craving for food which seems to come natural to all humans.

The nature of my employment being secretive, it was an ideal position for an actor who had to try to keep up appearances. And as I had only three weeks and one day's work as an actor during the next eight months, I hung on to that job with the tenacity of a bulldog. I had an office to myself in the St. James Building, and, when rehearsing, I could do my work at night, which I did.

In February, I had one week's work in support of Frank Keenan, in a one-act play at the Berkley Lyceum. It was an adaptation of or from the same source as 'Pagliacci,' and was called 'The Strolling Players.' My part was the lover. I enjoyed playing it very much, as it was all pantomime. Grace Filkins, a charming actress and a fine lady, did all the talking and I did the rest — to the best of my ability. I was on the stage during nearly all of the act. I was afraid some of our stuff would get laughs, but I was wrong. It held splendidly.

In April, I had one day's work with four weeks' rehearsals that paid me one hundred dollars. This engagement stands out in my memory as an example of what errors of judgment can be made in playwriting, and what slight happenings can change the destiny of an actor or actress.

The play was 'Love's Pilgrimage.' The author was

Horace B. Fry, librarian of the Union League Club, and a writer of distinction; the director, Edmund Lyons, a man of reputation and ability. The leading female rôle was written for an established actress, Carlotta Nillson, the object being to make her a star. The cast was composed of well-known men and women, including Guy Bates Post as the villain, and myself as the hero. Yet everybody concerned went straight ahead to destruction like a horse with the 'blind staggers.'

Post saw it coming, and so did I. As badly as I needed the hundred, I tried to quit twice; and twice Miss Nillson laughed at my fear and talked me out of it, saying, 'The play is a masterpiece — a sure triumphant success!'

There were two situations that filled me clean up to my throat with disquietude. The play opened in the penal settlement of Tasmania. The Governor's daughter (Miss Nillson) aids her lover (myself), an Irish political prisoner — a 'lifer' — to escape. In the second act the Governor's daughter, in the presence of her suitor (Guy Bates Post), explained to her father that she could not marry — that she was already married to the escaped convict, and when her irate parent justly demanded to know, 'Who were your witnesses?' she replied, 'The flowers and the birds.'

Before a house packed with celebrities, during a matinée at Wallack's Theater, this situation was enacted. Guy Post came into the dressing-room broken-hearted; the scene had been received with howls and shrieks of laughter. In the last act was to come the other scene which I dreaded. ... After a lapse of seven years, the young wife, now a seamstress seeking employment, with her child by the hand meets the hero, in the garden of his home. Before the final embrace there were inexhaustible 'flowers and birds' lines to be spoken that I had always felt it would be suicide to speak, and now, on account of the blowing up of the scene in the second act, I was sure of it!

Miss Nillson had gone all to pieces. As soon as they would get her up on her feet, off she would go into another fainting spell. . . . Something had to be done, and quickly. Both for the good of the lady and myself, I took a chance on an heroic measure. I saw the lady. I begged. 'Miss Nillson, please, for your sake and mine, do as I ask. When we meet, forget your lines — and I will do the same. Please, lady, for both of our sakes, do this. Our reputation, our future, our very livelihood depends on it. Silence in that situation is our only chance.'

She looked at me and nodded her head in assent. I was on the stage nearly twenty minutes before she came on. We were alone. We stared at each other.

I do not know whether Miss Nillson could have spoken or not — she acted as though she could not. She stood and stared, and I stood and stared — and then both of us stood and stared some more, neither one of us moving a muscle. Just as we were about to crack, it came! Thunders of applause that fairly rocked the theater! The audience had been trying to applaud all afternoon, and when they saw what seemed like an Ibsen effect in a ten-twenty-and-thirty scene, they went crazy!

The critics all gave Miss Nillson and me a wonderful send-off for this scene — 'Which tore off its hackneyed conventions and gave the audience a view of two bare souls.' Miss Nillson was immediately placed under a long-term starring contract by Charles Frohman.

But poor 'Love's Pilgrimage' . . . Alan Dale said, in substance: 'It was the best invention yet discovered to empty a theater in case of fire!'

About this time I received an object lesson — if Fate

rubbing it in on a threadbare actor can be called an object lesson. I had been offered the 'Hearts Courageous' production for one-night stands, to star as Patrick Henry, on a small royalty and no cash advance. I tried unsuccessfully to see Mr. Erlanger, to find out if he would book it. I could not get past the outside office. The next two mornings I was outside the entrance of the Amsterdam Theater Building at 7.45. The elevator boy finally took pity on me and told me Mr. Erlanger had been thirty minutes ahead of me each morning.

I wrote him what had happened. He would not book a play that had already failed; but he saw me ... and he grinned when he saw me, too! Doggone him!

In June, Fortune's wheel turned my way a bit. Hugh Ford, the stage director for the Proctor Theaters, took a vacation and engaged me to take his place. I played a starring engagement of three weeks at the Fifth Avenue and One Hundred and Twenty-Fifth Street Theater in 'The Lady of Lyons' and 'The New Magdalene.' I was paid one hundred a week and fifty dollars extra for using my own adaptation of Wilkie Collins's 'The New Magdalene.' It enabled me to send my mother and sister to Huntington, Long Island, for two months of hot weather.

What looked like a sure-fire engagement was an awful bloomer. A big melodrama, written by C. T. Dazy, titled 'Home Folks,' with Klaw and Erlanger and Joe Brooks as producers, opened at the Walnut Street Theater, Philadelphia, December 12th, played two weeks, followed at the New York Theater for four more, then took that sad truck route to the storehouse.

Again I was landed in the middle of winter, and my detective job that meant eats and sleeps for me and mine was gone. Some other 'professional,' working under cover, had it. (I think it was a lawyer this time.)

CHAPTER XII

CHILDHOOD DAYS REBORN

I was walking Broadway, broke, sore, and despondent. I had been doing the same thing for weeks. I met an English actor, Ted Emery, who had worked with me in 'The Christian.'

'Of all actors on earth,' he said, 'I would have thought you to be the first one engaged for this new Western play, "The Squaw Man."'

I had not heard of it. 'Who is doing it?' I asked.

He looked at me quizzically, as though he thought I was lying; then said: 'Well, there must be something wrong, Bill. George Tyler is doing a Western play which has a part that was written for you. It's a ranch foreman, or whatever you call it, and he is called "Big Bill."'

I doubtingly went to the Liebler Company's offices in the Knickerbocker Building. Mr. Tyler was a big man and it was very hard to see him, but I waited until I did. Yes, it was all true, but the cast was all filled. The first act of the play took place in England and was filled by Mr. Faversham's 'Letty' company. That cut down the cast — the Western parts had all been cast.

I said, 'I was told there is a part called "Big Bill" — who plays that part?'

He told me, and whoever the actor was, I do not recall his name even now — I had never heard of him. I turned away, thoroughly disheartened. I was at the door when Mr. Tyler called after me, 'There is a bit in the second act you might play — I'll pay you your salary for the three weeks' try-out.'

THE SQUAW MAN AND THE CHAPS

'No,' I said, 'I don't think I'll do it.'

As I was going out, he called again and said, 'Well, as it is a cowboy, I thought you might want to play it.'

I came back and said, 'Is it a sure-enough cowboy, and can I play it as a cowboy?'

'You can play it any way you please,' he said; 'he's a mean skunk.'

About half a dozen actors, including myself, reported for rehearsals at Buffalo, some time in April. Faversham was just closing his tour in 'Letty,' an English play and an English company.

I cannot imagine a more discouraging start than the opening rehearsals of 'The Squaw Man.' In the first place, the author, Edwin Milton Royle, while a really high-class dramatist, didn't know what a quirt was — he called it a whip! However, like all men of big brain and level head, he listened and acted. He called George Tyler on the telephone, and I was at once empowered to order chaps, quirts, spurs, etc., which I did by wire, from Pueblo, Colorado. The chaps they had furnished for us all to wear were made out of old rugs and doormats that had been lying around the storehouse. The legs were fur all the way round like an Eskimo's pants! And with Englishmen to wear them — it was tragic, but oh, so funny!

I recall one English actor saying to me: 'I say, old chap, you seem to be a bit of an authority on these uniforms. Why is it some of us wear *white* fur pants? Is it because we belong to the same regiment?'

At London, Ontario, the English assistant property man put rim-fire cartridges in a center-fire gun with which the squaw was to kill me by a shot fired off stage. Faversham was the star, but I had been looked to so much in all things that when the gun snapped and no explosion came, he said, 'What will we do?'

'Let's fight,' I replied.

We did — we rolled all over the stage. Finally, I said, 'Stab me! Stab me!'

Faversham had no knife, but he stabbed me just the same. The crowd rushed on, and the bewildered man said, 'I've stuck him, but I think he'll live.'

I don't remember what became of the assistant property man. I know I never saw him again and I doubt if Faversham did, either.

'The Squaw Man' played its scheduled three weeks on the road. It had practically an English company, who — while all excellent actors — knew nothing of the types they were playing. It had no advertising; it was just tagged onto the close of a season. And through it all — it made good! Mr. Tyler engaged me for the next season and asked me what I thought of the play's chances. I told him I didn't have one hundred dollars, but if I had one hundred thousand, I'd give ninety-nine thousand of it for a half-interest in 'The Squaw Man.'

To show how much Mr. Tyler thought of my judgment, he promptly made Charles Frohman a present of a half-interest. I do not know how much money 'The Squaw Man' made — I know it made several fortunes.

There were three months' idleness ahead. It was imperative that I earn money somehow. I appealed to my brother-in-law again, and again he secured me a position with the detective agency at the same salary; but this time I had to work outside. The nature of the work made it just as secretive. But through my lack of experience, when starting in I came mighty near getting man-handled, or something worse several times. My conscience is clear, however. I earned my salary several thousand times over. I stumbled onto a regular network of robbery that they had been seeking to get a line on for two years.

When we opened at Wallack's Theater, Cash Hawkins was the first presentation of a real American cowboy that Broadway had ever seen. And right nobly they responded. The critics and the public loved the devil, drunk or sober, as much as I did.

There is something about that which rings true that makes people know it is true!

We remained at Wallack's for the entire season.

W. E. Henley wrote: 'I am the master of my fate; I am the captain of my soul.'

Victor Hugo wrote: 'Man is neither master of his life nor of his fate.'

When these minds in calm reflection could not find a way out, except with opposite opinions, it gives me courage to confess that as a 'master of my fate' I was a sad failure.

There comes a time in every New York actor's career that for business reasons it is deemed essential that he become a social climber. While no amount of the taking up of an actor can improve his work or make an actor out of him, it can and often does secure him engagements and opportunities to show that he can act. Managers have very large ears and are very prone to listen to society. It means swell first-night audiences.

My fate in this respect was handed to me. I could not master it — I could not hold it. Every time I was boosted up a rung on the social ladder, I slipped back two, and always remained at the bottom.

I was ambitious. My soul was crying out its eagerness to succeed in my profession. The champions of my cause were steeped in that which I seemed to need, yet I never could make the grade. I never could wear the purple clothes of society. I knew that I lacked education, but I also recognized that I knew how to listen and not to talk. I knew that my parents were gentlefolk — born of gentlefolk — and that I had been brought up in an atmosphere of refined feelings, no matter how great the privation and lack of worldly goods. My youth had been spent in the open, but the open never spoiled anybody. It was in myself that I would not do! I did not expect any *boutonnières* nor jewels on my chest — I only wanted to slip through the gate, on account of my labors to please. I was a one-hundred-per-cent failure.

The loyal, loving helpers, who were trying to advance me in my profession, who were seeking to lift me out of obscurity and mold me to the form of fashion, were two ladies; two ladies who had reached such heights of perfection in themselves that they flowed over, and saw gold where even copper did not exist. Miss Giulia Strakosch, daughter of the former grand opera impresario, and niece of Mrs. Osborn, the leader of New York's so-called 'Smart Set,' was a member of 'The Squaw Man' company. Her schoolmate and friend of years' standing was Miss Ethel Barrymore, then starring in 'Alice Sit-by-the-Fire.' These are the two ladies who saw veins of gold in a baser metal.

Miss Strakosch had her brother go with me and help me choose two suits of clothes. I was invited to many parties at Mrs. Osborn's, where I met many delightful people. And then to try my wings a bit in strange surroundings, I was a guest at a big party given at a select Seventeenth Street home, where I really believe all of the celebrities then in New York were invited.

CASH HAWKINS AT A PARTY

I did my little recitation stunt and got by finely, but I wound up in the butler's pantry mixing punch and opening champagne for the servants; my only consolation being that working diligently beside me was Jack Barrymore. I have often wondered if Jack ever got any higher.

I received an invitation to attend a party given by Mrs. Jackson Gouraud. I wrote my regrets. The business manager of 'The Squaw Man' came to my dressing-room and told me that Mr. Tyler had been seen in the matter and would like very much for me to change my mind and go, as a matter of business. I still stuck to my guns and declined. Then Mr. Jackson Gouraud, escorted by the manager, came to see me, personally, and he was such a regular man that I thought I could get away with it and consented.

The party was held on a Sunday night. When I arrived at the house and was ushered into an elevator with liveried attendants, I thought, 'Golly, this isn't so much — it is just an apartment house!' When we went up several flights, the elevator stopped in a big room and the attendant at my elbow ushered me out, saying, 'Mawster's floor, sir,' which was not so good.

Here was a private home with elevators. I sat down and waited. No one else was there. Finally Mr. Gouraud came and gently broke the news to me that it was a costume ball and that I had been expected to come in my cowboy clothes. I would have given anything to escape, but again the charming personality of Jackson Gouraud won out. He sent his man in a car down to Wallack's Theater armed with a letter from me to Pat, the doorkeeper, and the man came back with everything in the dressing-room. And in due time, in the character of Cash Hawkins, I again entered the elevator and joined the party.

I cannot imagine anything being more gorgeous. The kings, queens, courtiers, and prime ministers of all periods seemed to be there. The Carmens, Cleopatras, and Queens of Sheba — all appropriately gowned and dazzlingly beautiful, just flooded the place. Victor Herbert's orchestra was faintly visible through a bower of foliage. I had never seen anything so beautiful before . . . I have never seen anything more beautiful since.

Cash Hawkins was a prominent stage portrayal on Broadway that winter, and after the seeming bizarre dress of the cowboy had been explained many times, and after I had done my usual recitation stunt, I was pretty much in demand by the Carmens and queens — and my steps often led toward the punch-bowl.

I could see that the rascals were aiming to have some fun with me, but I felt I was under complete control. I wasn't. Soon I saw that I wasn't, and I didn't care a doggone bit, either, if I wasn't. If they were determined to have fun with me and have me fill a hand-painted ceiling with lead — there was nothing easier. It could be done, and it was done. And I remember distinctly when the smoke of those forty-fives had rolled away, the kings, queens, and Carmens were not present, and the bushes that had masked the orchestra were all mussed up, too, and there was a fiddle or two lying 'round.

Mrs. Gouraud wrote me that I was the life of the party; that it was the greatest party that she had ever given; that she didn't mind the ruined ceiling in the least, although it was rather hard to locate the artist in Holland who did it; and would I please come again and be sure and bring my guns. And then followed a more intimate inquiry — would I please tell her if I had been serious in any of my proposals of marriage; that while all seven were dear

A RANGE RIDER OF THE YELLOWSTONE
Bronze statue at Billings, Montana, unveiled July 4, 1927

friends of hers and she must remain neutral, she would do her best to help me out.

I never was a frequent tippler of the cup that cheers. But when I dug up about six or eight ladies' handkerchiefs out of my few pockets, I realized that I had again 'failed to master my fate.'

I went on the water-wagon for five months; and although the Gourauds with a tallyho and six drove up to my little flat over a milk store — three different mornings — I remained true to myself, even if I had been false to the ladies of the seven handkerchiefs. I stayed home.

When the season of 'The Squaw Man' closed, I was engaged to remain for another year, and for the first time in my life I had a few hundred dollars ahead. I was determined that we should have a fine summer. I traveled to the end of the Long Island Railroad, Amagansett, and engaged board for my mother, my sister Mary, and myself, right down on the beach. We gave up the flat over the milk store, stored our bit of furniture, and were all ready to go . . . when the Amagansett boarding-place decided to delay opening for another week.

My mother and my sister Mary accepted an invitation to visit with one of my married sisters in Garden City for the week. The day before we were to start for our summer home, I was called on the telephone. My mother was injured; she had slipped on the hardwood floor and broken her thigh and hip, a compound fracture. I took my mother to the Mineola Hospital, one mile from Garden City, and I lived at the little village hotel at Mineola — nine dollars per week, room and board. My sister Mary remained as guest at our married sister's home.

When it was time for me to go on the road, I secured a

boarding-place for my mother and sister at Richmond Hill, Long Island. I exchanged my watch for a ticket, to settle the last week's hospital bill.

I remember how my mother suffered to keep from groaning when the auto driver and myself carried her past the 'wise' boarders who decorated the porch, while my sister Mary brought up the rear with an armful of blankets and rubber rings. Had I left my mother in the hospital, she would have died. My sister Mary and Dr. Sam Lambert kept my mother alive. Later on, my sister Mary moved our mother to another more comfortable Classon Avenue boarding-house in Brooklyn. How she did it alone and un-aided, I do not know. When the season closed and I came back from the road, I found them there.

My mother had suffered so much and her ailments were of such long standing that she knew she could not weather the storm very much longer. I knew she had a horror of being bedridden, or having a long siege of illness in a board-ing-house. She had just been through it, and her eagerness to get away from the possibility of such a thing happening again was pathetic.

I had nine hundred dollars in cash and I made up my mind it was now, or never, for a home. J. N. Marchand and Walter Gallaway, two artist friends of mine, had bought homes at Westport, Connecticut. I did likewise. I paid eight hundred dollars cash on an eighteen-hun-dred-dollar place, then borrowed six hundred from the agent who sold the place to me (Joe Hyatt is the agent's name)., I overhauled the house, made it livable, and we moved in. For the first time in my life I could sit under a tree on my own property.

Shortly afterward I was engaged to play 'The Virginian' for the next season at one hundred and twenty-five dollars per week. I loved the part of 'The Virginian.' It is a beautiful story and a beautiful play — a monument to the fact that a truly great writer can make the moon look like green cheese and get away with it. But I am afraid I offended Owen Wister and lost his friendship in saying so.

Owen Wister was a wonderful writer. His stuff was human, simple, and delightful. He loved the West. He loved to write of the West. But there was a lot that he did not know about the West. He was too big a man to hold resentment. Had this not been so, I'm afraid I should have been discharged instead of being engaged for a second season at twenty-five dollars a week advance in salary. I made a big hit as 'The Virginian' and the show made money everywhere.

Perhaps I should have remained quiet, but I couldn't and didn't. The truth of the West meant more to me than a job and always will! I never sought to offend any one, I never said my little say publicly, but I said it privately and to Mr. Wister, personally.

Fundamentally, the book, the play of 'The Virginian,' as far as the West is concerned, is at variance with cowboy life as I knew it. Two cowboys are partners; one is foreman, the other is a top hand. The top hand is caught by the foreman branding calves. The foreman tells his friend old dog Tray was a good dog, but that he got in bad company. The top hand is weak. He joins a bunch of outlaws and they run off some cattle. The ranch owners meet, form a posse, and decide to run down the thieves. There is only one man who knows the mountain trail. He is the foreman (the Virginian). They ask if he will lead them. He will and he does. He leads the posse of twenty men to the little camp of the three cattle rustlers in the mountains and hangs his friend, the top hand (Steve) to a tree.

In the first place, the foreman would have refused flat-footed to trail his friend, and the ranchers would have respected him for so refusing. In the next place, if he had led the posse he would have led them the wrong direction and the ranchers would have expected him to do so, and again, respected him for it. And if he had led them to his friend and found his friend, he would have done it for a reason. He would have stepped to his friend's side and said: 'Well, gentlemen, I have done my duty and brought you here, but if you hang him, you've got to hang me, too! And we ain't neither of us strong for being hung while we've got our guns on.'

And, also, it must not be forgotten that branding calves in the West was a hanging offense . . . maybe! The majority of owners didn't hesitate to brand a few, and the minority couldn't be trusted, either.

And, then, if necessary, a final reason. . . . There is an old adage in the cattle country, 'Never set a cow-puncher to catch a cow-puncher.'

In February, we played Great Falls, Montana, and my good friends, Charlie and Nancy Russell, met us at the train and took our leading lady and me to their home for dinner. After dinner Charlie uncovered his latest work. It was a splendid painting of myself riding a bronc through the sagebrush. Charlie had done it for me. It is one of my most prized possessions.

The summer of 1908 was a happy summer. My mother was not entirely well, but she could sit in her chair on the porch, and feel that she was at home. It made us all very happy. I spent many hours tramping over Old Hill and the surrounding country with my bulldog, Mack.

My Mother's Illness

Several more artists had come to Westport and, as it was hard for them to get models for Western stuff, I posed several times for them, mostly for Marchand and Fred Yohn. And in return they made drawings of me in characters which I had played and gave them to me.

When I left home in the fall, it was again like the old days in Asheville, only the bright, young face was not there — 'No touch of that vanished hand or sound of the voice that was still.'

My dear mother became frightfully ill during the winter. She was operated on at a hospital in Stamford and my sister made daily trips on the trolley to visit her. When she was brought home, she needed constant nursing night and day. Again, Dr. Samuel Lambert stepped in and made trips from New York, arriving at midnight, covered with the mud of heavy roads.

My mother pulled through, but she was still very ill when I returned in the spring and my sister was worn almost to a shadow from nursing and caring for her. Our one cause for rejoicing was that, on account of my season's salary at one hundred and fifty per week, I had been able to pay off the thousand-dollar mortgage. The home was all ours! It acted like a tonic to my mother. How eagerly she would look forward to seeing our village neighbors come in, and how her eyes would glisten as she would tell them that the home was all paid for!

Another tranquillized summer passed — so unruffled that it sort of lulled me into a false state of security. I had had a four years' run of luck and I began to believe in myself. I began to believe that I would receive offers; that managers would write to me and give me work. They didn't! So I caught the early train, and at 9 A.M. was once more doing the familiar round of the agencies.

177

Nothing had changed — everything was the same. I had merely been asleep for four years. That was all. Tired and footsore, I returned at night to the little white house on the hill, but the glad smile did not fool those who were waiting on the little porch. They knew! It was only the dog that did not know, and he was waiting for his walk, or he would have known, too. But I think even he knew when we climbed over Old Hill and looked at the setting sun. I think he knew how gladly I would have signed a twenty-five-dollar a week contract for life . . . to saw wood, teach acting, hoe potatoes! or any steady, honest employment.

My pride was hurt. I had startled Broadway and remained a whole season; I had toured the country and was lauded as an actor from coast to coast; yet I only imagined I had climbed — I hadn't climbed at all. It was the same waiting outside of a little rail fence while the fat occupant of a swivel-chair listened languidly to the whining, pleading, sickening inquiries of those ahead on the line as to the health of the chair occupant's son, or the inflammation on the left upper eyelid of the office cat: only to be dismissed after a half-hour, hat-in-hand wait, with a curt, over the shoulder, 'Nothing to-day.'

Actors are often happiest when poorest; actors love their profession. It is a good thing that they do, otherwise there would be more justifiable homicides.

I had grown weary and heartsick tramping the New York streets. I was at home mowing the lawn. The telephone rang. It was Mr. Brooks, of Klaw and Erlanger's office. . . . 'Will you play Dan Stark in "The Barrier"? — Come down at once.'

The actual train time between Westport, Connecticut, and Grand Central Station was one hour and ten minutes.

My Mother's Death

I was at Klaw and Erlanger's office in about one-twelve.

I had worked for Klaw and Erlanger in their biggest successes, yet I had been passed up for a Western part until one reputable actor had been let out, and another, after several rehearsals, had refused to play the part. Rex Beach wrote the part. Rex Beach knew the West — and the actors who rehearsed it did not. I played the part all season.

When I left home, the parting was sad. My mother looked at me wistfully when I kissed her good-bye. My sister smiled through a tear, and my comrade, the old bull-dog, followed me to the gate and cried.

We played a week of one-night stands *en route* to Chicago and opened at McVicker's Theater.

I received a wire from my sister — my mother was having a frightful attack; my sister doubted if she would pull through.

Tuesday, the spirit of death that had been hovering over the little white house on the hill, came. A broken-hearted girl, alone in her grief, was weeping over her mother's body . . . and a white bulldog that knew all, yet could not help, crawled under the house.

We had just opened the season. It was a new production — there were as yet no understudies. If I left, it would close the theater and ruin the chances of a new play. I did not go. Perhaps I was wrong — I do not know. I only know that it was my duty to have gone in spite of all the theaters this side of hell. Had I been stopped from going, I feel that I should have gone, but all was sympathy and kindness on all sides — just a silent entreaty not to injure them if I could help doing so.

I did not go . . . and the lone girl on the hill with our mother saw her placed in her last home with our father, and Lotta and the little Western boy, and when she came back to the little white house on the hill, alone, the old dog came out from the place where he had been for days in grief, and licked her hand.

Rex Beach, the author, and George Warren, the manager of McVicker's Theater, were very good and kind. They spent much time in my dressing-room with me.

At the hour when my mother was being placed in her last home, I went to an empty church on the North Side and said my prayers, as she had taught me, and as I had so often said them when a little boy kneeling at her side.

'The Barrier' remained at McVicker's for several weeks. Toward the end of the run some of the boys were going on a party after the show. It happened to be salary night, and three of them, who were all living at the same hotel on the North Side with me, gave me their unopened salary envelopes to keep for them. One took a six-shooter out of his trunk and loaded it and asked me to carry it. I had never packed a gun before and have never packed one since, but on account of an epidemic of hold-ups then taking place in Chicago and on account of having all the salaries, I took the gun. We were living at a hotel — I think it was called The Indiana. The shortest way to walk home, which we always did together, was over the Rush Street Bridge. Just before coming to the bridge was a very dark spot and there were many little blind alleyways. It was a decidedly hard neighborhood.

Right at the most favorable spot for a hold-up, an athletic-looking chap, with a cap drawn down over his eyes, stepped out and said, 'Do you mind if I walk across the bridge with you? I got a bit of money on me and I'm afraid to tackle it alone.'

His hands were in his sack coat pockets. Although it was a cool night, he wore no overcoat. I took a chance and jammed my gun against his short ribs and said, loud enough to be heard thirty feet away, 'Get your hands as high as your shoulders and keep 'em there. Walk ahead an' walk fast, an' if any one follows us, or comes within twenty feet of us on the bridge, there'll be six slugs of lead in your guts.'

My instructions were obeyed to the letter. There was a corner saloon on the other side of the bridge where we always stopped at the side entrance and had some sandwiches and beer before going home. When opposite this door, I stopped and spoke, 'Now keep right on goin'.'

'All right, Jimmie,' he replied. 'But, say, will you tell me somethin', where in hell did you git that gat from?'

I said: 'Don't worry about that. All you've got to remember is, quit your game, because there are loads of men floating around that are much faster with a gun than I am.'

He walked on, but, just as he was fading into the darkness outside of the rays of light thrown by the saloon, he said, half-turning, 'Yeah! What's their names, Houdini?'

Early in January we opened in New York at the new Amsterdam Theater. 'The Barrier' was an unusual play. It had only eight characters, and six of the eight were star rôles. It was a splendid drama and every part was beautifully acted. Therefore, I felt all the more happy when I was singled out for an ovation on the opening night.

In the early days when I spent many hours in the libraries, I read where Edmund Kean, after his first night in London, went home and told his waiting wife, 'They rose to me.' The audience at the Amsterdam 'rose to me.' At the final curtain I received an individual call that was an ovation, although I had just played a death scene.

The critics all spoke glowingly of my acting. But what pleased me most, they gave me credit for my knowledge of the West, saying, 'He supplies a welcome addition to his list of Western desperadoes that recalls no kinsman, near or remote.'

Mr. W. B. (Bat) Masterson, one of the greatest gun-fighter peace officers that the West ever knew, wrote editorially in 'The Morning Telegraph':

'The part of Dan Stark by William S. Hart seems to have been made to order for that clever impersonator of Western characters. Any one familiar with the character of the cool, calculating, and daring desperado, whose presence was a part of frontier life a generation ago, will instantly recognize in Mr. Hart a true type of that reckless nomad who flourished on the border when the six-shooter was the final arbiter of all disputes between man and man. Mr. Hart looks the part, dresses the part, and acts as if he were the real Dan Stark and had stepped out of the book upon the stage.'

After the New York run we went on the road, and I remember a most unusual happening that baptized and made a lasting convert out of me to the power of mental suggestion.

'The Barrier' company was a happy family. We were always harmlessly kidding each other. In the first act, one of our gang, Giunio Socola, had to deliver a tricky sort of speech to Theodore Roberts and myself. Theodore, in the dressing-room, on trains, or any old time, would twist the speech around and say to Socola, 'Now, don't you ever read it that way.'

Socola would just grin. Theodore kept it up and, after

a while, Socola asked him to quit, that the lines were commencing to worry him. Poor Socola came to a bad crowd for sympathy. I became one of the 'bull-baiters' also, and we could see we had him worried. And, by golly! It happened! And, furthermore, we knew it was going to happen, and when Theodore and I saw the sweat breaking through the make-up and the look of helplessness on poor Socola's face, we both involuntarily took a step forward, but we could not do anything, no matter how willing we were. Socola had started the fatal speech, and he read it with every syllable crying out suffering, just as we had hammered it into him for months: a silly mass of risqué stuff that had no bearing on the play, whatever. Roberts did not laugh — I did not laugh — no one in the company laughed. It was tragic!

When we returned to New York, Taylor Granville, an actor with whom I had worked some years before, came to me with a vaudeville act that he had tried out, 'The Hold-Up.' It had been a failure. They would not book it. He had a carload of scenery and two excellent railroad effects. I rewrote the act and we tried it out in Brooklyn, with myself as the star. It was a hit. We went into the American Theater for a run and it drew the first critics of the city to review it. We then went to Chicago for three weeks. The act was a big hit and very valuable. Granville quarreled with me. I parted with an interest in a fine piece of property for seventy-five dollars.

That summer my sister and I lived alone in the little white house on the hill. I acted as helper to a stonemason and we built a small addition to the little home. And at sunset I would walk over the hills with old Mack.

I was engaged by Charles Frohman for the following

season to play the part of Sherlock Holmes in an English melodrama of Conan Doyle's that had just finished a run of over a year in London. I was highly elated at securing the part, as Sherlock Holmes, while English to the core, is thoroughly Western in all his characteristics. William Gillette, an American, had given the best performance ever presented of Sherlock Holmes.

After the first few rehearsals I was heartbroken. Willie Seymour was an excellent director. But why should he, as Charles Frohman's director-general, worry about staging a proved success that had every bit of business written down in the prompt book, and with the English stage manager who was sent over with the play to keep all straight.

I stuck it out for one week and then quit. I was not big enough to give Seymour or Charles Frohman an argument; but I guess Charles Frohman wished that I had. The big successful melodrama that had everything had nothing. It opened and closed in Boston. If it had done anything else, I should have been *positive* that I was crazy. And yet they couldn't see it — 'It was a success in London!'

To me, 'Love's Pilgrimage' — of 'emptying a theater in case of fire' fame — was a classic by comparison to this big foreign success, 'The Speckled Band.'

I did not lose any time. I started right out in vaudeville with 'The Hold-Up.' William Morris would book the act for ten weeks, but not without me, so once more I allowed Granville to out-talk me. I took a salary of one hundred and seventy-five dollars a week. But it was work, and I needed the money.

At the expiration of the ten weeks, I was engaged by the Liebler Company for 'These Are My People,' another Edwin Milton Royle play — a sequel to 'The Squaw

Man.' It had been on the road and failed, and both Royle and George Tyler thought that by getting the old 'Squaw Man' cast we could save it. We couldn't. After playing it a week on the road, we closed, came into New York, rehearsed all night Saturday night, all day Sunday and Sunday night, and opened New Year's Day matinée, in a revival of 'The Squaw Man,' to fill in the time booked at the Broadway Theater.

While I was playing 'The Virginian' a few years previous, 'The Squaw Man' was produced in London. They wanted me to do Cash Hawkins, but I could not go. George Fawcett, the Big Bill of the New York cast, was the only one of the old principals available. George went and made a big hit — and justly so. He is a great actor! For some time it had been George's favorite indoor sport to tease me, his pet line being, 'Thought you raised hell as Cash Hawkins in New York, didn't ye? Well, if I'd had you in London, they never would have known you were in the show!'

All during our day and night rehearsing I badgered George to death about his London hit, and what would happen to it now! I was plenty nervous myself, for George Fawcett is some actor, but George didn't know I was nervous; nor did George know he was 'some actor' either — so he was nervous, too!

Cash Hawkins proved to be as popular as usual and, after the first performance, I went looking for George, but, although he dressed next door to me, I did not see him for two days, and when I did see him, it was only his head stuck through the door as he slammed a two-foot square by six inches thick, heavily bound book down on my dressing-table, saying, 'There, damn you, read that.' It was a book of his London notices!

There was a favorite Broadway comedian, Ernest Lambart, playing a British army major. He was an excellent actor. He knew his business thoroughly, but he had been 'gagging' in Broadway light operas so long that his antics were not exactly those of a British army officer, nor were they conducive to holding a serious dramatic situation with a drink-crazed cowboy. After a couple of performances, when I shoved my gun into his ribs, it meant nothing to him and he commenced to edge in his 'opera' comedy, which of course would be fatal.

I had a way of working the hammer of my gun with my thumb as a menace. Its clicking was quite effective. I didn't want it spoiled.

We all dressed along one hallway and were constantly running in and out of rooms. I placed my gun and bullets just where I wanted them, warned my room-mate to play straight for me, and waited! Soon in came Lambart with some of his usual English jokes — and they were funny, too! I listened attentively and laughed at the proper time; but somehow Lambart didn't put the same pep into the second joke; he kept talking, but his mind and his eyes were on me, as I slowly and carefully shoved five leaden pills into my six-shooter, keeping the barrel pointing to the wall and nonchalantly working the hammer. His voice died to a whisper. The story, if finished, was pointless — there was no laugh.

'Eh, eh, I say, old chap,' said he. 'Do you have those damn things in there when that twenty-one-ton thing is up against my stomach?'

'Why, sure,' I replied. 'Sure, a gun has to be loaded to get the proper metallic click. When I work the hammer with my thumb, you know how quiet the audience is and how effective it is.'

'Yes, yes, I know! I know! But when you let the hammer down, don't it strike?'

'No!' I replied. 'I always let it down on the empty chamber.'

'But, oh, I say!' he cried — his voice was high-pitched now. 'How do you know when it's on the empty chamber? You are always looking right at me.'

'I keep count of the clicks,' I replied.

'Oh!' he said, 'Oh.' He went away.

There were no more funny stories, nor did Lambart ever transgress the strictest rules of legitimate drama again. He watched me like a hawk, every move I made. He was game — but, golly, he was scared!

The run lasted only three or four weeks. Had it lasted longer, I should have told him — that I not only did not use lead in the gun, but I drew the powder out of blanks and used the empty shells.

I had brought my sister and the old dog down from Westport and we had taken a little apartment. It was another tough winter. Many first-class actors were out of work. Several of us used to go uptown in the subway in the early morning hours, after spending an evening at the Lambs, and many nights we discussed different forms of suicide, and not altogether in jest, either.

I was out of employment about two months in the middle of winter, when I was called by an agent to see a manager that was taking a show on the road. The play had made its first bow in New York, had just bowed and that's all, and then had gone to the storehouse. An actress thought she saw a part in the play suitable to her talents and her husband secured the play and had a route booked for it. Its Broadway name was 'My Man.' We played it as 'The Quality of Mercy.' After a few weeks on the road, the husband's name for it was 'Arlington's Folly' — his name being Arlington.

My salary for three years had been one hundred and fifty dollars per week. There was a big line of actors at the agency. I stated my salary with shaking voice and trembling limbs. Lord! I could have asked five hundred and gotten it.

'You don't know me,' the manager said.

I smiled weakly. I should have said I had known him for eighty years if I could only have thought of some possible place where I could have know him.

'I'm Eddie Arlington,' said he.

I was not enlightened. . . . After another long pause . . . 'Owner of the 101 Show,' he continued smilingly.

'God!' . . . and thereby hangs a tale. . . .

In April, 1908, I was playing 'The Virginian' at McVicker's Theater, Chicago. The Miller Brothers' 101 Show was at the Coliseum. The rival press representatives got to press-agenting a little too hard. I was saying, through the press agent of McVicker's, without knowing it — 'Wire fences have done away with all real cowboys.'

The cowboys, through the press agent of the 101 Show, were saying, without knowing it, 'Who is this guy Hart, anyhow? Send him out here and let him top off a bronc.'

The newspapers got tired of it, and at the same time saw a story and joined the pack, saying, 'Sure! There is your chance, Mr. Virginian, go out and ride a nice gentle horse.'

And when I declined with thanks, not wanting to get my head busted against a quarter pole, the 101 press men again slapped me in the stomach, saying, 'Maybe this stage actor don't want to trust his little self on a wicked pony that rares up and puts his ears back.'

Take it all in all, I was having a very pleasant time. I tried to smile it off and kid it off, but it would not be smiled off, nor kidded off. Something had to be done — and that, *pronto*. I hadn't been on a horse for years. I knew if I tried to bluff it through, I'd draw the meanest twister in the show, and any rider on earth has to be in condition to sit up on a bronc and take what that bronc wants to give. Don't ever let any one tell you different, because if they do they are lying.

But this wasn't helping me a bit — I was becoming a joke. I had to work fast. Finally it hit me! What a dog-gone fool I had been! I jumped up and down with glee, and then in the most self-satisfied, cold-blooded manner set out to take full advantage of the situation. It sounded hard, but it was easy, and there was no danger of getting smashed up. I sent for the rival press agents. I told them I was tired of all this four-flushing and badgering. I had a proposition to make, but I would only make it in the presence of representative newspaper men; they could pick the ones they wanted to handle it. They were back with their newspaper men in one hour.

'Gentlemen,' said I, 'I have never seen the 101 Show. I presume it is good — I don't know; but going out there and topping off a bucking horse would be too easy. Nothing unusual about it — dozens of their own boys are doing it every day. What I propose to do is something different. You gentlemen call at my dressing-room any morning, not a matinée day, and I will make up as an Indian in your presence, go out to the Coliseum accompanied by you, meet the Sioux Indians who are my red brothers, talk to them in their own language, ride bareback, BAREBACK, gentlemen, all through the show with them, and do every stunt that they do.'

Wow! Golly! They wouldn't think of letting such a thing be pulled off without the publicity which was its due.

A date was set one week ahead. The 'Chicago Journal' gave a prize of fifty dollars to the person that first sent in the number of the white man who was among the sixty Indians. He would ride in the morning parade, as well as through the entire afternoon show, so that all readers of the 'Journal' would have a chance to pick out the white man riding among the Indians.

It all worked out as advertised. A boy won the prize — a clever boy, too; he saw that I had blue eyes. All Indians have dark eyes.

I was very fortunate to get away with my 'way out.' It was not so easy. Making up for the newspaper men at the theater and riding out with them and meeting the Indians was fine — I enjoyed it, the Indians enjoyed it, and I know the newspaper men did, too. While my recollection of the Sioux tongue was only about ten per cent, my accent was such that the Indians gave me credit for one hundred per cent. I looked wise, threw in an occasional word, and let them talk their heads off. Besides, I caught a lot of what they were saying by their hand talk. A blanket Sioux Indian unconsciously uses his hands when speaking.

It was a raw, sleeting, cold, windy day. The parade, in a thin shirt, carrying a banner in one hand and handling a pony with the other, was no picnic. At one point I felt defeat coming sure. I wore a wig. It was a bit too large. On top of the wig I wore a big war-bonnet headdress, held in place by just a narrow chin-strap. The wind busted this strap. The pony, sensing that I was in trouble, as one hand

was holding the banner and the other hanging onto the
war-bonnet, started to jump a bit. But my 'rivals,' the
cowboys, were on the job. They quietly circled around the
pony until he quieted down; they did not touch him, nor
do anything to attract attention — it was all in a day's
work.

After that parade and hanging onto a bunch of feathers
in a gale of wind, the riding in the afternoon show was easy.
There was one number, when we were waiting to gallop
out, that Joe Miller took hold of my pony's head and
advised me not to try it, as it was tricky. But I was a bit
drunk with success (also I had been chilled to the bone
when we came in after the parade). I followed my leader
and came through all O.K. Many of the cowboys of that
day have worked with me in pictures. Fine men and fine
cowmen, all of them!

Yes, I could have gotten almost any salary I asked from
Eddie Arlington, the owner of the 101 Show. He had been
there when I had ridden all through the show with the
Indians in Chicago; and any man who could get away with
anything like that with a big circus was certainly a good
man to tie to — for a little dramatic company.

So Eddie Arlington *thought;* but as the weeks rolled by he
learned that a circus and a little dramatic troupe, no matter how small, were different games . . . and 'Arlington's
Folly' was born. He was wiser, but he was game. He
never whimpered a bit, and he must have dropped quite a
few of the thousands that he had just quit ahead with on
the closing of the 101 Show. We played as far west as
Minneapolis and closed in Chicago, giving us about ten
weeks' work.

The summer of 1911 passed without any engagement. I

was once more making the daily trip to New York and doing the rounds of the agencies.

Fred Watson (Nick, the Bartender) of 'The Squaw Man,' was rehearsing Devil Judd Tolliver, in 'The Trail of the Lonesome Pine,' for Klaw and Erlanger. Poor Fred sickened and died. I got the part. Prior to going into New York, we played the month of January at the Boston Theater.

I had my sister Mary and my old bulldog with me. I wrote to about twenty places in New York seeking quarters where they would take the dog, and received five or six favorable replies. Carrying two grips on a cold Sunday, sampling smelly boarding-houses, with a husky fifty-pound bulldog tugging on a chain, and a loyal sister skidding over iced pavements bringing up the rear, is not a pleasurable winter sport. Every place we tried was terrible. No wonder they were willing to take the dog! Poor old Mack's eyes fairly talked, 'Oh, boss, please don't let's stay here.'

The places were just plain awful. They reeked with cheap, shoddy hypocrisy and odors. A friend of mine in the company who had volunteered to help us find a place was fast weakening. In desperation, he tackled a hotel where he knew a clerk, the St. Margaret. My sister and I waited outside and shivered, and the old dog, with his blanket on crooked, looked anything but the conqueror of the mighty bull. Our friend came back with a happy grin. Eureka! And all sorts of ejaculations to express happiness!!! His friend, the clerk, happened to be on duty — he would take us in.

We entered, walking on our toes to avoid noise. The clerk took one look at the little pet dog that never barked. He flushed and fumbled, twisted the register the wrong way, dropped the pen, and finally managed to half-articu-late, 'Good God!'

All was lost. We were a tired-out pathetic group. I strode forward.

'Mister,' said I, 'I know this dog looks bad, but he is as gentle as a two months' old kitten. He is an absolute pet — wise, kind, and almost human.'

The clerk leaned quickly over the desk. 'Are you sure he won't make any noise?' he whispered. 'If so, I'll let you stay here for the night.'

'Mister,' said I, 'this dog has never been known to bark in a house in his life.'

Poor old Mack had known we were in trouble for the last two, or maybe three, hours. He knew it was all about him, too. The time had arrived for him to show his heartfelt in-terest in his master and mistress and the whole situation. He sat back on his haunches, raised his old majestic head as straight up as it would go, and opened wide the cave that the Creator had given him to receive food in. There was a long, sustained, dismal, weird roll of muffled thunder. I have heard the death cry of starving gray wolves, running in packs, in the dead of winter, but they were the feeble yelps of a coyote compared to that outpouring of the soul of poor old Mack. He would fight anything that ever walked on four or fourteen feet, and never falter! But here was something he could not fight. He felt the anxiety that his master and mistress felt. He knew they were in distress — they were pleading. His great bulldog heart would bend, too, he would plead . . . and he did!

After several seconds, when the echo had died away, I quietly told the truth: 'Partner,' I said, 'that's the first time, believe it or not. It looks like we're whipped, but, honest to God, he never did it before.'

And he never had. Poor old Mack's plea had won! The clerk took us in and let us stay three or four days. We landed at The Remington, on West Forty-Sixth Street. We were comfortable there, and the old dog had a good home.

Devil Judd Tolliver was one of those rugged, gun-fighting mountaineers that an actor could not go wrong in. I was credited with another New York hit. We played at the New Amsterdam for several weeks.

In the spring a prominent importer and breeder of Eng-lish bulldogs, B. J. Vandergrift, gave me a beautiful prize-winning female. She had been housed in kennels at Chest-nut Hill, Philadelphia, for a long time. Mr. Vandergrift had grown fond of her and wanted her to have a home. Golly! How happy I was climbing around the Westport hills all summer with those two wonderful dogs! It was the first home life that Ivy had ever known, and her grati-tude knew no bounds. Four full months she was with us. Her happiness, her devotion to my sister and myself, was remarkable, and her love of old Mack was nothing short of idolatry.

I was engaged to star in a new vaudeville act. My sister could not possibly handle both dogs, so I decided to send dear old Ivy back to the kennels for the winter. I had a carpenter come and make a big, strong, roomy box. I waited until the last possible day and then shipped her to Philadelphia.

I shall never forget her anguish at parting. I wish I could forget it, but I never can. She begged and pleaded like a human being. She cried; big, round tears ran off her lovable, homely old jaw. But the express wagon came and I sent her away. I can hear her cry still. In four weeks she was dead — she died of a broken heart. The owner of the kennel loved her. He did not tell me of her death until the following spring. He was a kind man. He knew she had no ailment but grief. Her memory will always be with me, and I am not ashamed to say that it hurts me greatly to think of sending her away. If there is a dog heaven — and I believe there is — I know old Ivy will be there, and I hope she will forgive me and know that, as I write, big tears are running off my homely jaw, too!

I opened in an act owned and written by Arthur Hopkins, called 'Moonshine.' My character was another mountaineer. It was a very fine act and I was considered good in it, but it lacked the snap or gunpowder that is necessary to put over a dramatic act in vaudeville.

Klaw and Erlanger wanted me to join 'The Trail of the Lonesome Pine.' It had opened in Chicago and they were not satisfied with my successor. So after one week at the Alhambra Theater, we shelved 'Moonshine.' Arthur Hopkins released me and I joined 'The Trail of the Lonesome Pine.'

In the latter part of March, my sister Mary joined me at Indianapolis; the following week was Cincinnati. It rained nearly all week. After Cincinnati came Springfield on Monday, and Dayton on Tuesday. The train passed through Dayton *en route* to Springfield late Monday afternoon. It just passed through and that's all. The railroad tracks at Dayton were two feet under water. The engine was enveloped in steam from the water hitting the fire-box underneath. It was raining heavily and the water was rising rapidly. We just did get out, and that's all. The sixteen miles between Dayton and Springfield was a lake, with the bed of the railroad tracks under water in many places.

Springfield, Ohio, is on a knoll; it was entirely surrounded by water. We played there that night in a deluge, a few half-drowned people for an audience, and remained, marooned in Springfield, for the next ten days. We suffered no hardships. The food never gave out. The town was under martial law with soldiers patrolling the streets night and day. There was no disorder of any sort, at any time. Depots were established to take care of all refugees who managed to get in from the surrounding country. There was no privation or suffering, although I was told that the food supply would have been exhausted in two more days.

On lower ground at the edge of the city ran a river. I saw it rise fourteen feet in one hour. All around was a lake of water. The roofs of one-story houses were visible, and the second stories of some others. Men in rowboats were trying to bail out the second floors of their homes through the windows. It was pathetic. It was like trying to empty New York Bay with buckets. Yet they worked feverishly, almost madly, shouting orders to their companions, as though they were accomplishing their purpose.

There was nothing to do but wait. We were far more cut off from the outer world than we would be if marooned in the Arctic regions to-day. The telegraph and telephone wires were out of commission the first day, and the radio had not been born.

One day the manager hustled us out at 6 A.M. A train was going to try to make Columbus. Our 'boats,' consisting of four coaches, 'sailed' all day, about two miles at a time. Once, when we anchored for an hour, I waded breast-high (when not swimming) over draws and coulees to a farmhouse a half-mile distant. The first floor of the house was covered with several inches of water. The lady gave me half a loaf of bread and about a pint of milk.

When I got back to the train, I was nearly mobbed, and I should have had real trouble had not my brother actors stood back of me. There were some gentlemen (?) who said that my bread and milk should be divided. I gave all of it to a woman with a little baby and my sister. The ringleader of the opposition disappeared on the back trail and we never saw him again.

A man had some sweet wine. On account of being wet and chilled, I drank all he gave me of it. It made me ill.

We arrived opposite Columbus, Ohio, just before dark. The river between us and the city looked like a spur of the Atlantic Ocean on a rampage. 'Way went the big railroad bridge. We missed certain death.... Had we been half an hour earlier, the bridge men would have let us try it! The train backed up through lakes of water all the way to Springfield. We arrived about midnight. I do not know how long it was before Springfield was relieved. I know we got out in about ten or twelve days.

A special train was made up for the president of the New York Central Railroad. He had been on a visit to his mother. He had to get out, and we benefited by it. We were about eighteen hours getting to Toledo. We passed broken bridges, trains in rivers, and in many places the tracks were twisted as though they had been over an earthquake. We would take an hour to make a mile.

CHAPTER XIII
THE GREAT OPPORTUNITY — PICTURES

At one isolated place there was a young man sitting beside a telegraph instrument, installed on an empty soap box. He was cold, thirsty, and hungry. He had been there without relief for four nights and days. The president talked to him ... the president meant nothing to him, he scarcely answered. The man was in a daze — he just knew he had to stay there until he was relieved and he was doing his duty. When the train reached Toledo, there were hundreds of people at the depot seeking information. We were the first ones out of the Dayton flood.

While playing in Cleveland, I attended a picture show. I saw a Western picture. It was awful! I talked with the manager of the theater and he told me it was one of the best Westerns he had ever had. None of the impossibilities or libels on the West meant anything to him — it was drawing the crowds. The fact that the sheriff was dressed and characterized as a sort of cross between a Wisconsin woodchopper and a Gloucester fisherman was unknown to him. I did not seek to enlighten him. I was seeking information. In fact, I was so sure that I had made a big discovery that I was frightened that some one would read my mind and find it out.

Here were reproductions of the Old West being seriously presented to the public — in almost a burlesque manner — and they were successful. It made me tremble to think of it. I was an actor and I knew the West. . . . The oppor-

TO-DAY ON THE HORSESHOE RANCH

tunity that I had been waiting for years to come was knocking at my door.

Hundreds of ideas seemed to rush in from every direction. They assumed form. It was engendered — the die was cast. Rise or fall, sink or swim, I had to bend every endeavor to get a chance to make Western motion pictures. Usually when stirred by ambition I would become afraid. But surely this could not be the valor of ignorance. I had been waiting for years for the right thing, and now the right thing had come! I was a part of the West — it was my boyhood home — it was in my blood. The very love I bore it made me know its ways. I had a thorough training as an actor. I was considered the outstanding portrayer of Western rôles on the American stage.

It was the big opportunity that a most high Power, chance, or fixed law, had schooled me for. It had been many years in coming, but it was here. And I would go through hell on three pints of water before I would acknowledge defeat.

The remainder of the season I visited all picture shows wherever possible. During the summer at Westport and on trips to New York, I did the same. I talked to my actor friends in The Lambs Club who were working every day playing Western parts in pictures being made over in Jersey. I was secretive. I told them nothing of my great plans. When it came time for 'The Trail of the Lonesome Pine' to open again, my reluctance to take an engagement before trying my pet scheme caused me to raise my salary to one hundred and seventy-five dollars a week. While waiting for their answer, I met an actor who was going to California to work in Western pictures.

'The Trail of the Lonesome Pine' was going to California. I was frightened! They might refuse to give me the part on account of the raise in salary. I was on the point of writing them that I would go for *any salary*, when they wrote me O. K.

The finger of Fate was pointing in the right direction. Fortunately, we came West immediately after opening, or I believe I should have gone nutty. At San Francisco I learned that all the principal studios were in Los Angeles; that the principal companies making Westerns were the Universal Picture Corporation in Hollywood, and the New York Motion Picture Company in conjunction with the 101 Ranch at Santa Monica.

When we reached Los Angeles, while a friend was registering for me, I went into a telephone booth, called up the New York Motion Picture Company and asked for Joe Miller. A man who said his name was Brooks answered, and said that Mr. Miller was not there, but that he represented him.

I then said, 'I am an actor and I want to see about making some Western pictures.'

He replied: 'Mr. Miller only owns the stock and the cowboy end of the company. If you want to see about acting, call up Thomas H. Ince — he is manager of the picture company.'

I did so.

'Hello, Tom.'

'Hello, Bill.'

The next day Tom called and took me out to the old camp. I was enraptured and told him so. The very primitiveness of the whole life out there, the cowboys and the Indians, staggered me. I loved it. They had everything to make Western pictures. The West was right there!

I told Tom of my hopes, of my plans. I told him everything.

A Big Opportunity

'Bill,' he said, 'it's a damn shame, but you're too late! The country has been flooded with Western pictures. They are the cheapest pictures to make and every company out here has made them. You simply cannot sell a Western picture at any price. They are a drug on the market.'

And to prove his statement, he showed me all the sets they were photographing on. The scenes were all laid in Ireland.

'But, Tom,' I cried, 'this means everything on earth to me. It is the one big opportunity of my life. Why all these cowboys? Why all these Indians?'

'Bill,' he said, 'it's a contract. Kessell and Bauman, the owners of this company, have a contract with the 101 Show that has another year to run.'

'Fine,' I said. 'Let me make some Western pictures and use these people.'

'Bill,' he said, 'I know you; I know, if there was any possible chance, that you could put it over, but it just can't be done. I made a picture when I came out here, a Western picture, 'Custer's Last Fight,' and I had all these Indians and cowboys. It was a fine picture, but it didn't sell.'

I looked at him, and he answered, 'Sure, Bill, I used the story you told me — that is why I'm telling you this — to show you that it won't go, that it cannot be done.'

I didn't have any more to say. We walked all round the camp. When we were leaving, I talked in Sioux to some of the Indians, and Tom was so astonished. He walked back and said to a young Indian: 'What did he say?'

The Indian just smiled and would not answer, until I told him in Sioux to do so, and then he replied, truthfully, that I had said that I was going away from here, but that I wanted to stay here.

I was late leaving (they had to hold the curtain at the theater for me), but just as Tom was putting me in his car he said: 'Bill, if you want to come out next spring and take a chance, I'll give you seventy-five dollars a week to cover your expenses and direct you in a picture myself.'

'Tom,' I replied, 'I'll be here as soon as we close.'

My sister joined me on the road in January and I told her of my hopes and plans. Just before the close of the season, Eugene Walters offered me the leading rôle in his new play, 'The Woman,' which was to be produced in Philadelphia, under the same management, as soon as we closed. I declined. He boosted my salary. Again I declined. Another boost! No, I was determined to go into pictures!

'Bill Hart,' he said, 'do you know what Erlanger says? He says he always gave you credit for having sense, but that all actors are crazy, and you've got 'em all skinned.'

We closed at the Grand Opera House in New York. An actor called to see his brother in our company, to say goodbye. He was leaving to take the train for California to work in pictures for the New York Motion Picture Company. He showed us his ticket and sleeper. I said nothing. No one knew I was going. I bought my own ticket and rode in a tourist car.

I had been wandering around camp, killing time, and seeing all I could see, as Tom had told me to do. I went to him and told him that my money was low and I was anxious to start. He said that he was sorry, that he had not thought of it, and he put me on salary at once. He said that he would like me to do a heavy part in a two-reeler, under an assumed name, before starting our picture, so I would get used to the camera — that he would cast me in a few days.

At that time the principal leading men or stars of the company were Frank Borzage, Charlie Ray, Tom Chatterton, Sessue Hayakawa, Dick Stanton, and Walter Edwards — the last two were directing also. The leading women were Clara Williams, Gladys Brockwell, Rhea Mitchell, Enid Markey, Louise Glaum, Tsuro Aoki, Gretchen Lederer, and others. The principal directors were Reginald Barker, Raymond B. West, Scott Sidney, Charles Giblyn, and others. E. H. Allen was general manager of the plant under Ince.

Allen had given me permission, and I was in the habit of going in my cowboy outfit to the chief of the cowboys and getting a horse to take a ride. As is usually the case, and as I knew would happen, each day the horse I got became a bit more spirited, and when I came in there would be the quiet, inquiring look as to whether I was going to say, 'I'd rather have the horse I had yesterday, etc.'

But I said nothing — I was enjoying the little play, too!

One morning they gave me a stubborn, wild little buckskin. I knew before we had gone a hundred yards that he was 'cold-jawed' and that there would surely be some fun. I headed him up a trail over the mountain, my object being to tire him so he wouldn't get salty and turn on. But he acted before he reached the tired stage.

We were well back in the hills, probably two miles from camp and mostly all down grade, when the buckskin decided to go home. In spite of his hard mouth, I could control him with quirt and spur and keep him from going back, but as soon as I let him feel the iron . . . down went his head and he started to buck, and on that mountain-side it was a certainty that either he'd break a leg, his neck, or go home with an empty saddle. I took a chance! I let him go back home with a full saddle. Doggone him! And when we hit anywhere near a level part of the trail, I made him like it; I hooked him good and plenty.

The camp is in a valley between the mountains. Down off the top we came. That pony had grown from a luke-warm to a boiling-over rage. He was indignant, sore, and almost blinded by his self-made passion — just as humans sometimes become. I do not remember how I felt. I do not think I felt much of anything, knowing full well that I had nothing to do with the immediate passing events. When we started to come off that hill, there could be no let-up; our pace was such that I could not admire the scenery or pick any flowers on the way down. I kept hooking Mr. Buckskin and he kept a-comin' as fast as his feet could hit the ground. Just as we hit the bottom level, we flashed past 'Whitey' Sovern, the chief of the cow-boys.

While I was unsaddling, Whitey rode up to the hitching rack. He did not speak, neither did I. There was nothing to say. He knew I was lucky to come off that hill that way, and so did I. He also knew the horse was running away, and that if I had attempted to hold him, he would have lost his feet and might have killed one or both of us.

That night I was talking to Tom Ince in his office and Allen joined us, saying: 'Here's a good one on you, Hart. Half an hour ago, Whitey came in and asked who the new hand was. I knew he meant you, but I said, "What new hand?" — and mentioned another new man. He said, "No! I mean that cowboy you been sendin' down to git a horse every day." I replied, "You mean that tall chap? Why, he isn't a cowboy. He's an actor — he just got in from New York." Whitey thought a minute and replied, "Look here, Mr. Allen, I been 'round here long enough to know actors. That feller just come down off the hill, kicking that buckskin colt like he was goin' to town for a new cook. It's none of my business, Mr. Allen, but that feller is kiddin' you folks! He's no actor!"'

My first picture (it is still playing) was a two-reeler. Tom Chatterton was the director and also played the hero; Clara Williams, the heroine; and I was the villain.

Chatterton was and is a clever actor, but he had never directed a picture! I did as I was told, but I felt terrible, and when I saw the rushes on the screen, I knew I was terrible. It was called 'His Hour of Manhood.'

At the completion of that picture, we immediately started another, 'Jim Cameron's Wife,' with the same director and cast. Again I was heartsick when I saw the rushes. When this picture was finished, still another one was handed to us. I rebelled. I felt too much hurt to talk, so I wrote Tom a letter. I refused to do the new picture and told him that I was not doing what I came out to do, and that unless he could do as he had promised I was going home.

Tom was very nice about it, and said he knew he was not keeping his word, but that it was his idea to keep me busy all summer and make up in that way for my coming out; that he was still afraid to do a feature Western picture. And that, furthermore, he had not been able to find a story.

He said, 'I've got a two-reeler that we made some time ago that I think might be built up, but we can't strike on a way to do it.'

I asked him to tell me the story. He did so.

'I like it,' I replied. 'Let me have it and give me three days. I think I can build it up.'

He gave me the story and in four or five days I gave it back to him, doubled in length. He gave it to C. Gardner Sullivan, the chief scenario writer of the camp, and Sullivan said that it was 'splendid,' and in a short time had turned out a beautiful scenario. Tom had Reginald Barker read it. Barker was highly enthusiastic, so Tom told him to go ahead and make the picture. I spoke to Tom about his directing the picture, but he said that he could not spare the time. Barker was satisfactory to me. I had been watching him direct and liked his work.

What an exquisite pleasure it was to work in 'The Bargain.' I rode five horses in the picture, but the principal one was 'Midnight,' a superb, coal-black animal that weighed about twelve hundred pounds. He was nervous, and had broken a director's arm and an actor's leg. But he and I got along finely together. We did skyline rides along the tops of ridges so fast that the camera man could not hold us, no matter how he placed his 'set-up.'

Although it would have taken every dollar I could raise, I tried to buy this glorious animal for one hundred and fifty dollars, and on account of his supposed meanness I could have bought him for that figure, only the 101 people were going to leave, and they did not want the New York Motion Picture Company to get any of their stock, and, on account of my known friendship with Tom, they suspected I was trying to buy the horse for the company.

The following spring Midnight won the saddle-horse championship of the world at the Columbia Exposition in San Francisco. Years afterward I heard he was working on a plow in Oklahoma. I tried to find him, but could not do so.

A Corking Trip to the Grand Canyon

I persuaded Tom to allow Barker to take a few people and go to the Grand Canyon for some scenes. What a glorious trip it was! I wore spurs and rode a horse at a full gallop on the worst turns of the narrow Hermit Creek Trail, on the brink of a straight drop of thousands of feet. It was the first time in history, and I doubt if it has been done since.

We camped for days down by the Colorado River. We could not use grease paint — the heat melted it in the make-up boxes. We got wonderful results at a minimum expense. I believe the trip cost about six hundred dollars, and, golly! what a corking trip it was — and how we all enjoyed it!

When we returned, Barker shot the scenes to match up with the Grand Canyon in Topango Canyon. We left camp at seven o'clock in the morning and arrived at Topango post office at noon. It was a narrow, dirt road, full of wash-outs. We boarded at McAllister's Tavern — a cook house and a few tents two miles beyond the post office. It was a primitive country. Land was worth anything you wanted to pay, and no purchasers.

I was much pleased with the scenes Barker was getting. We worked well together. When 'The Bargain' was finished, it seemed to be in the air that it was a success.

Tom came to me and said, 'Bill, I've got a fine part for you in another story Sullivan has just written. I want you to look it over.'

I did so. I wrote out some suggestions, stating where I thought it could be strengthened, and both Tom and Sullivan liked them, and Sullivan put them in the story.

'On the Midnight Stage' is still playing. It has also been called 'The Bandit and the Preacher.' I rode Midnight again in this picture.

I liked my work in 'The Bargain' and 'On the Midnight Stage,' and I told Tom I would like to stay if he would give me a year's contract. He said that he couldn't; that the company was taking big chances on these two pictures; that he would not make any more.

'Bill,' he said, 'why don't you take up directing? That is where the money is. I will give you a year's contract as a director at one hundred and twenty-five dollars a week.'

I replied: 'No, Tom. I have devoted too many years to acting to quit now. If I am to fail, I'll fail as an actor! Besides, I have no ambition to become a director.'

'Well, Bill,' he said, 'I'm sorry, but that is the best offer I can make and the best advice I can give you.'

I said: 'All right, Tom. I'm sorry. You know if I don't get back to New York now I'm likely to lose a season's work. I hope the company don't lose any money on these two pictures, because I know I talked you into making them. If they blame you, just tell 'em it's all my fault.'

At seven o'clock the next morning, September 1st, Cal Hoffner, who had charge of the automobiles, drove me and my trunk to the Santa Fé Depot at Los Angeles. I waited until Cal had gone ... and then bought a second-class ticket and a tourist sleeper for home. I had only a few dollars left. My trip had not been profitable.

When I returned home, my sister Mary and the old dog were waiting at the gate. I was cheered a whole lot ... they cared.

Some years before, when I was coming home, my sister had said to the old dog, 'Somebody's coming!' He had never forgotten it, and if those two words were ever spoken in his hearing, he would go and watch at the gate. No amount of coaxing could get him away.

In telling my story that night I tried to see the bright side of things, but I was like a boy going through a church-yard, whistling to keep his courage up. In spite of my sister's encouraging, hopeful smile, I knew that I had failed. True, my pictures had not yet been released, but those who employed me did not want me. I had been let out. It was an incontrovertible fact. I had failed. Selah!

Once more I started on the old sidewalk trails. Once more I visited the same old offices and saw the same old abdomens that looked like half-filled hot-water bottles. I thought of those lean, shad-bellied cow-punchers I had left behind. If what I felt could have reached them in sound, it would have burst their ear drums.

There was no work. I kept up the daily grind — it was my duty to do so. An actor seeking employment is as popular with the derby-hatted managerial gentry as a ruptured barnacle.

One night I went home; my sister was at the gate and the old dog raced down the road to meet me. He had a piece of yellow paper in his mouth. It was a telegram!

'Can offer you one-twenty-five per week as a star. One-year contract. You to direct your own pictures. Wire answer. Tom.'

... It had come! We did not talk much that evening. We thought and thought much. The little white house on the hill was home. The old dog sat between us looking anxiously from one to the other. He knew something of great moment had happened. He knew it affected us and him. He suffered! He was afraid the little home would be closed up; that we would go away, and that he would again be put in a box and sent to the kennels, and he knew if he was sent to the kennels any more that he would die.

His master and mistress did go away . . . the little white house on the hill was closed up. Annie, who used to steal small pieces of cake for him and feed him in the kitchen, followed to the top of the hill, threw her apron up over her head, and cried. But old Mack was not in a box; he was not going to the kennels; he was leading on ahead, tugging at his chain, taking his master and mistress to their new home . . . on the Pacific Ocean, where the mountains came down to the sea, and where his bones were to lie — while the little white house on the hill loyally waited alone, knowing it could never be the same little white house again.

Our money was low. We rode in a tourist car. The train stopped for meals. My sister would get me a sandwich and a bottle of milk. The old dog was such a gentleman in his habits that it was necessary to give him a good walk. Poor, dear old Mack, he was ninety-eight per cent perfect. His two per cent failing was that he had absolutely no idea of the value or the power of arbitration. He was the veteran of a hundred battles, and I never once could say to the other fellow, 'Your dog started it.'

Six weeks from the time I had gone away, I commenced work again. We rented a cottage at Ocean Park.

'The Bargain' had been shown in some little beach theater and was such a hit that it had been immediately purchased by Famous Players. The contract contained a clause that after three years the picture returned to the first owner. This clause was in all such contracts merely to protect the ownership of the negative; the life of any picture was never three years. When the three years had expired, 'The Bargain' came back to the New York Mo-

THE GREATEST ALL-ROUND HORSE THAT EVER LIVED

tion Picture Company and they made a great deal more money out of it. It is still being played. The success of 'The Bargain' was responsible for my contract and my return to pictures.

During my absence from camp, Bessie Barriscale had started as a star in five-reel pictures. George Beban, also, was making a feature picture. Tom started me on two-reelers. I was disappointed, but I knew I could win out.

After my first picture, 'The Passing of Two-Gun Hicks,' I asked Tom to make the assistant director, Cliff Smith, a co-director with me. He did so, and we worked together all the time I was with the company.

Dear old Midnight had gone with the 101 Show. In one of my first pictures I used a pinto horse named Fritz. He weighed only one thousand pounds, but his power and endurance were remarkable. We had a lot of desert riding to do. Our desert was the sand dunes, just below Playa del Rey. The action of our story called for Cliff Smith and myself to be attacked by Indians. His horse was killed and he mounted behind me, and we were chased for a long distance before my horse was shot while going at a full gallop, and we went down and fought behind his body. The combined weight of Cliff and myself with our guns and a heavy stock saddle was close to four hundred and fifty pounds, yet that little horse carried us for hours until all our scenes were taken. But when I was lying across his neck shooting Injuns, he rolled eyes at me that plainly said:

'Say, Mister, I sure was glad when you give me that fall.'

He never called me Mister again. He is on my ranch to-day, monarch of all he surveys.

My Life East and West

On Christmas Day, 1914, we did not work. I went to Hollywood to look at some furnished bungalows that my sister had selected as possibilities, our main need being an enclosed yard for old Mack, so he could neither attack nor be attacked by his canine brothers. I found one place that filled the bill perfectly. I asked the lady how far it was to the nearest restaurant. There were no restaurants in Hollywood! Not even a lunch-stand where one could buy a sandwich. Meals could be had at the Hollywood Hotel, but for guests only. I found quarters at 534 South Figueroa Street, and we moved to Los Angeles.

I worked very hard. I would get my breakfast at a little restaurant on Sixth Street, take the Edendale trolley, and at the junction of Lakeshore and Sunset catch the old Ford bus from the Sennett Studio, where our laboratory was. This bus took film to camp every morning and returned at night with the day's work. It meant fifty miles a day of travel, and getting up at five o'clock every morning to be at camp at eight o'clock. I never reached home, via the same route, before seven or seven-thirty in the evening.

After giving old Mack a walk, my sister and I would go to the Hoffman Café for dinner. Some evenings we would spend our two nickels at the Lyceum Theater, a few doors away, to see a picture show — but I usually fell asleep. When we reached home I would go over the story for the next day's work. For three years I worked sixteen hours a day and worried eight.

Several years previous I had attempted to write a poem. It was published in 'The Morning Telegraph.' I grew so fond of Fritz that I asked Tom to allow me to make a picture out of it. He did allow me to do so, and it was released under its title, 'Pinto Ben.' It has been shown under many different titles and is playing yet. . . . The little horse stole the picture from me.

All the actors and actresses in camp liked to work in my pictures. When working with other directors, they would often spend their spare time on our set.

The scenario department, of which C. Gardner Sullivan and J. G. Hawkes were the principal writers, could not keep all of the directors supplied with material. Many stories which had cost the company fifteen or twenty dollars, written in long-hand on a few sheets of paper, were handed to me to make a picture. That this was accomplished was not the result of brains, but of application, hard work, and a determination to succeed.

Early in the spring of 1915, after I had made over twenty two-reel pictures, the Triangle Film Corporation was formed. The new company absorbed the New York Motion Picture Company, the Reliance-Majestic Company, the Keystone Comedies. The owners of Triangle were Harry E. Aitken, Kessell and Bauman, and their associates. The director-generals were D. W. Griffith, Thomas H. Ince, and Mack Sennett. The Knickerbocker Theater, in New York City, was leased. Triangle pictures were to play at two-dollar prices.

Men, men, men! Women, women, women! How the New York office did send them! They came to the coast in droves — among them Eddie Foy, Joe Weber, Lew Fields, Hale Hamilton, Raymond Hitchcock, Willie Collier, Harry Woodruff, Frank Keenan, Dustin Farnum, Orrin Johnson, Billie Burke, De Wolf Hopper, Sir Herbert Tree, John Emerson, Douglas Fairbanks, and oceans and oceans of other stars of equal fame. It rained stars, like hailstones; and like hailstones, they melted under the California sun,

Doug being the only one I can recall who moved too fast for the rays to hit him.

Doug's picture, 'The Lamb,' opened the Knickerbocker Theater in New York City, at two-dollar prices. My picture, 'The Disciple,' followed the second week. I do not know what 'The Lamb' cost, but I know what 'The Disciple' cost. It cost $8000, including overhead! While I could make an affidavit as to the total cost, I am only able to quote from memory certain items. The story, written by S. Barrett McCormick, cost $75; star and director (myself), $125 per week; co-director (Cliff Smith), $30 per week; leading lady (Dorothy Dalton), $40 per week; leading heavy man (Robert McKim), $25 per week; the average cowboy actors that worked in the picture received $5 per week and board, the top hands received $6 and $8, and the foreman of the cowboys drew down $10.

'The Disciple' was an excellent story and the cast was excellent. Both Dorothy Dalton and Robert McKim made their first hits in this picture. The picture was a big success. As for me, such as I am, it made me in New York City as a motion-picture actor.

I went to Tom and told him that, while I knew my contract had four more months to run at $125 per week, it was a tough deal to ask me to direct and star for that money when all the new stars were receiving fabulous salaries. Hopper was getting $1800; Fairbanks, $2200; and Tree, $3500 per week, just for acting.

Tom doubled my salary on the spot, making it two hundred and fifty per week, and gave me fifty a week bonus, besides. I dove into my next picture head first.

One day Mr. Aitken, the president of the company, brought a party of ladies out to camp. They all wanted to see my horse. I had Fritz brought from the corral, but

DOUG MOVED TOO FAST FOR THE RAYS OF THE SUN TO HIT HIM

the little snoozer was stubborn — he wouldn't show off a bit. I was disappointed, as I loved every hair of the little scoundrel's hide, and I wanted to hear him praised. So I decided to give them a real thrill.

I asked the ladies and Mr. Aitken to promise me they would not move. They did so! I tightened up the cinch, mounted, took the little fellow back about two hundred yards, worked him a bit to get him excited, and then brought him toward the group at full speed. I headed right for the party and, as I came close, I could hear the ladies give little feminine cries. It was all over so quickly they had no time to run. They just gave one loud shriek and meant it. I had thrown Fritz right at their feet. My head struck one of the ladies on the ankle.

Mr. Aitken thanked me profusely for the thrill, and the ladies said it was the greatest experience they had ever known. It was unusual, and far more effective to see it in life than it is on the screen, for of all the stunts in pictures I regard it as the most dangerous to the horse. When he takes the fall, his whole weight hits on his left shoulder, and the danger is in fracturing the bone. I threw that little paint pony in almost every picture I used him in, and I am thankful that he escaped injury.

In July, 1915, there was an Exhibitors' Convention at San Francisco, to which all companies sent representative stars. Our company sent Frank Keenan, House Peters, Bessie Barriscale, and myself. I was wandering around the ballroom and saw a beautiful girl sitting alone in a box. I made all apologies for addressing her and asked her to dance. She smiled and said she would be glad to do so only it was the prize waltz, for which they were giving three silver cups.

'Well, please dance, anyhow, until they put us out,' I replied.

I was disappointed . . . a chap tapped me on the shoulder when we had about half-circled the floor. I told the young lady I was sorry I didn't last one lap, anyhow, and she explained that we had to dance again. By golly! We danced for half an hour — only the final couple beat us. It was Mrs. William Randolph Hearst. The lady I danced with got a fine cup for second prize. I never knew her name and I doubt if she knew mine.

I arrived home at midnight and found my sister Mary sitting on the ground in the yard with dear old Mack's head in her lap. He was dying. I saw it was all over, and started to find a veterinary to ease the old fellow's pain. I carried him upstairs and laid him down, but when I started out he struggled to his feet and tried to follow for his walk. The doctor came and the poor, nearly blind old dog put his head into the cone and breathed the fumes that took him to join Ivy in the next dog world. My sister Mary and I lost a friend that would have died for us. I took him to camp the next morning and buried him on top of a mountain overlooking the sea. Seven years later I dug up his little oaken box and his final resting-place is on my ranch where the same little white head-board marks his grave.

We had been anxious to move to an up-to-date apartment, but it was nearly six months before we could bear to leave the place where our friend had been.

One of the favorite sports of the cowboys and roughnecks on the lot was to kid actors who were to take part in a picture that had a fight in it, about the powers of their prospective opponent.

The Terrors of a Film Fight

I was making a picture titled 'Between Men.' House Peters, who played the heavy part, and myself, had to wind up with a fight and the story called for a smashing good one. It was a big situation!

As usual, the gang got busy. I had been through the mill so many times before that I didn't lose any sleep over what was going to happen to me. Whether Peters took it seriously or not, I do not know to this day; I only know that at the last minute he flatly refused to do the fight. He told me he was sore on the Triangle Company, that they had not treated him right, and he was damned if he'd take a chance of a bloody nose, or a black eye, for their benefit. I tried to talk him out of it. I told him that I had been in about eighty fights on that lot and had never been hurt, which was not 'the whole truth and nothing but the truth'; but he was adamant. He would not yield an inch.

I was in an awful fix. I had to have the fight, or the story was ruined. The extra cameras were set up, all was in readiness, but Peters would not budge. I went to Tom and asked him would I be discharged if I inveigled Peters on the set and then tore into him and we'd fight it out on the level — while the cameras were grinding. I called his attention to the fact that Peters was a heavier, more powerful man than I, and in all probability I'd get a licking; but if it so happened that I was the better fighter, I would promise faithfully on my word of honor to take the worst of it, as I really liked Peters . . . but we had to have that fight.

Tom not only would not give his permission, but he said, 'I'll be back in a minute' . . . and never did come back. He left camp.

I went up on the set again and talked to Peters for twenty minutes, and finally he said he would agree to what was called a furniture fight, that is, throwing things at each other, smashing chairs, and all that sort of thing. As we had never done anything like that, I told him to go ahead and order whatever breakable props he thought necessary. I called the property men and Peters did the ordering right there. Among the articles he ordered was a two-feet-high vase to stand on a pedestal. He told the property man to have it made out of glue and wax at the Sennett studio.

The next morning, promptly at nine o'clock, our set was ready. We started — we were doing finely. Drapes were being pulled down, legs were being yanked off tables and used as clubs (they were stuffed); chandeliers came crashing down when some thrown object hit them. Peters and I would clinch and roll and kick and bite, and never strike a blow or touch each other — outside of our loving bear-like hugs.

To our usual gang of roughneck scrappers who were watching, it was terrible. They went away in disgust. But I realized that Peters knew what he was doing and that we were getting fine camera stuff.

Then it came! We had just broken away from one of our embraces and were looking for an opening to repeat, when Peters saw the big vase in the corner. He made a lunge for it. I followed, to try to strangle with my bare hands the villain that would fight so foul; but the villain got his weapon. Up in the air it went ... and down out of the air it came, propelled by about two hundred and twenty pounds of muscle and flesh. The vase was NOT wax and glue — it was CEMENT! When the doctor had come and gone, leaving several stitches as souvenirs in the top of my head, it — that is, what remained of the vase — weighed twenty-two pounds on the scales. ...

218

'What? A first-class property man, that knows his business, ride half the night to get a vase made at the *Sennett* Studio. . . . What fer?'

Poor Peters was broken-hearted. He thought he had killed me. I thought so myself, but he hadn't — for which I know I was glad, and I'll gamble every nickel I've got in the world that House Peters was glad, too!

There was another little happening while we were shooting 'Between Men' that I recall. The Triangle Company had bought a large tract of land at Culver City and started to build a new studio. The flooring of the first stage had just been laid. My picture called for a big stock exchange scene, and my set was the first one built on this stage. Barker had just started a story (with Frank Keenan as the star) that also had a stock exchange scene in it. Tom told me to cut the stock exchange out of my story and let Barker have the set. Barker knew he was putting something over, so he arranged to shoot his scenes the next day.

I took Cliff Smith, Bob McKim, and a few other actors and my camera man, and went over to watch Barker shoot the first scenes at the new studio. Barker had a big mob to work with — he was in his element. When he shot his final big rehearsal, I had my characters, led by Bob McKim, working in the foreground on a different angle of the set with our camera man quietly grinding.

After the rehearsal we started away. Barker called out: 'Where you going, Bill? Wait for the big scene, and I'll show you horse-opera actors something.'

'Your rehearsal is big enough for me, Reg,' I replied.

I never saw the scenes in Barker's pictures, but his rehearsal was fine in mine.

Billie Burke was starring in a picture called 'Peggy.'

written by Sullivan and directed by Charlie Giblyn. I had always admired Billie Burke on the stage tremendously, and I cost the New York Motion Picture Company quite a bit of money arranging our work, regardless of its requirements, so that I could go to lunch when Billie Burke would be in the commissary. I used to ride Fritz up and make him act a little 'ornery' (which was easy to do), so I could show off. Tom caught me at it once and he didn't give me away — he just grinned. Billie Burke never caught me at it, at least, I hope she never did, as I'd rather be turned down than not noticed at all.

Sullivan wrote a story for me which I considered great. It was 'The Aryan.' The star rôle was one of those hard-as-flint characters that Sullivan could write so well, but this man had no motive for his hardness. I wrote a beginning for the story and talked it over with Tom and Sullivan. Sullivan gave me a great battle; his argument was that he wanted to create a character that was bad without reason. I finally convinced him that it would be stronger my way and better for the picture, and he allowed me to do it. It proved to be a gripping story. I regard it as the best story Sullivan ever wrote and one of the best Westerns ever made.

As there were three large studios under the Triangle banner, I got in the habit of borrowing actors. There was a part in 'The Aryan' that I wanted Mae Marsh for. She was tied up in a picture, but Mr. Griffith told me he had a young girl he thought very well of and was just waiting for an opportunity to cast her. When I saw her I grabbed her — she didn't have a chance of escaping. . . . Bessie Love made her first hit in 'The Aryan.'

Dear Bessie was a child — she was afraid of me. While the camera was grinding, her little mouth would quiver as she struggled not to cry and gamely fought for the rights of her people. It was just what the part required. It was one of the very finest performances I have ever seen on the screen.

Louise Glaum was also excellent in this picture.

We spent our Christmas at Felton, California, among the giant redwoods. We were doing a Canadian trapper story, 'The Primal Lure,' by Vingie E. Roe.

Tom called me on the telephone and asked me would I do two stories at once when I came home. 'Yes,' I said.

We did 'The Apostle of Vengeance,' in which I played a mountaineer clergyman, with Smith and myself directing. At the same time I worked, under another director, in another story, 'The Captive God' — playing an Aztec chieftain. Both stories were written by Monte Katerjohn.

Golly! It was tough work. It was the coldest weather I ever experienced in Southern California. We made a trip to San Diego to photograph the Indian cliff dwellings at the Exposition grounds. The railroads were all washed out, and we made the trip each way on a small coasting steamer. My costume consisted of half a pint of Bole Armenia Mixture and two feathers. Cold? Wow-wow-wow!

I remember one day we were working on an open set at camp. There were several girls gowned about as I was, and Allen, our manager, who was watching the work, had to turn up the collar of his heavy winter overcoat to keep warm.

Then, as an agreeable change, I had to do about two days of rain stuff in 'The Apostle of Vengeance.' I recall one whole day that we worked on a creek up the canyon back of camp, where the hills shut out the sun. There were two of us who had the hose turned on us all day long. It was really cruel.

I was particularly sorry for the young actor who was taking his medicine with me. He was one of the fifteen dollars a week extras, or, as we called them, actor boys, whom I had selected when we were doing 'Hell's Hinges.' I picked him out as the boy who wore the green shirt. I had noticed his avid eagerness to please and I could see he had training. I asked him who he was and where he came from. He told me his mother's name. She was a well-known stock actress. When I cast him for the part in 'The Apostle of Vengeance,' Tom gave me a regular bawling out. He said I was crazy; that the younger brother part was the best part in the picture and that he did not like this boy's work at all. He almost demanded that I take him out of the cast. I refused to do so and he said, 'All right, if he spoils the picture we won't release it and you lose your salary.'

I knew he didn't mean that, so I let him rave, and finally he went away. While I felt sure of my ground, I commenced to get shaky about the matter. I was so chilled I was shaking all over the place, anyhow.

In the story the young brother part was a regular fire-eater, and my much maligned choice for the rôle was thin almost to the point of emaciation, and being fully conscious of his shaking-to-pieces condition, he was frightened to death that he would lose the part. He was also actually shedding tears from the cold. It was really brutal. I went to him and said:

'Look here, laddie, we've got to go through with this, and we're going to do it. So just lock your teeth and "let's go"; and just remember you're making good and that no

MY COSTUME WAS HALF A PINT OF BOLE ARMENIA AND TWO
FEATHERS

one is going to do anything to hurt you or take the part away from you.'

We got our stuff, but it was bitter work. I still shiver when I think of it. The picture was a success. The young actor made a hit — his name was Jack Gilbert.

We were working on a picture, 'The Dawn Maker,' in which I played a half-breed Indian. The whole Triangle outfit, except my little 'horse-opera troupe,' had been transferred to the big studio at Culver City. We needed a library interior in my picture. The technical director told me there was one already up at Culver City studio that we could use. So we went over to shoot it. I was the only one in the scenes — there was just our working outfit that accompanied us.

We got our few scenes and went into the big restaurant to get some lunch. There were probably twenty companies working at Culver City at this time. We were not noticed. All our crowd being in rough clothes, we did not sit at the tables where the ladies were. We took high stools at the lunch counter. There was a tough-looking mug of a waiter, that we learned afterward had been a Second Avenue mixed-ale fighter in New York. He took all the orders of my 'Irish stew' partners with due attention. I ordered a piece of peach pie and a glass of milk. He just looked at me; and if there can be murder in a smile, there certainly can be murder in a look. It did not occur to me until afterwards that my order seemed at all incongruous, but perhaps it did. I wore a long black wig, and with my Indian outfit and dark make-up, probably a milk-and-peach-pie order was a bit out of place. At any rate, the waiter fed my friends, but paid not the slightest attention to me.

The affront had been so flagrant and the situation became so tense that my partners kept quiet. I meekly repeated my order. He did not hear — he started away. I called to him, not loudly, but with something in the quality of voice that made him very brave or rubbed him the wrong way. He walked straight back, picked up a heavy crock bowl, such as they serve breakfast food in, and without a word of warning brought it down wickedly on top of my head. The bowl busted to fragments. Had I not worn a heavy wig, there would have been a dead Indian right there; as it was I saw diamonds fly, as they did when I was a boy and my boss on the ice-wagon chopped a cake of ice.

I got on the counter some way, and some way I got over, and some way *he* was underneath. If I had worn boots instead of moccasins, I probably would have gone to San Quentin and suffered the death penalty.

An hour afterward, I was leaving for camp. I told Allen not to discharge the man on my account — to let him go back to work.

'Why, he's gone,' he said.

'Where did he go?' I asked.

And he looked at me as though I was joking, and when he saw I wasn't, he said, 'Why, Bill, you were looking right at the machine that took him to the hospital when it pulled out.'

That sort of scared me, as my head did feel queer. I went into a dressing-room and lay down. They sent for a doctor, but I was all right in a couple of hours; but I combed my hair with a towel for two weeks.

About this time 'Civilization,' a big special directed by Raymond B. West, was finished. It had been in the course of making for about a year. Tom owned the major portion

224

of this picture, personally, and he went to New York and remained many months exploiting it.

My little Western 'horse-opera' company and myself were supreme at camp. When I thought of my freedom and looked at those hills of throbbing hearts, full of the life of my boyhood, I was content, even if I failed to go higher. Success seemed to go with that which was transient. Those hills were mine, and had been mine since my birth. If I had seen farther than I had been able to travel in life, it was the fault of my vision. I had looked and dreamed honestly. If this mimic world of toil where I was earning a living and reproducing days that were dear to me was to be the top of my mountain, I was content. I was surrounded by no greedy grafters, no gelatin-spined, flatulent, slimy creatures — just dogs, horses, sheep, goats, bulls, mules, burros, and white men and red men that were accustomed to live among such things. If we wanted a snake, we could go out in the hills and catch one — one that would warn us that he was a snake, with his rattles. . . .

I was happy!

CHAPTER XIV

THE BIG SALARY AND THE BREAK WITH TOM INCE

ONE day I was highly elated. I had just accomplished a new stunt in pictures. I had jumped Fritz through a window. The little fellow had got only a slight cut on his nose and I wasn't hurt at all. A tempter could not have chosen a worse day for his purpose.

A man named Robert Kane, representing Paralta pictures, came to me and offered me five thousand a week, and, as a present for signing the contract, a big, new, highly painted Stutz car he was driving. I thanked him, but said 'No!'

A short time after this, the old gate man came and told me a lame man named Arbuckle wanted to see me. Our set was some distance away, and I didn't go to the gate, nor have the man sent in, as I could not recall any lame man acquaintance. A few hours afterward, when driving out on my way home, I saw 'Fatty' Arbuckle waiting. I was frightfully embarrassed. He had met with an accident and was temporarily lame — I had not heard of it. I apologized and meant it. Arbuckle had another man with him. They wanted me to sign with a man in New York with whom Arbuckle had signed, Joseph M. Schenck; that I could get four or five thousand a week. I told them I could not consider any offers. I did not want to change.

I wrote to Tom in New York of these and other big offers. I told him I did not want to leave — I was happy. The camp was home; that it was a sort of little kingdom to me . . . and I never wanted to go anywhere else; but to please talk to the heads of the company and tell them just

226

how I felt and explain the injustice of my working for three hundred a week.

Upon receipt of the letter, Tom said that such money was impossible; for me to do as he asked me to do — leave it to him, and when it was possible for Triangle to give me more money I would get it. He said he felt hurt; that it looked as though I did not trust him to do what was right by me.

There was much more along these lines. I wrote Tom immediately, thanking him, and turned a deaf ear to any and all offers that I was daily receiving.

There was a round table at the Hoffman Café that was real 'Bohemia.' It seated seven people. From 6 to 9 P.M. there were seldom less than fourteen dining at it. It did not matter if your tip was a dime or two bits (there were certainly none higher), Fritz, the waiter, played no favorites. And if there was any subject under discussion that he wanted to get in on, he did so, and stuck to it until some one of the family would cry out, 'Say! Do I get that "pig's knuckle and sauerkraut" for breakfast?'

Mack Sennett, Mrs. Talmadge and her daughters, Norma, Constance, and Natalie, Kenneth and Bessie Mc-Gaffey, Scoop Conlon, Edwin Schallert, Bill Keefe, Monroe Lathrop, Chet Withey, Bennie Ziedman, George Siegmann, Walter Long and his wife, Sid and Chet Franklin, Tod Browning, Eddie Dillon, Ray Griffith, Mary Hart and myself, were but some of the forty or fifty lovers of staunch comradeship who dined at the old round table.

May those who gossiped and wrangled and had the other fellow's soup spilled on their evening paper have much happiness in this life and in the life to come, and may they never forget the old round table!

George Fawcett came from the East. He was at once admitted to the circle of the round table. George unfolded stories of my popularity throughout the country that astounded me. He asked me what salary I was getting, and nearly expired when I told him the truth. I had a great deal of confidence in what George told me; but to this day I cannot see how I could be blamed for not being more wise than I was. I was working sixteen to eighteen hours every day. In addition, once we worked seven straight Sundays. My food was grabbed and gulped, not eaten. All my life I have needed eight hours' sleep and could do nicely with ten — I averaged six; and coupled with my other duties I was also appearing before the camera as a star.

The Eastern reports said that all of my pictures were making hits. I anxiously awaited the return of Tom. When he came back, I was awfully hurt. . . . He did not come to camp to see me.

I waited a couple of weeks, and then, more in shamefaced sorrow than in anger, I went over to Culver City — to shoot a scene we could just as well have shot at camp. Tom came on the set and smiled and gripped my hand. That was good for another two months of $300 a week, and it elapsed.

A representative of Mr. Spor, of Chicago, wanted to give me a big salary; Mr. Brackett, of the Brack Shops, in Los Angeles, had people from El Paso who wanted to give me forty acres of land and build me a studio in the city of El Paso and finance my pictures.

As the Brackett people pulled out of camp, Tom pulled in. He apologized for the delay and said that my salary was $1000 per week, but dated it ahead three or four weeks until Frank Keenan's contract expired and his $1000 a week was off the salary list.

I was grateful. My new salary started just before Christmas!

Kenneth McGaffey, one of our round table men, was publicity director of the Lasky Studio. He told me that Mr. Zukor wanted to see me and made an appointment at the Alexandria Hotel.

Mr. Zukor and I had a very pleasant chat. It was mighty pleasant to me. He started by saying he would have to consider the matter, that he hadn't figured it out yet, but he could pay me a salary in the neighborhood of four thousand weekly. I was flabbergasted! Here was an offer that WAS reliable.

A few days later, while waiting to hear further from Mr. Zukor, Triangle got busy. Mr. Quinn, the financial representative, started first, and he talked six or seven thousand a week, and asked me if I would talk to Mr. Aitken. Would I? I had to watch where I put my feet. I had to feel for the earth each step — like a blind man. I was not sure I was awake!

Mr. Aitken asked me to dinner at the Beverly Hills Hotel; he and his brother and a new vice-president of the company, Mr. Parker, who had just bought in at a reported price of one million dollars.

After dinner we bowled all evening. They all tried hard to get me to name a salary, but they kept boosting it so much themselves I did not dare speak. I kept right on bowling as hard as I could. Finally, Mr. Aitken said:

'Well, Hart, how about nine thousand, and we'll settle right now.'

'Mr. Aitken, I'll let you know to-morrow,' I said.

The next day I said 'ten thousand,' just on general principles, and they said, 'Mr. W. W. Hodkinson, our vice-president and manager of sales, arrives to-morrow morning. We will all meet at the Alexandria Hotel.'

I told them that I was working and had to be at camp at eight-thirty, but I would meet them at seven o'clock.

The interview was short. Mr. W. W. Hodkinson thought it over and figured some lump sums which worked out about ninety-five hundred per week the first six months, and a little over ten thousand the second, and the same was repeated the second year.

I had been up until 3.30 A.M. with Cecil de Mille in his office while he talked to New York to Mr. Zukor. Mr. Zukor would not go over six thousand per week, with some sort of an added arrangement, so I said to the Triangle folks, 'O. K.'

They instructed the vice-president, Mr. Parker, to make out the contract and they all left town. In about four days the contract was all drawn up and I signed it.

Three days later ... Zowie! Yowie! And then again — Zowie! What an awful roar! They could not fire Tom without giving me the chance of quitting. I felt sorry for Mr. Parker. He worked on me two whole days, but I was adamant.

Finally, he followed me into Tom's office and in Tom's presence said, 'Hart, my board of directors say I have made the blunder of a lifetime; they tell me they just lost Fairbanks through this same clause calling for Mr. Griffith's supervision. I will make you a present of a hundred-thousand-dollar certified check right now to cut that clause calling for the supervision of Mr. Ince out of your contract.' He continued: 'We understand that Mr. Ince has never supervised your pictures and it is apparent it was put in there for a purpose.'

'Mr. Parker,' I said, 'the one hundred thousand certified check doesn't mean a thing to me. I've got all the money I want in that contract. Tom Ince is my friend. That clause stays in.'

'Well, what in hell can I do with a man that doesn't know the value of money?' Parker said.

Tom grinned, but it was a teeny, weeny grin. Tom had been badly scared ... one hundred thousand dollars was a lot of money.

They had asked me to postpone my big salary raise three or four weeks so Mr. Hodkinson could get the booking prices raised. When that time had elapsed, they begged for four more weeks, just one more picture; they would start the big salary positively on the second picture.

'I'll do it on one condition, and that is that you sell me my horse Fritz,' I said.

Tom had always refused to sell him to me, as he knew the horse helped to hold me there.

They said they would give me Fritz. The picture was five weeks in the making, so it figured out that Fritz cost me $42,500. But he was worth it ... and the old snoozer is worth it still.

The 'Cold Deck' was one of those 'two sheets of note-paper written in long-hand' stories. Jack Hawkes and I built it up to feature length in two days. In addition to the two leading rôles, for which Alma Reubens and Sylvia Breamer were cast, we added a third girl part, a young sister of the character I played. I gave this part to a youngster who was a child playing around the sewing-room where her mother was forelady when I first went to

231

camp. The forelady told me she did not think laced shirts would be correct, and she got out a heavily bound book containing the different costumes of all periods up to date to prove her argument. The costume given of the cowboy as the correct thing had a laced shirt, one that my sister Mary had made for me when I played Cash Hawkins in 'The Squaw Man,' and the cowboy inside of the laced shirt was myself.

The forelady's little girl thought I was 'somebody,' having a pretty painted picture of myself in a big fashion book. And as I was wide open to a bit of hero worship, we became very friendly. She was a well-mannered, beautiful child. Some of the ladies used to do up her hair and dress her as a grown-up for fun, and she would visit my set and talk to me. She looked as quaint as a bit of Dresden china. I used to tease her and call her my sweetheart. . . . And now, three years later, I was able to give this little girl a chance to make a hit in what proved to be my last picture on the Triangle program. The 'Cold Deck' cost only $22,000, and Mildred Harris drew only $5 per day, but she made her hit.

Once more I was asked to delay the start of the big salary. They wanted me to make a trip around the country and appear in all the theaters. As they had already stalled nearly ten weeks, I loudly demurred. They called in Tom to put it over. He did! About May first I started on a tour that covered the country from coast to coast, thirty-four cities in thirty-one days.

It is hard to describe such a trip as mine and have the words accepted as truth. But unlimited imagination could never conjure up such experiences.

At Needles, California, the hand-shaking ovations

started and never stopped until I reached home, nearly five weeks later.

At Raton, New Mexico, when a tired man had turned in at midnight, a stream of exhilarated cow-punchers who had ridden distances from ten to a hundred miles thronged through the train. The passengers must have felt like lynching me.

Dodge City, Kansas, held the Overland Limited while the entire population and that of the surrounding country bid me welcome. Every citizen who owned one had a forty-five belt full of lead on his hip. The good priest of the town unstrapped his hardware and presented it to me in the name of the citizens of Dodge City. It was the gun and belt taken from the body of the last bad man killed on Front Street by Sheriff Chalk Beeson. I was then escorted to the site of 'Boot Hill' where reposed the many who died with their boots on.

The conductor stood watch in hand — the train waited — the passengers fumed. I gently reminded the mayor that the train was liable to pull out without me.

'If it does, it'll never stop in Dodge City again,' he said. Whether he meant it or not I do not know, but the train waited and the passengers fumed.

At Kansas City I received my first real baptism. I was in the city three hours, made about twenty speeches in depots, hotels, and theaters, and caught my train for St. Louis, with a cheese sandwich in one hand and a bottle of beer in the other.

I sent an S.O.S. to Tom, but he had been called to New York. No one could help me — the Exhibitors had me; and while they were a lovable, hustling, hard-working set of men, they were merciless in their demands. I clicked my teeth and resolved to stay with it until I keeled over.

Kansas City was bad ... but St. Louis was terrible. A regiment of soldiers was at the train before breakfast. The First Liberty Loan was on. I led parades and talked on horseback on different squares until I nearly fell off from exhaustion, then did my theaters, luncheons and dinners, afternoons and nights. One of the theaters was in East St. Louis across the river. It is the home of the stock-yards and was considered a hard-boiled town. The streets were jammed — dozens of young boys jumped on the running-board of the car.

'Say, Bill, can you whip Bill Farnum?' one yelled.

'Sure!' I replied. (I knew Bill wouldn't mind, that he would say the same thing under like circumstances.)

'Aw, he kin like hell,' said a second lovable, tousle-headed, bare-necked urchin.

'All right,' said number one, 'you're Bill Farnum and I'm Bill Hart.' And wham! Bill Hart landed on Bill Farnum's jaw and over went Bill Farnum.

When we came out of the theater there was a bunch of mounted cowboys waiting. I said 'Hello' to all of them. One was a dark chap. In the half-light I assumed that he was a Mexican.

'Bueno, amigo,' I saluted — which is just about my limit of Spanish.

He replied in Sioux, 'How kola! How! How!'

Oh! Lordy! Lordy! Lordy! Didn't I splurge! That half-breed Indian cowboy hadn't had a chance in months to speak his mother tongue. But he didn't have a thing on me — all the big newspapers had their star reporters right there. I repeated every phrase I could think of in Sioux about fourteen times. The newspaper men were delighted. The Sioux boy was delighted, and I was delighted a heap!

234

A Great Reception in New York

Two such small cities as Indianapolis and Cincinnati were played in one day, the former being the matinée town. I was almost tumbling over for want of sleep. My right hand was swollen to three times its normal size, but I was happy. It was glorious! I was astounded, appalled at such tribute. It may have been the excitement or the weariness, I do not know. I only know the inside of my eyelids were often mighty damp.

In front of a theater in the Bronx at New York City, the crowd tore the top clear off a seven-thousand-dollar limousine.

At the New York Theater, downtown, the reception was so great that I could not speak for many minutes, and Marcus Loew presented me with a huge silver cup, inscribed:

To William S. Hart, Greatest Screen Actor.
As an indication of the esteem in which he is
held by millions

I was appearing in New York, Brooklyn, and surrounding cities for three days. Tom was there. He told me that Triangle was trying to force him out; that his lawyer and J. Parker Read, his personal representative, were trying to effect a settlement. I begged him to stick to Triangle. I told him of my love of the old camp, and how it would hurt me ever to think of leaving it. He said he would do his best to patch it up.

I had worked all evening and was leaving for the Boston midnight train. Daniel Frohman wanted me to appear for a few minutes at the Actors' Fund Fair. There was a big parade. I had the honor of walking with Lillian Russell. We busted up the parade. I had to make my train. It was impossible to get out, and the soldiers were called. A husky chap with muscles bursting through his jacket was the apex of the wedge just ahead of me. I was thrown about like a cork, but he bored through like a trained-to-the-minute football player. At the door, with sweat streaming off his face, he gave me his hand and said, 'Good-bye, Bill.' It was Kid McCoy.

Beautiful Marjorie Rambeau threw her arms about me and, living up to the players' adage of suiting the action to the word and the word to the action, said, 'Kiss California for me.'

I wasn't in the least bit of a hurry to catch that train.

The trip West from Boston covering all the big cities was a whirlwind of travel and work. I was in Chicago three days. At a banquet I sat between Mae Tinee and Louella Parsons, each representing their respective newspapers. These ladies were mighty kind to me. I shall never cease to be grateful.

The waiters were dressed as cowboys. They all had their sleeves rolled up — the usual mistake — and often made by actors, also. I explained in my little talk that the only man in a cow outfit that ever rolled up his sleeves was the cook, but that he was the overlord of the whole works, the one hundred per cent boss.

The morning of the third day in Chicago, I received a wire from Tom. He was on his way from New York to see me on the Twentieth Century Limited. Half an hour later came a wire from Mr. Aitken. He was on his way from New York to see me, traveling on the Pennsylvania-Broadway Limited. Neither seemed to know of the other making the trip. It looked as though I was in for a pleasant morning. Mr. Aitken arrived first.

Mr. Aitken's talk was lucid, logical, and apparently sincere. He told me that, in view of my known friendship for Mr. Ince, he had made the trip to tell me that Mr. Ince was to sever his connection with the Triangle Company; that Triangle was about to close a contract to buy him out for a very large sum of money; that he (Mr. Aitken) was there personally to advise me of the facts and further to state that my big salary would commence as soon as I reached home; that the name of the old camp had already been changed from Inceville to Hartville; that I would continue to work there with my own company and be in complete control.

He explained that it was believed that Mr. Ince had never directed or supervised me in a picture, and that therefore I must have insisted on the clause calling for his supervision through friendship, and for the protection of Mr. Ince; therefore, now that Mr. Ince was voluntarily to settle with the company, he wanted my assurance that I would stick to Triangle. The talk he made was not only forceful in its directness and simplicity, but it was appealing in its seeming sincerity.

I told Mr. Aitken that if Tom was forced out I would still consider that I had the right to quit, if I so desired, but if Tom willingly made a settlement I would think it over seriously — that the old camp pulled on my heartstrings mighty hard.

And then came Tom. I had always given way to the charm of his personality, but this time I gave him a great argument. I explained briefly that I had been in pictures three years; that I had been told on excellent authority that my pictures had made millions of dollars, and that I had nothing to show for my work, outside of my popularity; that now was my chance to become a rich man —

$9500 per week to start on — and I did not own $5000 as a result of my life's work.

I explained to him that he *had* his money — that I had mine to get. I told him all that Mr. Aitken had said. And then Tom talked. He talked for an hour. He gave me a document to sign. I signed. He called in Bert Lennon from the next room and asked him to sign it. He did! And when the door had closed on Tom hurrying to catch his train, Lennon looked at me blankly, saying, 'What in hell is in that thing?' 'Damfino,' I wearily muttered. 'Damfino either,' Lennon replied.

Such was the personality of Thomas H. Ince.

Our little troupe consisted of four men, Bert Lennon, his assistant, whose name I do not recall, Don Keyes, the photographer, and myself. Both Lennon and Keyes had been on tours with real celebrities, such as Mr. Roosevelt, Mr. Bryan, and others, where there was a certain amount of dignity maintained and where the 'tourists' were expected to have an hour or so sleep every three or four days. Our tour was different, and my three companions were as badly used up as I was.

In addition, after leaving Chicago, there was added to our usual traveling and fifteen or twenty speeches each day, long-distance telephone calls from New York, Boston, Philadelphia, and all points East. I could not go to the telephone; I was talking almost every minute. I would send Lennon to answer. He would come back with sweat streaming from his face, 'It's Mr. Ince,' or 'Mr. Aitken,' or 'Mr. Somebody else.'

I would reply, with the sweat streaming off my face also, 'Tell 'em, for the love of Mike, to let me alone.'

And then I'd go on trying to make good talking to

several thousand people. I remember in one town — I think it was Spokane, Washington — Kenneth McGaffey, representing Mr. Zukor, called me from Los Angeles. Mr. Zukor wanted to know if I had signed a contract with Mr. Ince. I said, 'No,' but if I left Triangle I would join with Mr. Ince and that we would make pictures together.

At San Francisco, Tom nearly stepped over the line. He called me from New York and told me rather peremptorily not to go home, to remain in San Francisco until I heard from him again. It was an order, but when I resented it, he quickly switched to pleading and I quickly forgave him. But I kept to my schedule and went home.

I soon discovered the cause of Tom's uneasiness. All of the principal producers and distributors had their representatives in Los Angeles to see me. I could not only write my own ticket; I could write as many tickets as I wanted to write. There was no offer under $10,000 per week. Triangle had sent old neighbors that I had known in Asheville, North Carolina, to see me. One of these men was Mr. Lynch, the man who later tied up the South for Famous Players.

Mr. Lynch was a keen business man. He presented an angle which I did not think possible, but which six months later was carried out. He said that if I quit Triangle, they intended to flood the country with my pictures.

This was done. In addition to their regular releases they sold to newly formed companies all of my two-reel and some of the five-reel pictures. These pictures were released under several different titles, some two-reelers being built up to five-reelers. Then there was one five-reel picture made entirely from cut-outs (discarded film) of various pictures and released under the title of 'A Lion of the Hills.' I never knew who was responsible for this picture, nor did I ever work in any such picture.

That I was able to maintain the confidence of the public through this siege is good for me to look back upon, as it was heart-breaking to receive letters from little boys and girls all over the country telling me how they had saved their pennies to go and see my picture, only to find that they had seen it before, some being victimized three and four times on the same picture. One of these companies called themselves 'W. H. Productions.' I received on different occasions their bills and rental receipts at my studio, which was The William S. Hart Productions.

Of course, I went after the offenders, and while it cost me a great deal of money, my attorneys were influential in getting an order from the Federal Trade Commission that does away with this practice. All pictures must now display in equal-size type the former name of the picture should its name be changed.

Tom had quit Triangle and I had sent in my resignation. Tom was calling me from New York every day or night on the telephone begging me 'to stand by him.' The Triangle Company was sending Mr. Quinn, or other representatives, once every week with bags of gold containing $9500, my weekly salary, which I declined to accept. One week — two weeks — passed; three weeks — four weeks — passed; still I was salaryless, and still I was turning down bags of gold and the biggest producers and distributors in America. Friendship was costing me dearly.

I would tell Tom over the telephone when he called me:

'Mr. (whoever it might be) is out here offering me $10,000 per week.'

He would still beg for time and say that he was negotiating with Mr. Zukor.

Tom Ince and Famous Players

My friends, Joe Weber and Arthur Hopkins, and many other friends in New York made urgent appeals for me to do business with them, but I stuck to Tom.

And then it came!.... Tom signed a contract to deliver me to Famous Players within thirty days. He also signed a contract for himself to make two pictures a year with a $50,000 guarantee for each picture; and a second contract involving three other stars with a guarantee of $35,000 for each picture.

My contract was for sixteen pictures with a guarantee of $150,000 for each picture. Each of the other contracts contained a clause which made them void, provided a contract was not made with me delivering me to Famous Players within thirty days. This fact I did not learn until three years later.

I felt a bit hurt at Tom going in for wholesale producing, but I knew from my previous experience I could make the pictures myself, the same as I had done. The worst thing I had to face was the 'I told you so' of dozens and dozens of men who had predicted just what happened.

I had a talk with Tom and told him I wanted to work by myself.

'Certainly,' he said. 'I never intended anything else.'

But I had no story — Tom had nothing for me. I had a story in my head I had long intended to do. I worked on it three days, turned it over to Harvey Thew of the Lasky Studio, and he in turn made the continuity in another three days.

While waiting for this continuity, Bert Lennon advised getting some new action photographs of Fritz and myself, so we went to the barn on Washington Boulevard, where I had been forced to keep the old fellow in a box stall for many weeks. Golly! He was mad! He was fighting mad! He could not understand why he should have been cooped up for so long and see me so seldom.

The proprietor of the stable told us that there were a couple of vacant lots about a quarter of a mile distant. I walked and led Fritz, much to the amusement of Lennon and Keyes. They didn't know the animal — they had only seen him on the screen when he was being a good horse. Before mounting, I made a little talk to the 'funsters.' I explained to them how Fritz had been taken from his personal corral at camp and shut in an indoor box stall for over a month, and that he always demanded his little morning play when I got on him, whenever he felt like it. I told them that he was going to buck and buck hard as soon as I started to mount, so for them to stay clear of him; no matter if it was too long a shot, not to come close.

We all got ready and I put one over on the little fellow. I made out that I was going to give him a tidbit, and, instead, vaulted into the saddle. Oh, golly! He was mad before, but he was madder now. Any first-class rider could stay on Fritz when he was bucking his hardest, as he bucked straightaway, he did not weave or sunfish or spin. But, Lordy! how high he would go, and every jump was accompanied by a kick!

I yelled and yelled at the boys to keep away. But I had to quit yelling and ride, for the little fellow was getting real rough. My hat went, my quirt went, one stirrup went, and things were not looking so mighty rosy for me, personally, when there was a dull thud behind, and out of the corner of my eye I caught a glimpse of a body flying through the air. . . . The doggone little divil had landed one of his flying kicks on Bert Lennon and he took a ride of

MY WELCOME TO THE LASKY STUDIO

Left to right: William S. Hart, Mary Pickford, Jesse Lasky, Cecil de Mille

thirty feet and lit on top of an ash heap. And after Fritz had finished his playing hell and allowed me to get off, the impertinent little rascal followed me over to see what was the matter. Bert Lennon walked on crutches for three months.

My first picture, 'The Narrow Trail,' was made at the Lasky Studio; and my first big quarrel with Tom was about my horse. For some unaccountable reason Tom, who always could see anything that had a money value, could not see Fritz. He just did not like the horse and I was never able to find out why. 'The Narrow Trail' was conceived and written in my love for Fritz, and when Tom wanted me to use another horse, I began to doubt either his or my own sanity. The horse made the picture a great success, and it is still playing.

In the next fifteen pictures, although Tom tried in various ways through Allen and Sullivan and others to get me to use Fritz, the little pinto never earned another dollar that Tom shared in. That is why the little fellow was idle for fifteen pictures.

Perhaps our row about the pony might have been patched up had I not found that I was being charged a proportionate share of the overhead expense of running Tom's own studio. I was dumbfounded. I went to see Tom immediately, expecting him to make some excuse and rectify the mistake at once. He did adjust the matter, but instead of an excuse, he attempted to justify his position.

This busted the breach wide open. Tom and I were never friends afterward. During the two years that passed in the making of the sixteen pictures, I never saw him but three or four times of probably five minutes each. All our quarreling — and there was a heap of it — was done through E. H. Allen, my studio manager.

We leased the old Mabel Normand Studio in East Hollywood from Mack Sennett. I remained in this studio for four years.

CHAPTER XV
WAR WORK

ABOUT Christmas time, 1917, most of our cowboys had been called to war. We were doing a picture, 'The Tiger Man,' that called for an unusual number of expert riders. We needed three bands of horsemen, a company of soldiers, a band of outlaws, and a sheriff's posse; and the riders that could come off cliffs and race at full speed over rough, unbroken country were in training camps or had gone overseas.

Mr. Allen advertised, and made it positive that all men must be first-class riders. They looked all right, but when out on location and it came to riding, eighty per cent of them admitted they had lied to get the work, the only saving grace being that they were game to a man. They all would try. A straightaway chase on level ground was tried first. It was hopeless! There were soldiers, cowboys, and sheriff's men scattered all over the mesa; one of them, a colored boy, who claimed to be an Indian, having a badly damaged leg.

The scenes had to be taken. There was nothing to do but double. The men on the working staff of a Western outfit can all ride. We used all of them except the ones turning the cranks of the cameras. As the outlaw, I first did my own rides, then I changed clothes, joined the sheriff's posse and chased myself, then changed again to a soldier man and joined in the chase of the sheriff's outfit.

In February, 1918, we were on location at Donner Lake, near Truckee, in the heart of the Sierras. It was here, seventy-one years agone, that over half of a party of eighty pioneers perished while following the very trails in that wilderness of snow that we were trying to follow. It was on these very trails that poor, crazed creatures made their death camps, and where two volunteer guides, men of the red race, were killed and eaten by men of the white race. These trails are still unmastered. Rough cairns of stone stand alone in defiance over their unburied dead, undaunted and unknown.

I had to drive a dog team in 'Shark Monroe,' the picture we were making. I discovered that it was just the same as driving steers — I had no difficulty whatever. If I were broke, I believe Sam, the Alaskan musher who still owns and operates dog teams in the Sierras, would employ me as a driver. I drove over many of those tragic Donner party trails.

There were four motion picture stars selected by the Government to tour the country and speak in behalf of the Third Liberty Loan, Mary Pickford, Douglas Fairbanks, Charles Chaplin, and myself. Mary, Doug, and Charlie divided the territory from Kansas City east. When I received my letter from Mr. McAdoo, I was told to report to the Pacific Coast Committee at San Francisco. They arranged my four weeks' tour to open at San Diego, then east to Salt Lake City, north to Butte, west to Seattle, and south to Los Angeles — taking in all cities between those points. My railroad fares and hotel bills and those of my manager, Mr. Allen, a camera man and a publicity man, were paid by the Government, although Mr. Allen informed me that in many cities the hotels would not accept any money.... It was all for Uncle Sam, and Uncle Sam for all. Our contribution was the overhead of the idle

MAKING A MOTION PICTURE FOR THE LIBERTY LOAN

Left to right: Bill, Doug, Mary, Julian Eltinge, and Marshall Neilan

studio at Hollywood, which was considerable, as all employees received full salary during my absence.

The opening day of my tour at San Diego came mighty near being my closing day. During the war I was godfather of the 159th Infantry, then located at Camp Kearny. Colonel Farrell, of the 159th, came to San Diego and took me to Camp Kearny to make a talk.

Whether it was the usual daily drill or not, I do not know, but Colonel Farrell had arranged to have all the soldiers at Camp Kearny lined up at 5 P.M. Thousands upon thousands of those lithe, bronzed specimens of young American manhood were standing at attention, eyes straight ahead, when I mounted a horse they had waiting for me and rode up to speak.

There are moments in one's life that are too big for words. ... I could not talk. My brain functioned, but it was centered on that ocean of manhood, back-lighted by the setting sun. Who and what was I, that I should be chosen to talk to the flower of my country? These men of youth, brains, and guts, standing in front of me like granite walls ... I felt infinitesimally small.

In terrible silence, for full two minutes after Colonel Farrell introduced me, I sat my horse with every muscle paralyzed. Then, God allowed me to speak and say things that were in my heart; and I will always be thankful to God that he did, for many of those ranks upon ranks of fighting men liked what I said and remembered and wrote me from overseas that they remembered. That is why I know God directed my tongue.

At Salt Lake I was greatly impressed by the staunchness of the Mormons in support of the war. I talked at a private meeting of venerable old gentlemen, held in their marble sanctum. They appeared to be charged with war. They were so full of warfare that their long white beards seemed fairly to throw out electric sparks. I never made a talk to any body of men that needed it less. I think the leader was addressed as President Smith.

For a little diversion and to get material for my talk, I was taken out to Fort Douglas and shown the camp of the alien prisoners. The grounds seemed to cover many times several acres. There were rows upon rows of wooden barracks and regularly laid-out streets with signboards at the corners, printed in German. Surrounding the same two thousand inhabitants was a high wire fence, and at each corner was mounted, on a high pier or platform, an ugly-looking gun with attendant gunners.

As we entered the gate a voice called out, 'Hello, Bill!'

I kept right on telling what I considered a funny story to Colonel Byram and his accompanying officers, and then a voice from an opposite direction — 'Hello, Bill!'

My mind was wandering — 'guns mounted high with gunners' — 'wire fences' — 'many, many soldiers' — 'and officers' . . .

Another and louder call, this time with a pronounced German accent — 'Hello, Bill!'

My story was gone — it was too much! It might be a joke, and it might not, BUT —— 'Look here, Colonel Byram,' I began without ceremony, 'you haven't known me very long, and before going any farther I'd like to have it understood, and know that you realize, that these men calling out to me are not friends of mine.'

Colonel Byram liked a joke. I'm glad he did. I was beginning to feel just a little bit queer.

I cannot remember just where we ran into that scholarly

gentleman and splendid American, United States Senator
William S. Kenyon. He was a trouper like us. We were all
doing our bit and traveled on the same trains. We soon
gathered in two more comrades, Major Gordon (Ralph
Connor), and Major-General Swinton, of the British
Army, he who invented the British tank. What a quartet!
Senator Kenyon, with his frock coat and silk hat; Swinton,
in his smart English uniform, his breast just smothered
with medals; Major Gordon, with the bare legs and kilts of
the Highlanders — whom the enemy dubbed 'ladies from
hell'; and me bringing up the rear in my cow-puncher outfit. We could have sold bonds or run a medicine show just
on our looks!

We were together for some weeks. I was sorry when we
parted. I'll bet the Secretary of the Treasury was sorry,
too! We sold millions and millions of bonds. We were a
merry party. My three partners used to have great fun
getting back at each other in their speeches, picking each
other up on certain points. Golly! they were clever! It
was a delight to hear them. I always spoke last, and I
know they used purposely to leave me openings, so I could
take an occasional slap at them and be in the running.
Fine men they were! Fine men! If I ever envied any one,
I think I would envy those men their stock of brain-stuff.

One thing I am sure I envied them, and that was sleep.
They could take off their clothes and go to bed. I had to
pull off my boots, stretch out, and let it go at that, for
every time the train stopped during the night, the engineer
would 'hold her' for a couple of minutes, which meant five
or even ten, while I crawled out, sometimes with a boot in
one hand, and did my talk.

I am not saying I didn't like it — I did. I loved it! I
loved the Cause, and I loved every man, woman, and

child who remained up nearly all night to say hello to a man that they could feel loved them.

At Portland, Oregon, in addition to my regular work, I was asked to speak at a high school. The crowds were so great and the enthusiasm of those wonderful boys and girls so ardent that the authorities declared a holiday for all schools and announced a mass meeting at the auditorium for two o'clock.

When I looked out over those youthful faces, it seemed as though they extended miles and miles. They were in the aisles, on the window-sills, on each other's shoulders. Everything but the chandeliers was covered with young life, light hearts and a high flow of spirits. A sweet-faced lady beside me sang: 'There's a long, long, trail a-winding, into the land of my dreams.'

The light beams came through the windows and met the sunshine that was in her voice. The thousands of young faces became a little blurred. It was such a gathering as angels would have grouped. I am sure that God loved it and smiled.

At San Francisco we had to fight, or rather the soldiers and police had to fight, to get us into the auditorium. Bully Major Swinton! His medals were found all over by every one. He almost lost his dignity, too! But it only strayed — it came back of its own accord and the General made merry with the rest of us. Much of my apparel was gone, but, unlike the Major's medals and dignity, was not found and did not come back. They took all of my handkerchief, half of my coat, and nearly all of my shirt.

There were a million kids stormed the doors at the last minute when the hall was packed to the roof. They came down those broad aisles like juvenile dervishes. The police and firemen captains marshaled their forces to crush back slowly those half-dirty, joyous, eager faces, whose every movement was pleading to stay. The order was given. The dejected retreat was commenced.

A sharp, shrill whistle pierced the air. I half-turned and saw behind me on the platform a stalwart man taking an ivory police whistle from his lips, and then he spoke:

'Let them stay, Captain. I'll take the responsibility.'

And as Mayor Rolph sat down I heard him mutter, 'To hell with the fire laws — those kids stay!'

I reached down and gripped the mayor's fist, and I've been gripping his fist ever since and hope to do so as long as I live.

When we arrived home, it was put up to my pinto pony (Fritz) to do his bit. The ladies of the Red Star Animal Relief wanted to raise some money. I led Fritz through the principal business streets of Los Angeles. I doubt if there ever was such a tribute paid to a horse. Traffic was blocked wherever we went. Passage through the streets was next to impossible. We had about twenty cowgirls working their way through the crowds with baskets, in which the donations were placed. When the baskets were full, the girls would empty them into panniers fastened to the saddle on the little horse's back. These panniers held nearly two bushels each. When we finished, they were filled to the brim with twenties, tens, and five-dollar bills, and many pounds of silver and coppers. It required several ladies two full days to count the donations, the amount running into several thousands.

Sam Rork was handling my publicity. He had been with me about three months. He was the first publicity man I ever had. Sam was helping out on our street work. Anything Sam undertakes, he does it; if it's work, it is never beneath his dignity.

Sam crushed past me during an enforced halt, saying, 'Here's a hot one, Bill. Just met an old New York friend of mine.

'"What you doing out here, Sam?" he called.

'"I'm Bill Hart's press agent," I replied.

'"Hell!" he answered. "What a snap! Bill Hart's horse has got twenty million press agents, without salary."'

I was shipping several boxes of tobacco and cigarettes to the boys of my regiment at Camp Kearny.

'How about the officers?' asked Sam Rork. 'Don't they smoke?'

Of course it was said in jest; we could not send the officers tobacco. It would be fine if they were in the trenches, but hardly the gift for a training camp.

I cannot remember whose suggestion it was; I am inclined to think it was my own, for I could never shake off that indescribable feeling when I thought of those soldiers all lined up the day I talked to them at Camp Kearny. It was decided that I should give a ball and week-end party to the officers of the 159th and their brother officers, to be held at the Coronado Hotel, with everybody my guest.

It was a glorious success. We took a party that occupied two Pullmans down with us, mostly girls, and the prettiest girls we could find. I never shall forget Bessie Love's mother bringing little Bessie down to the train by the hand and placing her in my sister Mary's care. It was Bessie's first experience. And I never shall forget little Bessie walking on the sandy beach with one of the tallest, best-looking young officers of the bunch — also Bessie's first experience, and, by golly! how little Bessie did enjoy it, too! Bless her heart! Omigod! If Bessie's mother could have seen her then! But sister Mary was not far away . . . neither was another soldier.

What a ball! I do not believe there ever was anything more picturesque. The Grand March, led by Colonel Farrell and Katherine MacDonald, was a sight long to be remembered. I was proud of it then — I am proud of the memory of it still. I received a letter from Major-General Strong, commander of Camp Kearny, in which he said that it was the finest gathering he had ever seen.

Lambert Hillyer, my director, will always remember our party too. He and I took nearly all the money from Coronado and San Diego, playing some sort of a foolish game called 'stud poker.'

I had seen an actor play a heavy part in a Universal picture. I liked his work very much and had asked Mr. Allen to find out who he was. In casting my picture 'Riddle Gawn,' there was an ideal part for this actor. I asked Mr. Allen to send for him. The next day Mr. Allen came up to my office and said:

'Well, your actor man was here. I thought he wouldn't do, but to make sure I called in Lambert and he agreed with me. He has a strong face, but he is altogether too short to play opposite you.'

'Where is he?' I asked.

'He's gone,' he replied.

'Perhaps you're right,' I said, 'but please get him on the telephone and ask him to come back. I'll wait here to-night until he comes. I'd like to see him.'

The actor came back and I saw him. There were quite a

few inches difference in our height. We were alone in the room. He turned away regretfully, saying, 'I didn't think you were as tall as you are. They told me I wouldn't do, that I was too short.'

'Inches never made an actor,' I replied. 'You're an actor. You get the part.'

It was Lon Chaney.

The first time Chaney and I met in a scene, Lambert directed us. When the scene was over, Lambert looked at me questioningly. He felt it was wrong. I shook my head. We took the scene over. Again I sneaked in a negative shake of the head when Chaney wasn't looking. We tried it once more, but it just didn't measure up. I took Chaney by the arm and we walked a few yards away.

'That scene is all wrong, Lon,' I said. 'There is no question about your ability to play it. You can play anything. You just haven't got the idea. Do you mind if we change parts and rehearse the scene over? I will play your part and you play mine. I want to show you just what I mean.'

'Come on, come on, let's do it,' he replied quickly.

My part was a real type of the dominant gun-man. Chaney's part was made of the same steel. It should be 'diamond cut diamond.'

After we rehearsed the scene, Chaney said to both Lambert and myself, 'Is that the way you want it?'

We both nodded 'Yes.'

'Well,' he said, and his voice quivered, 'do you mind if we lay off this scene for a while and come back to it later in the afternoon? I can't realize it; boys, I'm up in the air — it's the first time I've ever been allowed to play a scene when the star was in it.'

The scene in the afternoon was a pippin.

254

A Kangaroo Court

We camped on location for four weeks at Brent's Crags. Of course, a kangaroo court was held every night, whether any one deserved a chapping or not. Business was not so good, so people were chapped for being too good! Chaney got his medicine one night for chopping wood for the cook, or dancing too much with Mary Hart, the star's sister, or some such terrible charge. And the cow-puncher that swung the cowhide knew his business. . . . It was noticed that Chaney did a lot of walking — some standing — but doggone little sitting down, for the next few days.

About this time in the picture I had to run out of a ranch house, hit the top rail of the porch, land on my horse's back, and make a fast get-away. I had a good horse — Jack was his name — but he got scared when he saw me coming and started away. I was in the air and so close to him that I foolishly tried to make it, but the best I got was both spurs cutting a deep furrow in my saddle. I came down in a sitting posture and the ground was hard, awfully hard. I did the scene the next time, but the added thump in the saddle didn't do my injured part any good. That evening, of all evenings, I got mine. I was found guilty of loaning the leading lady five dollars with which she shot craps and took away the money of honest cowboys.

Lon Chaney was appointed by the court to swing the chaps. He had not been with us on location that day — he knew nothing of my studies concerning a new seated attitude. He had been scorched a few days before. The judge of the court didn't think him so husky — he wouldn't be so tough on the star. Therefore . . . let him swing the chaps.

The judge didn't know — the judge was positively ignorant. Husky? Oh, garrote and garroters! That man Chaney was raised, went to school, and graduated in a boiler shop, swinging an eighty-pound sledge. It would never do to show the white feather! I had to take my medicine! So there was one man more that it was 'noticed' did a lot of walking — some standing — but doggone little sitting down, for the next few days.

Near the end of the picture when I was supposed to be running down the villain, the villain plants himself behind a boulder, waits until I am within revolver distance, and then uses a rifle to make a good job of it. He shoots my horse — the horse falls dead — I crawl behind the horse and shoot back.

The black horse Jack was not a falling horse, so we had a falling horse (a bay) sent out to double for him. Bays, blacks, and sorrel, all photograph black — it is no trouble to double them. It so happened that the day we were to shoot these scenes a New York newspaper man, representing — if I remember correctly — the 'New York World,' came out to see us work. He wanted to see something exciting, and Mr. Allen had picked the day for him.

I looked over the falling horse. He was a bay colt, called the 'Sovern colt' because he was owned and had been broken to fall by a cowboy named Clarence Sovern, the younger brother of 'Whitey' Sovern.

Certain cowboys always doubled for actors in throwing horses, but they all knew I did my own work. They expected it and did not mind it in the least, as I always gave the cowboy who owned the horse the money he would have received had he thrown him, himself. When I entered pictures the price was two dollars; it is now twenty-five dollars, or even higher. On the day I am writing about, the price was fifteen dollars.

I asked young Sovern if his horse was cold-jawed, or hard to throw, whether he fell best coming fast or not, etc.

He answered my questions, and then added, 'Sometimes he's some stubborn.'

All was ready. The members of the company were perched around on boulders to see the falling-horse scene. It usually attracts a little attention, and this day, it did especially, on account of the newspaper man being there.

I took the colt through the scene a couple of times. Lon Chaney had tested his gun and was set behind his rock. All was ready.

'Camera!' called Hillyer.

Down through the boulders came the bay colt running like a deer. Bang! went Chaney's gun, but, instead of my horse going down, he spun around like a top.

Oh, well! — the first time. That's nothing; we seldom get a scene like this the first time. Try it again. We did. And then again, again, and again, and again.

'Sometimes he's some stubborn.' I'll tell the world he was. Not 'sometimes,' but all times. I was in a devil of a fix. I never beat a horse in my life ... but, oh! how I was tempted to give that pony a licking! Finally I did worse — I tightened up his chin-strap. He would either take the fall or have a broken jaw. The snoozer knew it. It may be that the chin-strap should have been tightened in the first place, and that was what he was waiting for, I do not know. I only know that every time before, he ran like a deer. This time he ran like an antelope. And while Fritz was one of the fastest falling horses I ever saw, this pony hit the ground this time even quicker. He caught my whole leg and came near busting it.

The newspaper man asked for a car and was sent into town. He saw no shortcomings in our 'horse-opera.' He remarked to Katherine MacDonald when leaving: 'That man gets cartloads of money, but he earns trainloads.'

'Sovern,' I said, 'what in thunder was the matter with that horse? Why wouldn't he fall?'

'I dunno,' he said. 'That's the first time he's ever been throwed 'cept by me.'

'Anybody else ever try to throw him?' I asked.

'Uh, huh! Oncet! Shorty Hamilton tried oncet for an hour, but he couldn't get him down.'

Shorty Hamilton, since deceased, was one of the very best stunt cowboys in pictures. Take it all in all, I was lucky to get away with my stunt ... when the newspaper man was present.

'Border Wireless' was a semi-war picture. We had to go to San Ysidro on the Mexican border, where the Eleventh Cavalry of the United States Army was camped, to get some of our scenes. The action called for me to come to this army post to enlist, but, being recognized as a fugitive outlaw, I jump my horse over a fence and escape; the army officer not being in sympathy with the informer, almost looking the other way and allowing me to do so. I had to use a jumping horse, and again Jack could not jump, so we left him at home. The only horse I ever knew in pictures that could do and did do anything and everything himself was Fritz, and he was in temporary retirement.

Captain White, of Troop L, had a fine jumping horse that would double Jack nicely, and he did. But for the scenes where I arrived at the post, the army boys had a handsome black three-year-old stallion, and while he was some two hundred pounds heavier than Jack, otherwise he was his counterpart. He had a beautiful flowing mane and tail, the same as Jack. The soldier boys apparently were all much interested in the horse; they were all there to see those scenes shot — officers and men.

THE LADIES' PET THAT BECAME A BLACK DEMON

The Ladies' Pet Becomes a Black Demon

There was a pretty shot where the scene could open empty and I could make my entrance coming up over a cutbank. At the bottom of this cutbank was a space about one hundred feet wide with a barbed-wire fence on the far side.

I don't know why I walked to where I entered the scene. I was not in the least suspicious of the horse. He acted like a ladies' pet animal, and was nosing me all the time. But I did walk, and, when all was ready, I mounted.

Gee! What an awful shock! That black 'ladies' pet' became a black demon. Oh, how he did buck! The first jump caught me absolutely unawares. The saddle horn hit me right in the pit of the stomach. It was an ugly bruise and looked ugly for months afterward. The blow dazed me. I was really 'out' for a few seconds. When I got a grip on myself, I was scared of being killed. A wire fence on one side and a steep bank on the other, and the young stallion was bucking viciously and squealing like a killer. When his head was toward the bank, I risked it. I sank the irons into his sides, deep. Up the bank he went. Emboldened by my success and knowing that the worst I could get now was a nasty fall, I hooked him good. And while I broke all rodeo money riding rules, I put up an honestly wonderful ride — at least, the soldier boys thought so. They cheered me so lustily that it could be heard in Tia Juana, where the horse lived, three miles away.

The imps! They had framed me! They wanted to see Bill Hart ride, and they journeyed across the border to get the horse to do the trick.

Practically the same thing had happened at Camp Lewis when I was on the Liberty Loan, only there they gave me a runaway scoundrel with a broken bit chain and yelled themselves hoarse as he tore through the middle of camp before I could go out on his side and get his cheek strap in my hand.

Great boys, those soldier boys. . . . Golly! How I loved 'em all!

'Branding Broadway' was my next picture. It was the story of a Westerner going East and being engaged by a rich father as a sort of caretaker for his wayward son. An important scene was supposed to take place in one of the Great White Way restaurants. The young man in the case was in the habit of imbibing freely and then starting a rough-house. It was the duty of the Westerner, the character I played, to protect him and fight his battles. The Westerner refused to be this kind of nurse, but while he was in it he earned his hire. There was the big fight in the swell Broadway café.

The night that we photographed these scenes, the fighting boys whom we always had for this work brought in a newcomer for me to look over. One glance showed me that he was a boxer; he wore the ear-marks that so few fighters escape. The other boys vouched for him and said he was all right.

In all fight scenes the boys who were accustomed to the work used to tear right in. This had three advantages. It kept them in the foreground where they were photographed a lot, their pep pleased the director, and they got theirs from the heroes and were finished quickly.

The newcomer was not only new to our studio, but was evidently new to the ways of fight scenes in pictures, for he did not take advantage of any of the old-timers' tricks. He stayed in the background milling around through hours of scenes, to the extreme discomfiture of a lot of our extra people. However, as he was acting as a waiter and was one of the restaurant crew, he had to be finished, and as I was the only hero left (my charge having become *hors de combat* early in the *mêlée*), he had to be finished by me.

Just before the scene for his retirement, I walked over to him, as I always did before fighting a new man, and said:

'Partner, of course you know your business, but as you and I have never fought before, I want to explain how we try and work it. We never rehearse any blows. We find they always look planted. We just take a chance and fight.'

He looked at me calmly, attentively, and penetratingly, his six feet something of proportionate build never moving a muscle.

'You see, brother, we've got to get a real fight scene, as one would actually happen — so just tear in. Of course, time your punches and pull them as much as you possibly can. Neither one of us is aiming to get hurt; but if you hurt me, it's all right, and if I hurt you, it's all right.'

He had not stirred. Somehow his thirty-year-old eyes looked sort of steely, too!

'Another thing, *brother*. Now, this is most important. When I judge we have enough for the scene, I'll take the first good opening I can get and land on you. Of course, I'll pull the punch as much as I can, but you'll feel it; also, just as the punch lands I'll say, "Go," and you go down, just as you would in a knock-down.'

Still the calm, steely stare! Doggone it! It was uncomfortable. I looked at Lambert Hillyer.

'Oh, one more thing, BROTHER!' (Loud enough for Lambert to hear.) 'When I say, "Go," the director will also holler, "Go," and you go down so we can't make any mistake.'

Still no move. The man was embalmed, mummified, or something. What in thunder was he driving at?

'Camera!' called Hillyer.

At it we went. Oh, gee! How that fellow did punch! He wasn't so awfully fast at first, but he hurt. I soon had enough of his game. I saw an opening. I slammed one in, and it was none too easy, for I was getting what was not beneficial.

'Go!' I cried.

Go nothing! He charged like a mad bull. Oh, Lordy! He was plenty fast now, and he had just been gently tapping before. Now every time he hit me, I let out a grunt that was almost a roar of pain. Wham! I hit him again.

'Go!' I yelled with all the breath I had left. 'Go — go!'

'Go down!' frantically screamed Lambert.

Gosh! The man was a murderer. He threw all semblance of boxing to the winds and slugged like a maniac. That was the only thing that saved me. Had he kept on boxing, I couldn't have got him in six years, but he was wide open and swinging wildly.

I had been having (through Allen) a lot of quarrels with Tom Ince. It flashed through my mind, 'This is a frame-up to get me whipped.' The irregularity of the man coming in, a stranger, his stony silence, and seeming sarcastic glances when I talked to him. Yes, thought I, that was it — it was a job to get me thrashed.

Stung by the blows I was taking, enraged at the plot against me, I became desperate. I knew there was only one way to end it with honor, and that was to fight and get knocked out. In I went. The onslaught was so sudden and so contrary to all rules of fighting that I got right in where I started for and placed an upper cut with every ounce of my dying strength right under my opponent's chin. Down he went!

There was no triumphant gladiator-of-Rome pose, with my foot planted on my fallen adversary's neck. No, sirree! I jumped on my fallen adversary, punching, kicking, gouging. If I hadn't been cursing, I would even have tried to bite! I was crazy with anger at the injustice of it all. I knew if he got up, he would probably kill me, and I wasn't taking any chances of his getting up. I was feeling mighty mean, too, and sore on the whole crowd. They finally pulled me off and held him (I looked and made sure of that). Then I started in on my faithful boxers.

'What do you fellows mean!' I cried. 'You are a lot of ingrates! What have I ever done that you should try to double-cross me and get me knocked out?'

I talked a streak. Every time they would try to cut in, I'd turn on worse than ever. When I was nearly run down from exhaustion, one of the leaders said, 'But, Mr. Hart, it's all a mistake.'

'Mistake, hell!' I yelled. 'Look at my jaw.' (It was lopsided.)

'Wait a minute, please, Mr. Hart. Listen just a minute,' he pleaded. 'You're all wrong. We forgot to tell you that this man is stone deaf. He can't hear a thing.'

My opponent and I visited the doctor together. I paid the bill and I bought him a suit of clothes. But he never came back.

I was simply crazy to go to war, and although over a year previous one of the greatest Americans our country ever produced had been denied the privilege, I applied to the War Department to allow me to raise a volunteer regiment of cowboys and Western men, with myself as a private; the regiment to be officered by United States Army officers. Times were much altered since Mr. Roosevelt's offer had been rejected. The country had been drained by three Liberty Loans, and I had just received instructions from Mr. McAdoo to report to the Speakers' Committee at New York City for the Fourth Loan.

Such a regiment as I proposed to raise would have been the biggest possible help in putting over a loan. It would have been a laudable, public stimulant, and all who worked on Liberty Loans knew how badly we needed such stimulation. Besides, I had found out that horsemen were badly needed as dispatch bearers right at the front when wires were torn up between the main body of the army and the front-line trenches. My heart beat high with hope.

On the Fourth Loan I was assigned to cover the territory that had been taken care of by Mary, Doug, and Charlie on the Third Loan — from Chicago east. It was a stupendous job. In addition, I had two stories for which I could get exteriors: 'Branding Broadway,' in New York City, and 'Breed of Men,' which was to be my next picture and had scenes laid in Chicago. So we took quite a few people East with us.

When I went home one night and told my sister Mary to pack her trunk, that she could go along, Natalie Talmadge was with her. Dear Natalie almost had a fit. It gave her the jumps to think of a trip East. The boy she afterwards married was overseas — she was lonesome, and going to New York would make him seem a bit nearer. Natalie went with us ... and I got a big kiss.

My Liberty Loan tour started in New York City. How wonderful it was to stand on the steps of the Astor Library and talk, and have all traffic for four blocks, between

THE GATHERING ON WALL STREET

TALKING TO THE CROWD ON WALL STREET

Thirty-Eighth and Forty-Second Streets, made to stand still! How great it seemed! How fast it made my heart beat! Often as a hungry actor I had haunted this same library seeking historical knowledge for use in my profession; and just above, on the northwest corner of Broadway and Forty-Second, I could see an old hotel, the Westminster, that was there when I was a messenger boy years and years gone by.

But it was at the gathering on Wall Street that my eyes became moist. I was to talk at twelve o'clock noon. I was late. I had so many places to talk that I did not arrive until one o'clock. The crowd had not only remained, it had grown and grown, until it became what some of the newspapers described as the largest body of people ever brought together. For blocks up and down Wall Street, for blocks up and down Broad Street, and even around on Pine Street, the streets were jammed with humanity, and every building seemed to be alive — all windows being packed with people.

When I took my place on the Treasury steps to speak, and heard the roar of welcome of sixty-five thousand Americans, my knees shook, my voice trembled. I thought of my father and mother and how proud they would be if they could only have lived to see me so honored . . . and I talked.

It seems there must be a humorous side to everything, no matter how tremendous the occasion. The laugh provoker in this instance was one of my camera men, although he did not join in the laughter personally. A native Californian — it was his first trip East. In spite of all the protection, we had become separated. He got lost in the crowd. He also 'became separated' from his purse, containing some couple of hundred dollars. A sorry, but wise, Californian walked all the way uptown.

My dates for Philadelphia, Washington, and Boston were canceled at the last minute; the cities being quarantined on account of the flu. But that meant no let-up in work. I was kept busy doing all the neighboring cities around New York.

When I spoke at Brooklyn, the whole City Hall Square was packed with over twenty thousand loyal Americans, all with upturned, eager faces, ready and anxious to do their bit.

An example of the war's cruelty was carried to the platform. One of the committee informed me. 'Here's a poor, mangled guinea. Show him to the crowd.'

I looked at the 'poor, mangled guinea.' He was an American Indian — and they did not know.

There are many different Indian languages, but I took a chance. I spoke to him in Sioux, the language of my early boyhood. It was the language of his people. He straightened his bent body; his blue, sweated, trembling chin stood still; a heavenly light came into his clear, brown eyes. Tears came forth and they must have come from heaven, too! I asked him in English if he was in pain.

He replied, with a pitiable attempt at smiling, 'She feel better sometime, when she stop hurtin'.'

I could not speak. My hand gripped his shoulder. He looked at me and saw my weakness. And to this broken boy soldier of the trenches must have come a vision of the far-away prairies and the stoicism of his people, for he said in Sioux — slowly, deliberately, proudly:

'A ta, nena O he ta ka.' (Our fathers were brave men.)

The flu was everywhere. I often wonder if a record of this dread disease was ever made known. Dear Natalie Talmadge was down with it. We kept her with us in the hotel, only she and my sister had temporarily to quit rooming together — the doctor said Natalie had to be isolated.

On a trip to Providence, Rhode Island, we were shunted off on a roundabout branch of the New Haven Railroad. We traveled through many towns that had coffins piled up at the stations like cordwood, awaiting shipment to their burial places.

At Providence I received a letter from the War Department, signed by the Assistant Secretary. They appreciated my offer and were passing it on to the General Staff for their consideration. If they found that there was a method by which it could be done, they were sure that the General Staff would be interested in my offer.

How my heart thumped in anticipation. I wrote to the officers of the General Staff and begged hard.

Billy Sunday came to see me. I remember realizing after he had gone that he was a clergyman. It had never occurred to me during our visit. Of course, I knew he was a clergyman, yet his personality was such that I treated him as I would have treated a brother cowboy — which suited him fine.

I have often wished I could recall how many bonds I sold at the Turk's Head Club banquet at Providence. Anybody who bought a one-hundred-thousand-dollar bond was a piker. The Governor of the State sat next to me. Whenever there was a slight let-up in trade, I would sell him another half-million. These men were not doing it to show off. They would call their partners aside, and with set faces and low voices arrange to carry this and that, then return and buy all over again, as though they had just started. They had lost sons and nephews, their own flesh and blood over there. They meant business and were backing their hand. Grim-visaged war was being waged right there at that table.

I was getting into my cowboy clothes to keep dates at surrounding towns near Providence when Allen came in hurriedly. New York had ordered us by telephone to return at once. The President was to talk that night at the Metropolitan Opera House and I was to introduce him. We just caught the train. My — my — my, but I was proud!

But it just was not to be. At the last moment the President received some message in his box and he did not appear on the stage. There were rumors of important developments overseas which prevented his making the expected speech. There were rumors of the discovery of a plot against the President's life. What did prevent the President speaking I do not know. I only know my instructions from the secret service officer in charge were for me to remain on the stage after the President's entrance and not to leave the stage until after he did. The back of the stage was full of tiers of seats and every seat was filled by foreign soldiers. It was a thrilling sight.

I made my little appearance. But, oh! how disappointed I was that I lost the opportunity of introducing a President of the United States. The occasion was a huge Italian benefit. Many artists appeared. Caruso sang, Kreisler played, and Will Rogers talked.

I was working so hard on the Liberty Loan and the police had shoved me through crowds so much that they began to look upon me as a regular thing, and when I wanted to shoot some scenes for 'Branding Broadway' they fell right in with it as though it was all in the day's work. Police Commissioner Enright gave orders for me to have anything I wanted. I was greedy. I took a whole lot. I shot scenes at Forty-Second Street and Fifth Avenue at four-thirty in the afternoon. The cameras were in taxis parked at the curb and in second-floor windows on two corners. I never saw more natural New York scenes.

During the shooting of this stuff there occurred a shining example of the unwritten comradery that exists between screen actors and their fans. The action called for me as the big Western plainsman to become rattled in the traffic and ask an officer to take me across the street. It was done. The cameras were grinding — the officer was leading me by the arm. When in the middle of the street, with traffic being held, I'll be doggoned if an energetic lady didn't grab me, whip out her book and pencil, and say, 'I'm going to get the first autograph that Bill Hart has written in New York.'

She thought that I had just arrived and that the scene was on the level . . . and, by golly! she got the autograph. There was nothing else to do, and, besides, it was the quickest way out of it. The good-natured cop said, 'Hell, Bill, that dame is worse than my kids.' . . . And we took the scene over.

I had to have another double for the horse Jack that was left at home 'way out in California. I was supposed to grab a mounted policeman's horse, chase an open taxi up Sixth Avenue, and catch the man I was after in the park. Lambert Hillyer, after a great deal of difficulty, found a big horse with long mane and tail. He was another 'gentle baby' of fourteen hundred pounds that had been cooped up in a box stall near the park for six months.

We shot our stuff at six A.M. to avoid the heavy traffic.

I mounted my steed at Fifty-Fourth Street and Sixth Avenue, under the elevated railroad. The two cameras were against the park wall on Fifty-Ninth Street, to get the taxi dashing up Sixth Avenue and turning west on Fifty-Ninth Street, with me following.

I saw Lambert wave the signal and I hooked Mr. Big Black Horse. The taxi was a block in the lead, with only two blocks to go. We nearly ran it down. The big black rounded that corner so fast he tore a hind shoe off on the car-track. The taxi served one purpose — it helped me to stop my fiery steed. I couldn't get past it. The horse was taken to get a new shoe on while we set up inside the park at the Seventh Avenue entrance for our next shot.

The shoeing of the horse delayed us. Great crowds were gathered, which meant much to the big black horse. He was a Kentucky thoroughbred race-horse. He had sailed past many grandstands to the cheering of the multitude. He heard those cheers now when I mounted. And in a few jumps he felt the dirt of a race-track under his feet.

Oh! Oh! Oh! How that horse did run! We passed the taxi that I was to catch as though it was some sort of a June bug. The early morning wind cut my face. The big black laid down to it. He lengthened his stride. Faster and faster he went. The bridle path of Central Park vanished under his flying feet as would the track at Belmont Park. I knew it would be folly to work on him at once. I let him run a little and then started in. Golly! the things I TRIED to do to stop that horse! The big snoozer had a straight bar bit in his mouth. He ate them for breakfast, and it was just breakfast time. I did everything I had ever known or ever heard of; I even crossed the reins under his neck and sawed on him. It was all to

270

no purpose. With my waning strength, every effort became more futile.

God! It was horrible!

Once more I tried. It was no use — I couldn't budge him. The big exit was just ahead. I could see the tops of moving vehicles through the trees. I could hear the growing roar of the traffic. I sat idly and waited. . . . Was I going to play the woman and faint? I could feel him stopping. He was easing up — I was afraid to move, afraid to breathe — he kept slowing up — he came to a lope. I slid off and sat in the middle of the bridle path. The little strength I had left held the end of the reins. The big black stopped with a jerk. He circled round me and stood still directly over me — my head was touching his belly. I could not move. My heart was too full of gratitude . . . and I sat there and cried!

An hour afterward a big black blanketed horse was being led back to his stable.

'Why don't you ride him?' I said.

'I'd rather walk, Bill,' the horseman chirped. 'I need the exercise.'

'I got twenty bucks that's waiting to change owners if you'll slip that blanket off and ride him home.'

'I can earn money easier than that, Bill,' he called.

And the big black horse disappeared around some trees. He was owned by a wealthy man who had taken him out of his racing string for a saddle-horse. He was kind and gentle, but in spite of all thunder he would run away. They told Lambert that the boss said that if Bill rode him it would do the horse good; and if Bill didn't ride him his number would be six, as five had tried and failed; the boss being proud of the fact that his number was one, wanted to see a lot more numbers added, but now he'd be disappointed, as Bill had won out. But they didn't tell Lambert any of this until it was all over.

Whether it was the Mexican border, the Canadian border, or Central Park, New York City, they all wanted to see Bill Hart ride. A park police officer loaned me his horse . . . I caught the man in the taxi, as the story required.

A gentleman called on me one night at the hotel. How glad I was to see and know him personally! We talked for two hours and it seemed like five minutes. The owner of a soft, low voice; the wielder, if the occasion required, of a virile, audacious pen; a quiet, unostentatious gentleman; a great American citizen . . . William B. (Bat) Masterson.

I always loved Chicago — I love it now. It is an American city, typically American. I can remember Chicago when wide-brim hats were worn on State Street and high-heeled cowboy boots were not an oddity; when one could hail a passer-by and seek a direction to any given point without speaking a foreign language. May such conditions be restored!

Chicago was a hard city to sell bonds in. There were two classes of people: those who would and those who wouldn't. I won't say it was pro-German, because I do not know, but in many sections it was pro-un-American.

It was the last day of the Fourth Liberty Loan. It closed at midnight. By the time I reached my last working place, the Chicago Athletic Club, it was about 9 P.M. What a wonderful band of men! How they did work! They had all bought to the breaking point days before, and yet they all buckled right in and bought all over again. Their zeal was such that they got the salesman going. I bought again

— more than I could carry, but I hung on to them. I held them until they went to one hundred, the price at which they were purchased, before I sold. I hope all the good, wonderful, fine Americans who may have been influenced by my urging to buy did likewise.

When those Government securities that were even more stable than American money were down to eighty-two and eighty-four, it hurt me terribly because I imagined hundreds of thousands of poor people who could not hold them would lose. I hope I was wrong. I hope that every man, woman, and child that bought a bond through me, or any one else who sold them, was able to hold on and reap the benefit of a valuable investment just as they showed their one hundred per cent Americanism in buying, when in many cases they could ill afford to do so.

CHAPTER XVI

THE FORMING OF UNITED ARTISTS

WITH the Liberty Loan work closed, we started full speed ahead to get the scenes of our picture, 'Breed of Men,' the principal ones being in the stockyards. Lambert Hillyer went out to see the officials to get permission to work, and received not only a discouraging reception, but one that came mighty near being the toe of a stockyards boot.

Some seven years before (they told Lambert) they had granted permission to a company to shoot some exteriors and the company matched up their scenes with studio interiors showing all sorts of frightful stockyard stuff that was as revolting as it was untrue. The story used was an adaptation of a popular novel that had an enormous sale, and it had done them an incalculable injury.

That night I called up the main superintendent of the whole yards, and I begged so hard that he yielded. We got permission to shoot.

Miss Mae Tinee, of the 'Chicago Tribune,' the lady who had been so kind to me on a previous visit, joined our party to watch us work. It was a man's party — just our working crew — as I was the only one in the scenes. The camera men became discouraged and some of our outfit suggested turning back, but Mae Tinee stayed right with us. Golly! she was game!

The antipathy of the big bosses to picture people was carried right on down along the line throughout those hundreds of acres of cowpens and tangled horns. Many of those cowhands had good memories and were bitter at what had taken place in the past. They crowded around

274

us, a milling mob, that just would not be ruled or denied.
We could not get anything approaching a clear space to
work in, but were just shoved here and there at their will,
slipping and sliding on cobbled pavements several inches
deep with bovine excrement. Rather tough on a lady of
refinement — to say nothing of her neatly booted feet.
But the lady was game. Boys! she was game!

I climbed a fence and amidst occasional 'boo's' and
'baa's' told my little story as straightforwardly as I could.
I was putting it over them (but they did not know it), for I
know the innate fairness of any man who has ever worked
among or around cattle. They listened — they wavered —
and then one big, rubber-booted chap called, 'All right,
Bill, if you can make as good at workin' as you can talkin',
it's all right. Come on over here. We got a bull we want
you to top off.'

To attempt to ride a bull in that footing was just plain,
unadulterated suicide. But I didn't DARE weaken, nor attempt to put forward the slightest excuse. Those men were
tough, and as straightforward as they were hard.

'Where's the animal?' I said, and started with them.

Sure enough! There was a big walloper in a pen a short
distance away. He must have weighed an even ton. I
never learned how mean or ornery he was or might have
been. I climbed the fence and threw off my coat and sat on
the flat board top and started to take off my spurs.

'You win, Bill!' the big man called. 'You win! Go as
far as you like!'

The act of removing my spurs had shown them that I
had ridden bulls before and that was all they wanted to
know.

We got our scenes and delivered Mae Tinee back to town
safely.

There were two happenings in one day that I recall with conflicting emotions. Examples in point:

In the late afternoon, without knocking or without ceremony, a woman of seemingly unquestionable respectability opened one of the doors of my suite and walked in, nearly frightening Natalie Talmadge and my sister Mary to death. I was resting, lying on the sofa. Straight over to me the visitor came and, looking at me with calm, reproachful eyes, said, 'I've come to take you home.'

I spluttered something, but I couldn't speak.

'To take me home?' I finally managed to gasp foolishly.

'Yes,' she quietly resumed. 'You've been away long enough.'

My eyes followed her movements as those of an animal would when fascinated by a snake. Slowly, deliberately, she opened her handbag and inserted her right hand. Natalie involuntarily ducked behind a doorway. My docile sister Mary unconsciously reached for an empty mineral-water bottle on the table. I arose as easily as I possibly could and, taking the lady who wanted to take me home gently by the arm, moved her toward the door. She did not fight. She obeyed like an obedient child. She was through the door and it was slammed and LOCKED. . . . I never knew what she had in that bag, and I never wanted to know — I was convinced plenty. I telephoned downstairs at once. The house detectives got busy, but they never found her — they never saw her. Where she came from or where she went, we never knew.

The second happening was in the evening. I was walking to the elevator. I saw two sailors stop three different men ahead of me and ask for and examine their enlistment cards, by which all men subject to draft were classified. I hurried past. I had no card. I had gained the elevator and pushed the button, but it was long in coming. On came the sailors with heads down, almost guilty-like, as though having an unpleasant duty to perform. I did not have long to wait.

'Let me look at your card, buddie?' the foremost sailor asked.

'I'm sorry, partner,' I replied. 'I'm too old to have one.'

His eyes seemed to start at my feet and were slowly, incredulously raised. When they reached my face, his mouth was open, all set for words of unbelief and fight. He looked . . .

'Oh, my God! Bill Hart!' he gasped. 'Oh, Bill! Forgive us, Bill, please, please, forgive us, Bill!'

I groped for their shoulders, but they were gone. I called after them. They would not stop. I wanted to tell them — oh, how badly I wanted to tell them of my plans and my hopes! But they were ashamed of what they had done — and they had done no wrong. I did not follow them. I was ashamed, too, oh, so ashamed! I was not to blame. I knew I was not to blame — yet I was ashamed. And oh, how I longed for that message from Washington!

Days passed that seemed like weeks. I waited. My message did not come. . . . But there came a joyous message to the whole world — to white men, red men, and black men; a message that made mothers and fathers, sisters and brothers of those soldier boys 'over there' dance and jump and laugh and cry; a message that caused strange women and strange men to rush up and kiss each other in the public streets; a message that made joyous bells ring out peal on peal throughout the land and siren whistles shriek their shrill tones until they reached the sky.

It was the eleventh day of November, 1918. . . . 'Cease Firing! Cease Firing!! The Armistice is Signed!!!'

What was to have been the Fifth Liberty Loan became the Victory Loan. It was oversubscribed before it was issued. Its salesmen were little white doves that carried God's message —

'Peace on earth and good will to men.'

It needed no ballyhooing, no organizing, or the sending of more machine-gun or bursting-shell fodder across the seas to feed the maw of war. And the real heroes, those mud-spattered, blood-spattered men of the trenches, who had lain out in the heat and the cold with lice and with rats ... *They* were coming home!

About New Year's time, while working on the Oakland California ferry, shooting scenes for 'The Poppy Girl's Husband,' I met Mary Pickford. Mary was there to welcome home the regiment of which she was godmother.

Mary told me that Douglas Fairbanks, herself, and Charlie Chaplin, wanted to get D. W. Griffith and myself to go in with them and form a distributing company of our own. A few weeks later, Doug came to see me at my studio and we had a long talk.

Then began many meetings held at Miss Pickford's home, or Doug's home, or at Charlie and Syd Chaplin's home. Arthur Wright, Charlie's attorney, was present quite often, but as a rule, it was just ourselves, which also included Mrs. Pickford (Mary's mother) and Syd Chaplin.

Mary has always been considered as having a great amount of business acumen and soundness of judgment in addition to her million other admitted charms. Mary is a mighty level-headed girl, straightforward, fearless, and honest; but I believe the credit for the business sagacity of the Pickford family should have gone to Mary's mother. In my opinion, in all big business deals, Mrs. Pickford was overlooked, which probably helped out, as it saved the aircraft guns of the enemy from being trained on her and allowed her more freedom to work. It is certain that in engendering plans for the formation of 'United Artists,' Mrs. Pickford pointed out many dangerous shoals that might have wrecked the ship. And I remember that later, when all the big attorneys and Mr. McAdoo got into the game, the arguments and opinions of Mrs. Pickford carried weight and were listened to with much profit.

I do not remember whose idea it was for us all to congregate one evening publicly in the dining-room of the Alexandria Hotel, but whoever was responsible, it was an excellent idea. All of the representatives of the big distributing companies were in town. They knew something was in the wind and were all seeking information. Golly! They got it! Mary, Charlie, Doug, Griffith, Mrs. Pickford, and Bill Hart all dining together! What fun we all had!

At our 'family' meetings the next few nights, Charlie had us all screaming with his imitations of the different scouts and their principals who would enter the dining-room for the most apparent silly reasons. In their excitement they forgot what the dining-room was for — they never ordered any food. Our little fun did not end with imitations of others. We were all working, and if coming in from location would show up for our meetings in all sorts of regalia, and we did not spare each other in our caricaturing. Charlie was always the leader in this play — he enjoyed it immensely.

I remember one night Charlie and Syd fixed the telephones at their home and had Tom Ince call me. I fell for it, hook, line, and sinker. Of course, Syd and Charlie were Tom's representatives on the wire and kept it up until I was all set to hear Tom's voice on the telephone. They sure had a lot of fun with me. I was so worked up, I just spluttered — I couldn't speak.

It happened that Tom at this time was even more neglectful of me than he had been. I had no story, and was forced to write one for my own use. I was lucky. It made a good picture, 'The Money Corral.'

I cannot conceive of any one trying to accomplish more than I was just then. I was also working on a series of books for boys. The success of a little volume, 'Pinto Ben and Other Stories,' had piled up more tasks on me.

The forming of United Artists meant work for all of us. Our little gatherings were held at the expense of much-needed rest and sleep.

By this time all of the big motion picture distributing companies had their officers on the coast. They were all bidding for United Artists, and United Artists was giving them all an audience. One evening we would meet Mr. Zukor at Mary's house, and the situation would be thoroughly discussed. Another evening we would meet the officials of First National, also at Mary's home. The 'Big Five,' as we were called, seemed to be in entire control of the situation. On account of my liking for Mr. Zukor and the excellent treatment I had always received from him, I was strong for an alliance with Famous Players and talked for it on all occasions. I was practically alone — I do not recall any one of the others being in favor of it.

Mr. Zukor was in the habit of calling on me quite frequently. He usually came very early in the morning, when I was making up. On some occasions he would be waiting at the studio for me as early as seven-thirty.

Mr. Zukor was always most fair in his business talks with me. He stated just what he would do if I would continue to release my pictures through his company, and never once tried to influence me, except in terms at which no one could cavil. He told me how the work of his life had been about to be crowned by success, and that now it was in serious jeopardy. He stated quite simply and plainly that my remaining or going could seriously affect Famous Players. In all our talks Mr. Zukor had my friendship and profound regard, but we both regarded the situation as strictly one of business. All of my brother actors in United Artists knew of this condition. I never failed to tell them of the pleasant relationship that existed between myself and Famous Players, and of my visits with and high regard for Mr. Zukor.

The main element for discussion at our meetings seemed to be whether we should be financed by outside capital or furnish our own money. At first we were more or less divided on this issue, but finally I was the only one that stood out for outside financing by any responsible group. All of our New York attorneys came out for the big wind-up. My attorney, William Grossman, brought with him a certified check for $1,000,000 as a deposit that he could make in behalf of a Boston group of bankers who wanted to finance us. But after several meetings which were attended by all principals, their attorneys, and Mr. McAdoo and Mr. Oscar Price, it was decided that we should finance ourselves. This did not appeal to me or to Mr. Grossman. I was then being financed by Famous Players, and they were eager to have me re-sign at a guarantee of $200,000 per picture, which would be an increase of $50,000 per picture over my expiring contract.

Under the proposed arrangement with United Artists, I would have to put up $125,000 as my share of the $500,000 necessary to establish exchanges, and, in addition, finance the cost of making my own pictures; this without any guarantee as to what my gross would be when the picture was distributed.

Charlie had always called me all through our meetings and negotiations 'Silent Bill,' as I was usually a listener. But now I talked, I talked freely, and when I finished, Mary, Doug, Charlie, and Griffith offered to add $25,000 each to their share and let me come in without helping to finance the exchanges. This fine offer I promptly refused, stating as the reason, that I refused to eat any of the cake if I didn't pay for my slice.

I spoke as eloquently as I was able to do. I at least put my whole heart into it to try to get them to accept outside financing for all of us when it was knocking at the door in the shape of million-dollar certified checks, but they were determined to go ahead their way. I bade them all an affectionate good-bye and withdrew.

Mr. Zukor immediately renewed his offer for me to sign with Famous Players, but I told him I'd rather wait; that, although I could not agree with our little United Artists group, they might change their minds. Mr. Zukor said that was perfectly agreeable to him; that he admired me for fair dealing, but not to forget that he was waiting.

Again I had no story. C. Gardner Sullivan, who was working for Tom, came to see me. He outlined a story for me to consider. I told him the brief outline of a story I was going to write myself to use as my first story on my new contract. He liked it so much, and, as I needed two stories to finish my contract with Tom, I said, 'Sullivan, if you will promise me to write your story and do this one, too, before doing anything else, I'll give it to you.'

He took me up. We did 'Wagon Tracks,' the story I gave him first, and I finished the William S. Hart Productions contract, of which Tom was part owner, with Sullivan's story, 'John Petticoats.'

While we were on location doing 'Wagon Tracks,' Douglas Fairbanks came to see me. He said that United Artists was now fully formed, with William G. McAdoo as counsel general, and Oscar Price as president; that they had unlimited capital behind them and wanted to know would I negotiate. I said 'Yes'; that if they were financed, that altered the matter entirely, and for McAdoo or Mr. Price to communicate with Mr. Grossman.

Mr. Price and Mr. Grossman promptly started negotiations which lasted for three or four weeks. Meanwhile, I was on my last story, 'John Petticoats.' We had to go to New Orleans to get some Mississippi River scenes.

A short time before this, Marguerite Clark was doing 'Uncle Tom's Cabin,' and two doubles were drowned at a bad spot in the river. Of course, this had to be the location that Lambert picked for our water stuff. Although I had heard of the accident, I thought the folks around the hotel and on the docks were kidding me a little, but when just before we had to do our little act the captain of the harbor police came to me and warned me, I knew it was no joke.

We had a New Orleans professional girl swimmer to double for the girl of our company that I was to save from a watery grave. I explained to her in the presence of the captain just what had been told to me, and said, 'It's up to you, young lady.'

The young lady replied, 'It was up to me — now it's up to you.'

In we went. It was a bad spot. There was a swift current and a nasty undertow, but neither one of us had the slightest bit of trouble. The girl was a regular water-nymph. We were both fully clothed, and that didn't make it any easier. After I had brought her to the surface, as the story called for, I said:

'I don't feel anything, do you?'

'No,' she said; 'this is fine.'

So I couldn't play the hero even a little bit when, after saving the girl, I was pulled onto the dock.

Mr. Grossman wired me that he and Mr. Price had worked out a contract and that he was leaving for California. When he arrived, Mr. Price arrived with him. The contract called for United Artists to finance me for the making of nine pictures; to release my pictures on a 75–25 basis and to guarantee me $300,000 as my share per picture. And as a guarantee of their ability to carry out and fulfill its terms, they agreed, on the signing of the contract, to put up the full amount of the guarantee of the last picture, namely, $300,000, on which I should draw the interest until the money was turned over to me in full.

Even with my inadequate business head, I could see that this was a marvelous contract; its face value meant a fortune. As I look back, I am convinced that had William Grossman not known me since my kid years and had he not been accustomed to seeing me do all sorts of crazy things, he would most surely have taken steps to have a lunacy commission appointed to give me the once-over. I never shall or can forget the look of bewilderment and blank amazement that would spread over his face when I would talk of Mr. Zukor's offer. But he would say:

'Bill, I also am a friend of Adolph's. I have known him for many, many years. We were once partners in a little picture show theater. Adolph is a fine man. But, good Heavens, Bill, as your attorney I must point out to you that this is a matter of business. Here is a gilt-edged contract, backed by one of the biggest banking firms in the world, that guarantees $900,000 more profit and five per cent more in percentage than the contract of Famous Players. As a business proposition, you cannot refuse it.'

'All right, Bill,' I said. 'Only wire Mr. Zukor again. Give him a chance to meet this or see what is the very best he can do.'

Mr. Grossman wired. Mr. Grossman told me, Mr. Zukor's answer was in substance that he could not do any better than his former offer — seventy per cent of the gross, and a guarantee of $200,000 per picture.

There was nothing left for me to do but sign with United Artists. I walked the streets at night. I worried. I cussed myself. I had my constant adviser, my sister Mary, walking the floor of her room, as she was in sympathy with what was in my mind. The United Artists' attorneys were waiting in New York for the wire from Mr. Price saying the contract was signed.

I busted into Bill Grossman's room, saying, 'Bill, wire Mr. Zukor I accept his terms.'

My contract with Tom came to an end. We had a final directors' meeting at the William S. Hart Productions Studio; Tom, Mrs. Ince, William Grossman (my lawyer), and Ingle Carpenter (Tom's lawyer), and myself being the directors of The William S. Hart Productions, Inc. The meeting accomplished nothing. Tom claimed some hundred and twenty-five thousand dollars more than I considered him entitled to, and my attorneys had been tying up the money in the bank for some time to prevent Tom as treasurer from taking it. It meant a law suit.

There was quite a nervous tension throughout the pro-

ceedings at our meeting, and yet I had a hard job to keep
from laughing. . . . Tom and I sitting on opposite sides of
the table ignoring each other. It seemed so funny. Dear
Mrs. Ince — it was not easy for her. She was, of course,
loyal to Tom, but I thought she looked sad that all was as
it was.

I retained my same studio for the William S. Hart
Company. 'Sand' was the first picture made on the new
contract with Famous Players. This picture marked the
return to the screen of my pinto horse Fritz. With the
exception of some little one-reel pictures which we made
for the Government, he had been idle for fifteen pictures
and the motion picture public was clamoring for his return.

During his long lay-off, Fritz had formed a great attach-
ment for a mare named Cactus Kate, owned by a cowboy
and used only for bucking contest scenes in pictures. She
had no value outside of this work, as she was a regular
'outlaw.' On account of the affection of Fritz for the mare,
I bought her and told the foreman of my ranch if he could
break her for use under the saddle I would not allow any
one else but him to ride her. He saddled her up one day for
the first session, and I rode Fritz beside her. My cowboy
foreman went up into the saddle carefully, all set and ready
for her to 'turn on.' She never made a single jump. She
loped off alongside of Fritz like a high-school mare. That
was eight years ago. She has never attempted to buck
since. . . . And there are those who say that horses do not
understand.

There was another member of the Fritz family that had
been gathered in — 'Lisbeth,' a giant mule. She had been
on one of the mule teams we used in 'Wagon Tracks' and

Fritz, Lisbeth, and Cactus Kate

I picked her out for a pack mule. I first named her
'Jupiter,' but I was wrong and had to change her name. I
had some night camp scenes with my horse, and dear old
'Lisbeth' horned right in and played them with me, too!
Her grading-camp days and working on dirt wagons were
over . . . she came under the pinto pony régime.

How proud Fritz was when he and Cactus Kate and
Lisbeth were loaded in trucks to go on location! The little
rascal knew what it meant and he knew his ability to
show off in front of his family. I know I am right in this
and submit the following as proof.

The first time we used him was on the desert outside of
Victorville. We left Kate and the mule at town in the
corral. Fritz had been led out to location, as I never allowed any one but myself to ride him. The scene was
ready. I went to mount him. He fought me. I fooled with
him, talked with him, walked with him, unsaddled him,
saddled him up again. I was convinced there was nothing
wrong but his temper. I did all the little tricks I knew to
get his mind off his grouch. No, sirree! Every time I went
to mount, he would fight. I whipped him a little. Oh,
golly! It was worse! He was snorting and seeing red.

So I said, 'Well, old-timer, if you must fight and buck,
let's go.'

I caught him unawares and mounted. He made no attempt to buck, but he sure did fight. He kicked and ran
wildly sideways. I saw he would throw himself. I spurred
him and gave him the quirt. Golly! Now it was a battle!
He shut his jaws down on the bit and flew right at the
cameras. Joe August, Dwight Warren, and their assistants
had no chance to save the big cameras. They just barely
ducked out of harm's way themselves. Smash! Crash!
Away went the cameras, propelled by flying hoofs.

287

I saw that the little follow was going crazy. I took a chance and jumped off. He stood beside me trembling with anger, but made no further move while I bawled him out. He just glared at me. It was a serious piece of business. The cameras and camera boxes were collected from all over the desert. We held a consultation.

'Boys,' I said, 'I may be a damn fool, but let's try it. Send for Kate.'

Kate came . . . Fritz rubbed noses with her. She watched him work as only he could work; just as she had to watch him work in every scene afterward. Do horses understand?

I had written a story years before, but could never find an ending for it. It had a big climax near the end, and then it was a case of 'nowhere to go.' I had tried several authors, and offered one well-known man a thousand dollars to suggest a way of 'carrying on,' but he gave it up.

At Victorville my sister Mary came to me and said:

'Will, I think I have an ending for your story, "The Toll Gate."'

Golly! I was happy. She had it — it was a corker. It was my next picture.

For the location scenes on 'The Toll Gate' we went to Sonora, Tuolumne County, in the beautiful old Bret Harte country. The little pinto horse and myself nearly lost our lives on this location. About sixteen miles from Sonora we found a swift-running stream which tunneled right through a mountain. It was the most wonderful place in the world for an entrance to our bandit cave. The tunnel was about one hundred yards long. At the entrance there was an overhanging ledge which made a roomy cavern. At the back of the cavern was the round hole through the

288

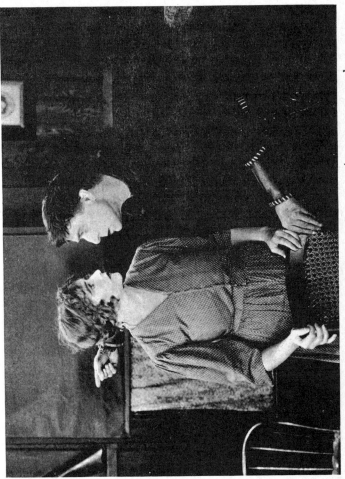

ANNA Q. NILLSON AND WILLIAM S. HART IN 'THE TOLL GATE'

mountain, varying in size so little that it might have been the handiwork of man, but it was made by nature, and in it my little friend and I shook hands with death.

Lambert, my director, and Joe, the camera man, and their assistants had looked over the place the day before. Joe had stripped and followed the swift stream through the mountain on a raft, sounding for depth with a long pole. He reported about eight feet of water, except in one strip some thirty feet long where he could not touch bottom. There was some six feet of width on the water-line, and the arched roof was about the same distance in height at the center. The camera men were to place their cameras at the upstream end of the tunnel where we were to come out, and we were to swim against the current and carry heavy torches to give them sufficient light to photograph us as we made the trip.

There were nine of us to go through, single file, eight feet apart. There wasn't any talking — we all realized that it was a mighty serious piece of business. I told the boys, as we loosened our cinches, that any one who wanted to draw out could do so. No one did.

I was to go first. The second man was not to follow until I had gotten across the strip where Joe had not been able to find bottom. I am positive that this decision saved the lives of at least two horses and two men. The thirty-foot strip was a bottomless whirlpool or well. Once an animal got into it, he could neither swim out nor climb out. There was no bottom for his hind legs to reach and he could only get his front hoofs on the ledge which was six feet under water.

Almighty God! How Fritz did try! He struggled. He screamed. He looked at me with the eyes of a human being. He actually climbed the arched side walls until he turned himself over backwards. Twice we went down in those cold, whirling depths and twice we fought our way to the surface again. I knew the next time would be the last. Fritz spoke to me — I know he did. I heard him, and I spoke to him. I said, 'God help us, Fritz.' . . . And God did help us!

My little friend could not struggle any more, his eyes were glazed with coming death, and as we were going down for the last time the strong current we had been fighting carried us over the ledge back toward the way we came in, and as we sank we touched the bottom and regained our feet.

We were saved! God saved us! I know He did, and I know my little horse knows He did, because when we came out of that dark gripping pool of death and reached the sunlight where the heavily branched fig trees were glistening on the mountain-side, and the topknot quail were calling, and the wild doves were cooing to their mates, we sank down on our knees and said a little prayer before the sun stopped shinin' an' we were asleep.

'The Toll Gate' was nearly finished when I received word that I had to go to court. I rebelled against it, but, after investigating, my lawyer informed me that a subpœna would be issued if I did not go voluntarily. There was a woman in the county hospital who had made serious charges against me and had turned over to the court various letters I had written to her.

It happened that on the day set for the trial we had a special train on the Salt Lake Railroad between Los Angeles and San Pedro, and about one hundred people working. To charter a train with an electric generator in the baggage car and get a free track for working, arrangements had to be made some days in advance. If I did not use the train on the day it was contracted for, it might be some time before I could get it again and it would hold up my picture.

I had never heard of the woman in the case and I was angry. I went ahead with my train work. We had a car waiting and when my lawyer telephoned to a near-by station, I started for court in my make-up and cowboy clothes. The judge had every reason to call me down for my apparel, but he did not do so. I was there half an hour before my case was called. The woman was brought in. She was a trained nurse about thirty-five or forty years of age. The doctors on the committee who had had her under surveillance for some weeks were present and had turned in an opinion that the woman was sane. One of the three doctors testified that she had nursed him through an attack of the flu.

The judge made a short talk to the woman and asked her to again tell her story. She did so. It was very simple and was to the effect that three years previous I had met her at Syracuse, New York; that under promise of marriage I had seduced her, brought her to California, and then had deserted her; that she had earned her own living since that time, but that now she was ill and needed support.

It was necessary for the woman to identify me. When the judge asked her if I was the man, and if she knew who I was, there was a roar of laughter, in which the judge himself almost joined. I was in my cowboy clothes. The bailiff of the court had to hammer still louder when the woman replied, 'Certainly, I know him. Everybody knows him. He is William S. Hart.'

But the laughter quickly subsided when she added, 'He is the man.'

I was then sworn, and the judge took me in hand, in — as well as I can remember — the following manner:

'Do you know this woman?'

'No, I do not.'

'Have you ever met her?'

'No, I have not.'

'Were you in Syracuse three years ago?'

'No, I was not.'

'Are all of her charges untrue?'

'They are all untrue.'

'Were you at the automobile races on [a certain date] at Ascot Park?'

'I was.'

'Did you meet this woman there, as she has testified?'

'I did not.'

'Have you ever written to her?'

'I may have done so. I signed hundreds of letters daily that were prepared by my secretary and that in her opinion needed personal signatures, but I have no recollection of ever having written to this woman, nor can I recall her name.'

The judge then again centered his attention on the woman. He called her attention to the entirely opposite testimony as to the facts in the case.

'I cannot help that,' she replied. 'My story is true.'

The judge continued: 'Now, Miss ——, you know I have been your friend. I believe this is the third time I have had you tell me your story. You are a professional nurse. You know I have appointed these medical gentlemen to make a report on your physical condition. One of these gentlemen tells me you nursed him through an attack of the flu. Is that true?'

'It is.'

'Now, Miss ——, it seems to me you thoroughly realize

what your charges mean to this man here, and I am going to ask you again ...'

And here the learned jurist and judge of both law and human nature talked for many minutes. In the most delicate manner he introduced the most intimate subjects that could take place between a man and a woman, and then, after many minutes of this masterly talk, he propounded a simple, straight question in plain, but not offensive, language. The face of the kindly judge came slightly forward, his eyes looked into the eyes of the woman steadily:

'Do I understand you to tell me that this took place?'

The face of the woman also came slightly forward, her eyes looking into the eyes of the judge, steadily. A soft, almost whispered, answer: 'Well, not in the flesh, your Honor.'

'What's that?' (Sharply, but still kindly.)

'Your Honor [now closely and confidentially], he and I live in the spirit world.'

... It was all so kind — so humane. It is a great thing that we have such men to sit in judgment in our courts, especially where dethroned reason is involved. There was not one word of publicity. The kindly judge must have been responsible for that, too. The case was closed. The court adjourned. The judge gave my attorney the pitiable little packet of letters. They were all signed by Mr. Allen, my manager, or my secretary, in their own names.

I patted the woman on the shoulder as they were taking her away. She smiled at me. The judge saw, and his expression seemed to say, 'Sad, isn't it, Hart?'

Then, looking toward the medical group, with a twinkle in his eye, he said, 'Doctor, how about you? Do you live in the spirit world?'

A man must be brave, gentle, learned, and human, to sit on the bench in such a court — Judge Sidney N. Reeve was all of these.

Famous Players liked 'The Toll Gate' so much that they put it out ahead of 'Sand.' They made it the first release on my new contract. It was a big hit! It has played to more money up to date than any picture I ever made.

The fact that 'The Toll Gate' was the third story that I had written for the screen, and that stories were so hard to secure, emboldened me to attempt to write some more. Ever since I had played the part of 'Patrick Henry' on the stage in the long ago, I had been working unsuccessfully on a one-act play for vaudeville, with 'Henry' as the central figure. I managed to turn out what I thought was a good little play, but I knew it was not suitable for vaudeville. I now rewrote all that I had done and turned it into a story for the screen. I sent it East to have it copyrighted. Mr. Grossman wrote me that The Britton Company wanted to publish it in book form.

I was frightened; I knew it was in bad shape, so I asked him to return it, so I could do some more work on it. He did so. I had it printed in Los Angeles for copyright and then let it rest, as it was a story that required more time than I could then give it for research work. I did not put this story out until 1923, and then it was published as a novel, after I had received splendid help on it from a dear friend and accomplished authoress, Vingie E. Roe. It has been republished in Great Britain.

While we were producing an excellent story of a returning soldier, 'The Cradle of Courage,' written by a young author of Providence, Rhode Island, I wrote another screen story, 'The Testing Block,' and followed this up with 'O'Malley of the Mounted.' Both of these pictures were highly successful.

In my opinion, it is much easier for a man of limited education to write for the screen than to write fiction for reading, as brilliant dialogue and proper atmospheric and descriptive language is not necessary in pictures. It is the plot and action that count. I attribute my luck at having turned out some successful screen material to this fact. I believe many successful screen plays are written by stars who have had a dramatic training. I know of one instance where an actor has written as many, if not more, stories for the screen than I have.

Our location work for 'The Testing Block' was done at Ben Lomond, up in the big-tree country. We were there during March and April. Once it rained for over ten days without our shooting a single scene, and we carried in the neighborhood of a hundred people. The first scenes we did were night work, and even then it drizzled intermittently, with big drops of rain constantly dripping from the giant trees. We commenced work at seven o'clock and quit at five in the morning.

The action of the story (and I could not blame the author) called for me to fight eight men of my bandit gang, one at a time. The battles took place around a camp-fire. Those who fought first were the lucky ones. They were finished. Those who were kept waiting were unlucky. They nearly perished with the cold. They were in every scene and could only sit there and shiver and watch the fight. It was not so hard on me, as I was getting exercise — 'exercise' that left its mark, too!

It was not necessary to put any make-up on me between

scenes. It was all there. I was a sorry-looking spectacle. One of the first men I had to fight was on his wedding tour; his bride, bundled up in a big coat, was watching her husband act. He was an ex-heavyweight champion of the Pacific Coast. He could play with me boxing, and he did play with me. I am supposed to have (for an amateur) what boxers call a good right hand. Big Mac kept teasing me and calling, 'Where is that right, Chief? Where is that right?'

He got more and more playful. He left himself wide open and called again: 'Oh, come on, Chief. Come on with that right hand.'

I thought surely he would block it. He did; but he blocked it with his eye. From then on he was on his wedding trip, not only with a beautiful black-eyed bride, but the owner of a beautiful black eye of his own. It was all in the night's work. Mac didn't get mad. Lucky for me he didn't. I got mine later. No one escapes.

The very last man I had to tackle was an Indian, Wolf Verduga. The title I spoke and which was to appear on the screen was: 'Come on, Wolf, you're next.'

Wolf and I were very friendly, but Wolf had been there all night, nearly dying of cold. Wolf was twenty-five years of age, a star player on the Riverside Indian School football team, carried two hundred and ten pounds weight, and no excess . . . AND . . . in an imbecilic or evil moment I added certain words in Sioux to my spoken title, words which would make a fighting warrior out of an Indian squaw. Allah be praised! An' everything else . . . I was not killed!

My horse Fritz was supposed to be a colt running around the camp loose during these night scenes. The man who played the villain, Gordon Russell, was supposed to become annoyed at him and hit him with a club. He masked the blow and threw the club at the little fellow as he was running away. In the last part of the story, Russell was to steal Fritz and make a getaway. After following on another horse and being unable to outrun Fritz, I was to call him and he was to stop. The villain was to dismount and run away on foot, and when I came and mounted Fritz he was to jump off a bank after the villain and trample him to death.

They were the easiest scenes to get that we ever photographed. Russell is a fine, kindly man and a lover of animals, but Fritz had to be held when Russell mounted him, and when I called to him to stop, he not only stopped, but he bucked, and Russell left in a hurry, and the little rascal ran thirty yards toward me in the scene and I changed horses in motion. It was wonderful stuff . . . and all on account of the resentment the little rascal held for Russell for going after him with a club. Yes! They understand!

'O'Malley of the Mounted,' which we were making in the mountains up Chatsworth way, had a fight in it, also. But other things happened which made the O'Malley fight a bit out of the ordinary.

At a certain point in the story I was a captive tied to a tree in the camp of an outlaw band. The heroine came, supposedly to abuse me, but in reality slipped a knife into my palm with the whispered warning to watch her movements just at dark. As soon as the sun disappeared behind the mountains, I was on the alert, and, when she came dashing down past the tree, kicking her horse at every jump, I went up behind the saddle and we made our escape. I had held my exact position and the outlaws had no suspicion that I was free.

The heroine was played by a beautiful girl, Eva Novak, the younger sister of dear Jane. It was too much of a stunt for Eva, or any leading woman, so we doubled her. I never saw a cowboy double for a girl who didn't go one hundred per cent nutty when he got the skirts on, and Hank Potts was no exception. Hank was small, but he was dynamite. Everything went well. Hank worked splendidly until I went up behind him. Then the long, blond curls, the skirts an' everything, gave him his one hundred per cent nutty feeling. The docile Eva's double became the wildest 'cow-jane' that ever came off the prairie.

I was riding on that big black mare's rump and had my troubles in chunks. However, I could have gotten away with the mare jumping, but the wild thing in front of me with all sorts of never-mentionables now flying in the air was heading the beast right along a dim trail that ran under the spreading branch of a tree. The crazy he-female could lean forward and duck the branch, but I being a head taller could not do so, and, besides, the yipping fool in front was occupying the space. I could not duck. I did the only thing I could do. I swung off, lit running, and tried to hold my feet. I was on the uphill side; my feet were not fast enough. The mare started to kick and she kicked me plenty.

After I had my grunt and roll, all the cowboy surgeons took a feel, and we decided the patient was bruised considerable, but not badly damaged. I finished my day's work. Before turning in that night, Wolf Verduga, having had experience in football, rubbed me with some white liniment out of the first-aid kit and bandaged my body. My right side pained me so much in the night that Wolf had to come and cut the bandage off; and when daylight came we discovered that he had got hold of the wrong bottle in the dark and rubbed me with honey almond cream instead of some 'Doctor Cure-all-ills' liniment.'

I was in terrible pain and whimpered like a kid every time we went over a rut on the twenty-mile trip. The M.D. said: 'Two broken ribs,' but took a picture just for good luck before bandaging me up. The picture was a failure, the plate was fogged, but the M.D. being certain in his diagnosis, my pain being a whole lot better — 'Why take off all that wide plaster bandage for a picture?' It was not taken off. I went back to work and put in two mighty uncomfortable weeks.

We held the O'Malley fight until the picture was finished, to guard against being held up if I got hurt, which in my present condition might happen. As it was a night scene, to make it easier for me, we duplicated our outdoor location for the fight at the studio. Leo Willis, the most reliable screen fighter I ever worked with, was the character with whom I had to battle. But even Willis was up against it this time. He did not dare hit me in the body, on my right side — it would have killed me. But, oh, Lordy! That man hit every spot on my face four hundred times, and I, being stung, hit back a whole lot. Oh, gee! At times we had a regular fight. I had all of him to hit at and he had to keep above my chest, and we slugged until three o'clock in the morning. One of the hardest of the hard-boiled crowd we had for outlaws said:

'That's the toughest fight I ever seen in pictures.'

At two o'clock in the afternoon of the same day we were all at the studio to see the fight stuff run. It had been put through the laboratory special. Every doggone, single, damned scene had static, and was ruined.... It was a cold night. Allen had failed to have X-back film which is used in such cases, and Joe, the head camera man, took a chance with straight stock. The whole fight had to be done over again.

Was it done over again? It was! That night! Was it slighted? It was not — it was just as vicious as the night before! When it was finished, two crippled-up men sat down and almost cried. As the outlaw spokesman of the night before was leaving the studio with his ten-spot in his hand, he was heard to say:

'I said last night it was the toughest fight I ever seen in pictures. I was wrong. It is the damnedest, punishingest fight I ever seen, in pictures or out of pictures.'

At daylight I was X-rayed and rushed to the hospital. The two broken ribs had rebusted, and there were two more that, owing to the fogged plate, had never been set. I was at the studio again in five days, but I didn't do any more fights until — my next picture, 'The Whistle.'

Bob Kortman, a fighting machine, who, had he lived fifty years earlier, would have been the Charles Dickens model for Bill Sikes, did the fight with me in 'The Whistle.' Some big English motion picture magnate, who was looking over the making of films in America, was present to witness the scrap. When we were fighting, he was so astonished, all he could say was, 'My word! My word!'

This tickled Bob immensely, and while he was listening for 'My word! My word!' I would soak him hard. Then he didn't listen any more — and I didn't soak him any more.

CHAPTER XVII
WILL ROGERS

A LARGE sum of money had been tied up in the bank for about a year. My attorneys had filed a suit against Tom Ince for moneys due me. Tom filed a cross-complaint, which brought his suit to trial first. Because of many postponements, this trial dragged along for about three months; the evidence presented consuming seventeen volumes of court reporters' transcript.

During a three weeks' lull in the Ince trial, a suit that J. Parker Read, Tom's confidential friend and business associate, had brought against me was tried, Read claiming I owed him a commission on the Famous Players contract. This took eight volumes more of clean white paper and the reporters' time. Meanwhile a five-thousand-dollar expense each week was going merrily on at the idle studio of the William S. Hart Company.

Tom was on the witness stand for many days in the Read case, and it looked mighty bad for me, as both Tom and Read testified to many alleged meetings with just the three of us present. If the trial had lasted long enough for me to have to present my side of the case, I should have been up against it. It would have been two against one. But after making Read admit that he received a percentage from Tom's other contracts, and forcing Tom to produce these contracts in court where their contents were made known for the first time, each contract stating that it had been induced by the signing of my contract and could be terminated at any time if my contract was terminated, my lawyers made a motion for a non-suit. The court sustained the motion. The jury was discharged, and Read's suit was thrown out of court.

Tom lost his suit, also. The court upheld my contract which Tom for some wild reason had been seeking to change. I won without presenting my side of the case, but the overhead of my studio and legal expenses ate up all the money I gained. The two trials must have cost Tom a lot of money.

One of the greatest joys I have ever had from my picture work is the affection bestowed upon me by children. The little son of Admiral Cary T. Grayson, physician to the President, and the sturdy young boy of Will H. Hays, the Postmaster-General, were unswervable Bill Hart fans, consequently their daddies, in spite of the burdens and affairs of State, were compelled to use valuable time in writing many human letters to a motion picture actor. I hope they and all fathers and mothers will always know and understand how grateful that motion picture actor was to be so honored; and how much more he understands now that God has given him a wonderful man child for his own. How I treasure a letter of Admiral Grayson's which tells me not only of the genuine admiration of his little son when my pictures were displayed at the White House for the recreation of the President, but of the often expressed appreciation of the President himself on the excellence of my riding and the sincerity of my acting.

It was almost impossible to secure suitable Western stories. I had just produced 'The Cradle of Courage' and 'The Whistle,' which were not Western, and while they pleased and were good money-makers, the exhibitors called for more Westerns. So while the court proceedings were going on I put in part of my days and most of my nights working out stories. My good luck remained with me. I was fortunate enough to turn out two more successful screen tales, 'Travelin' On' and 'White Oak.'

While doing 'Travelin' On,' we were working on the stage at the studio one day shooting the interior of a barn. The scenes were hard to get, as Fritz had considerable work to do with a monkey. On account of the difficulty of getting a horse up a narrow stairway into the studio, we did not bring Cactus Kate. That settled it. The little horse would not work a lick, and his rising temper did not augur well, either for the quality of our scenes or the welfare of the monkey. Kate was sent for immediately and after quite a bit of trouble landed safely by the side of her lord and master. The world immediately took on a lavender hue. The scenes were shot almost as fast as the camera could be set up. The little spotted rascal even voluntarily kissed the monkey.

Then suddenly there was a rolling roar that beggared the wildest sounds that ever came out of a circus menagerie. Our studio occupied the full space of a triangular-shaped block. Around and around this building this tragic ear-splitting, screaming volume, of the sound of dying things, traveled. Workmen dropped their tools, electricians scrambled down from their stations overhead, actors ran hurriedly to the exits. We were all on the sidewalk. . . . The monster was coming! The circling, wailing cries grew nearer. Around the corner the monster came! Head up and jaws wide open, a torn, bleeding chest, and blood-red eyes, trumpeting in weird, discordant tones her woes to the world . . . It was 'Lisbeth,' the giant mule. Lisbeth had been left alone, Lisbeth was lonesome. She had broken through a stout corral, with her flesh against jagged timbers, had traveled a mile through traffic, and come to her family.

There was quite a bit of cost added to the making of 'White Oak'; one cause being too much water, the other, too much wine.

The story called for many scenes on a Mississippi River steamboat. The interiors were taken at the studio, the exteriors on the Sacramento River. We landed at the city of Sacramento with one hundred and twenty-five people, twenty-five more than we had at Ben Lomond — and, like Ben Lomond, it rained, only it rained days and days longer, and when it did clear, it was plain that the elements were just kidding us a little, so we worked as though our lives were at stake. As it turned out, mine almost was.

I had to ride a horse along the river-bank, pass a steamboat, dismount, swim out, and head off the big stern-wheeler. For the necessary suspense in the story there had to be a number of scenes taken of me swimming, before the captain ordered his engines stopped and a rope thrown to haul me on board.

It was late in December. The water was like ice, and if it is possible for mental suggestion to lower the temperature of water, it was even colder. The swiftly running Sacramento was covered with fuzzy, snow-white cakes that it gathered from the flooded rice fields on its journey to the sea. All that was needed was Eliza and the trusty bloodhounds, and 'Uncle Tom's Cabin' could have been picturized right there. To any one who belonged outside of a lunatic asylum, those river scenes should have taken three days in the photographing, but with menacing skies and visions of the fast disappearing bank roll, we shot them in one, with myself as chief lunatic.

Tanking up from a Tank Car

When we returned to Los Angeles, I should have gone to bed; instead of that we went to Victorville for our desert scenes. The river scenes were only the start of the story, but they came mighty near finishing it, for at Victorville my sister Mary made me smoke that little glass cigarette and it registered one hundred and three. Dr. Garcelon, from ten miles out on the desert, came in and pulled me through. I was in bed three days. The company could not work.

Cowboys are children — from eight to eighty, age makes no difference. They are boys just the same. Idleness is bad for children.

A heavy Santa Fé freight was side-tracked to allow a passenger train to go through. One of the cars of the heavy freight was to all outward appearance an oil-tank car. But it wasn't an oil-tank car! Appearance was all wrong. It was a camouflage. I never knew who put it there, nor who was responsible for it, but ninety-seven million gallons of the finest Mexican wine ever made from grapes was in that car. Where it was going, I do not know. I only know it never arrived there, and that through the medium of several short pieces of garden hose, enough wine was siphoned out of that oil car to irrigate the Mojave Desert. Only it was not used for any such purpose. At the end of every piece of hose was an endless line of cowboys, each with a receptacle; said receptacle being every movable thing that would hold liquid — wooden buckets, tin buckets, milk pans, garbage pails, horses' canvas nose-bags, washtubs — every repository imaginable or available within two miles of Victorville was on that line. The heavy freight and the sadly depleted oil-tank car passed on.

For two whole days and nights the carnival lasted. The streets of the town became a public dance-hall. Innocent and harmless — yes! But to those who knew not the way of the cowboy — menacing. The more timid citizens telephoned to San Bernardino, forty miles away, for help. The sheriff and twenty deputies, all armed to the teeth, arrived on a special train. They did not need guns. They needed many husky men and many stretchers. The merry-making had ended. Every foot of available space outside or inside at Victorville was occupied by a sleeping cowboy. The courthouse was full — the jail was full. Nothing was sacred to those Bacchanalian inebriates.

There were no 'good Indians.' They were all alike, from the manager and the director down. I was ill in bed, but I can make an affidavit that it was good wine, and said affidavit can be supported by a reliable witness — the sheriff was in the room at the time. The sheriff was a real sheriff; no one had been harmed, no damage had been done. He returned with his deputies to San Bernardino.

I often wonder what some of those old desert-rat prospectors think when they uncover some of those lost board-covered buckets that were cached during those two days of revelry and the location forgotten. I'll bet they don't try the contents on the burro first!

'Three Word Brand,' the last picture of my contract, was completed. I was to give up my studio and take a long rest. We who had been together for four years — ahungered to make good pictures — were to part. While there had always been an undercurrent of freedom and a spirit of levity in our little family, we had driven ourselves hard. Our efforts had been honest in labor, hardship, and mental concentration. Our pictures had been highly successful, but success had never spoiled us. We stuck doggedly to our work.

WITH BAT MASTERSON IN NEW YORK

When, one calm spring morning, the last truck pulled away from the old place, I felt that something had gone out of my life. Nor was I consoled when, alone in the little bare dressing-room, I looked at the engraved copper-plate inscription on the inside of a new rawhide trunk:

A token of esteem and love from
the greatest Hart fans in the world
His Own Company

In September, when my affairs were pretty well straightened out, I took a vacation and journeyed to New York. I had some never-to-be-forgotten visits with Mr. Masterson. One day we had our picture taken together on the roof of the Telegraph Building. When we came downstairs to Mr. Masterson's office, he said:

'Bill, sit in my chair at my desk for one more. I want to have one taken like that.'

I did so, and he stood beside me. Mr. Masterson was sitting in the same chair eighteen days later when he heard the last call.

To know Mr. Masterson was to love him. What he did for the Western frontier is recorded. May flowers always nod their heads and the winds blow gently over the graves of this man and his kind! May never a tired horseman ride by that does not stop and wish well to those who sleep!

Will Rogers was playing with the Follies, so I spent many of my evenings in his dressing-room, and when the show was over we would go around to Dinty Moore's for a bite to eat. It was like the old stage days. Bill, when with the Follies, always finds keen enjoyment in introducing folks to the audience, and if any one will go back at him a little, he just loves 'em for it. On all of my trips to New York, I never failed to call on Bill, and, if I became brave and essayed a little mental badinage, I never failed to take a licking.

On this trip to New York I was so impressed with Bill's success that I wrote back home to the 'Los Angeles Herald' that in my opinion Will Rogers was proving himself to be the greatest humorist since Mark Twain. I am glad the last few years have proved my judgment to be true.

On one of my visits East, Bill got going so strong and I was taking such a trouncing that I stayed away from the theater for two nights. Brandon Tynan, a member of the Follies, came to me and said:

'Bill Hart, Will Rogers is all busted up over your not coming around. He says if you'll come to-night he just swears you can stay upstairs in the dressing-room while his act is on.'

Of course I went — I was dying to go. I would have gone, anyhow. Bill kept his word. But when he came up to the dressing-room after his act, he was unmistakably blue. Assuming my best blustering manner I made a little talk, winding up with 'See here, Bill, I am going back to California Sunday. Now, to-morrow, Saturday night, I am coming up here with my cowboy outfit in a suitcase, I'm going to put that outfit on, and when you walk out on that stage I'm going to walk out with you — and doggone you — look out for yourself' . . . the last being said with lowering brow and serious mien.

A bright glow came over Bill's mug that immediately developed into a radiant grin. 'Will ye? Will ye, sure enough, do that, Bill? Gee! That'll be fine!'

I had thrown a scare into Will Rogers.

BILL HART AND BAT MASTERSON ON THE ROOF OF THE TELEGRAPH BUILDING

A Night with Will Rogers

I thought up a whole lot of what I considered witty sallies, and Saturday night out we went. As soon as the members of the company had seen me in my cowboy clothes, they knew a battle was on. The word was flashed, and every human being back of the curtain line was in the wings by the time Bill and I made our entrance.

I got along fairly well while the so-called bright thoughts I had stored up lasted — then my licking started. But I had thought out a good story for a clean-up, and it was a good one, too. I knew it was, for I had tried the main part of it on hundreds of Liberty Loan audiences and it never failed. I told the audience of my boyhood days among the Sioux Indians; how I once knew an Indian that took off his moccasins, stood with his bare feet in the snow, and gave the moccasins to his friend who was going on a long trail. I made the hand talk signs the same as the Indian had done, and then explained to the audience what they meant. I then told the audience that I now knew the reason why I always sought the society of Will Rogers. It was because he was one of my own people: it was because he had Indian blood ... Will Rogers was part Indian.

There was a tense silence. My heart stood still. How would they take it? And then it broke forth. The house rocked and re-rocked with applause.

I looked slyly at Bill, trying to say with my eyes: 'Now, doggone you, beat that one.' ... And I ran away.

Bill pawed at the stage with his right foot a minute, and then he said, in substance, in his inimitable way:

'Yes, folks, what Bill Hart says is true. So far as I know, that's the first time it's ever been told — but it's true; both my father and my mother have Indian blood, and I'm proud to be their son.'

309

My thunder was stolen right there. But the snoozer had to rub it in.

'I'll tell you all one thing, though, folks,' he continued. 'In spite of my Indian blood, I never could learn to talk with my hands as good as Bill can. Bill is good at it, and while Bill lived with Indians when he was a little feller, I lived with 'em and among 'em until I was a grown man, right in the middle of all that hand talk stuff. I've had better trainin' than Bill, for years and years. And, besides that, folks, look at the trainin' I've had for the last five years. There ain't no finer trainin' on earth. It's the greatest hand talk school in the world right here on this stage.'

He hunched his shoulders, with bent elbows and both hands extended, palms upwards. He stopped the show!

Passing through Chicago on my way home, Jack Dempsey invited me to attend a dinner that was being given in his honor by the newspaper men of Chicago. After the dinner Dempsey poked me in the ribs and said, 'Let's make a getaway.'

We did. We tramped all over Chicago — wherever there was a boxing night being held, we were there. We would enter in the dark, and in some places leave before the lights were thrown on at the end of a round, and Jack would thereby escape ring introductions.

At one place there were a pair of lightweights battling. One was completely outclassed in all except gameness. He was taking an awful licking, and about the head, too. I was just about sick. Again I got a poke in the ribs and we worked our way out through the dark in silence. The fresh air of late fall hit our faces — we inhaled long breaths and walked blocks, still in silence.

JACK DEMPSEY AND FRED STONE

'Gosh, Bill, I can't stand to see a boy get beat up that way. That fellow is liable to be goofy all his life from a beating like that.'

The voice was Jack Dempsey's.

Fred Stone was playing at the Colonial Theater. Jack had never met Fred. It was between acts. I left Jack on the stage and went into Fred's dressing-room.

'Fred,' I said, 'I'm up against it. I've got a man here with me that I'm responsible for. I won't attempt to explain. I know you've got only a few moments, but I must have an answer right now. The man is waiting outside. I've got to go through to California to-morrow and I want to leave the fellow in your care.'

'What is he, Bill?' said Fred.

'He's a prize-fighter, Fred.'

Bully Fred Stone! He never batted an eye.

'Bring him in, Bill,' he said.

I brought in Jack Dempsey. We were soon joined by Jim Corbett and Walter Kelly. We parted when the streets were light.

I was married to Winifred Westover December 7, 1921. We separated May 10, 1922. Our wonderful son, William S. Hart, Jr., was born September 6, 1922. Mrs. Hart obtained a divorce on the grounds of desertion at Reno, Nevada, February 11, 1927.

In this narrative I have expressed my admiration for men — judges at the top of the legal profession. It is my fondest hope that, when my son grows to young manhood, he will follow in the footsteps of one of his great-grand-fathers, and show an aptitude for the profession of law. It is a manly, honorable calling, one that can always be

311

used for good. Its pathway and training lead to the highest gifts of our Republic.

The time is fast approaching, however, when this honorable profession will be forced to clean house and through their Bar Associations kick out an element that must hit the nostrils of all upright men. The profession of law must clear away the scum that floats on the surface of its honorable calling — unregenerate traitors who have learned in their legal training how to hew close to the line and dish out libelous scandal, introduced with such phrases as 'It is reported . . .' 'A suit will be filed . . .' 'Charges will be made . . .' etc.

The press is eager for news. It is their right and privilege. The newspapers print what is given them in good faith, waiting for what is to come next. There is no next! There is never any suit filed nor any charges legally made — the scum has played the one card held in its filthy fingers. The damaging news has been spread all over the world. They sit back and smile, and through other channels let it be known that for more American dollars they will turn back or go ahead. When defied, they snarlingly retreat into their holes, their fingers subconsciously clawing into the dirt, for dirt is all that they know.

It is not my purpose to record any lies that have been launched against me, then denied under oath after three years' silence by the one person who could deny them. This is a record of my life as I have lived it.

In the early summer of 1922, Will H. Hays, the president of the newly formed Motion Picture Producers and Distributors Organization, made his first official trip to California. The stress of many conferences and public speeches made it necessary to get Mr. Hays away for a restful week-end. Cecil de Mille's mountain ranch was the chosen spot. Mr. Hays requested that I be invited to join the party, as he had been forced to be a Bill Hart fan for a long time, whether he wanted to be or not—by his young son. It was my first meeting with Mr. Hays and I enjoyed the party very much. It was composed of the host, Cecil de Mille, his brother, William de Mille, Mr. Hays and his two friends who were traveling with him, Jesse Lasky, and myself. Mr. Hays went up there for a rest. We all gathered in the big living-room and talked until the early hours both nights of our mighty pleasant outing. Mr. Hays got plenty of rest, but not much sleep. Cecil de Mille calls his ranch 'Paradise.' It is an appropriate name.

The big 'get-together' meeting of the Association was a public dinner with all the city officials present, held at the Ambassador Hotel. It was a mighty impressive affair. Mr. Hays made a comprehensive speech, outlining the aims of the new organization. He gave as one of the principal reasons for his resigning the position of Postmaster-General of the United States to enter motion pictures, an illustration that was mighty flattering to two actors, one of whom was myself.

He said: 'You know it took me about a year to decide to enter the motion picture industry. Like many others, I had given no thought to its great possibilities. A small incident fetched me insight to the great power of pictures. I was going home to Sullivan, Indiana, from New York, and I had taken my little son and his cousin some cowboy suits. After the lads had invested themselves in the new regalia, I overheard a conversation between them. It was this:

'"I'm going to be Bill Hart."

'"Well, if you're going to be Bill Hart, I'm going to be Doug."

'As I listened to the conversation of those two lads, I was suddenly made aware of the influence of motion pictures. Here, I thought, in little Sullivan, two boys are governed in their thoughts and play by characters introduced to them through the screen. If this be true of these two lads, what about the millions of persons throughout the country and the other millions throughout the world? Then the idea came to me of the tremendous power for good to be wielded through the medium of motion pictures. That is what largely induced me to enter the realm of motion pictures.'

I had, at this time, attained not only success, but a position respected and honored in my profession of actor and in my production of pictures. I was endeavoring to 'hold the mirror up to Nature' and giving out the best in my own nature in the effort.

Now, as it is only necessary to breathe upon a mirror to dull it, so it is only necessary to blur with scandal a public character and that character is lost. Those who had been stalking me, and failed hitherto, belched and spewed and spawned. The result was horrible. I wakened one morning to find the papers blazoned with my ignominy. A woman had been discovered who claimed I was the father of her child, and a record of her claims was on file at the office of the Los Angeles district attorney. It was true that this woman existed; it was true that she made such charges five years before. It happened in the following manner:

In December, 1916, my sister Mary, who in those early days was taking care of my mail, informed me that an Eastern lady of superior education, who had written beautiful letters about my pictures, was in town. She urged me to see her. I said, 'All right, invite her to dinner.'

The woman dined with my sister and me one evening at our old round table in the Hoffman Café. She was a woman of very plain appearance, about forty years of age, a brilliant conversationalist. It was nearly two years later, in November, 1918, that this same woman called again on the telephone and said she was in town and had the baby with her. I made some joking reply.

'I am not joking,' she answered.

'Well, if you're not joking,' I replied, 'it's tough on you, lady, for you're crazy.'

And then I forgot all about it.

About two weeks later there was a telephone call in my box for me to call up the district attorney's office. I did so, but as it was nearly midnight I could not get in touch with any one. The next morning I mentioned it to Mr. Allen at the studio and asked him to find out what was wanted. He came back and reported:

'The district attorney wants to see you personally. He says he has a woman that claims support from you for a fifteen-months-old child.'

I told Allen to explain to the district attorney that I knew nothing of any such matter; that it must be a joke, or an act of insanity, and to tell him that I could not spare the time to come in the daytime, as it would hold up our work. It was arranged for Allen and me to go that night. We met the district attorney and the assistant district attorney. I briefly stated what little I knew of the matter.

A short time after this, Allen told me that another interview was required; this time I was to go — and did go — alone. A statement of the woman's was read to me. I pointed out all its absurdities. I was asked to face the woman. I did so, and I did what I never did before and have never done since — I cursed a woman.

After one more trip to the district attorney's office, I refused to go again. The all-night sessions, combined with a long day's work, were wearing me out.

The poor woman herself had no story, no proof — nothing! The case could not be moved either way. It was at a standstill. The woman, fearing an investigation, had no facts that she dared present. My attorney could make no investigation without at least some alleged facts. There was nothing to start on, nothing to investigate but the woman's word. . . . The woman disappeared from whence she came. . . .

This was the accusation that had been torn from dead archives and thrown at me. I didn't at first grasp the devastating effect of this publicity. Then letters and clippings poured into my office — the news had circled the world. The people who loved my work were shocked. They believed the damning thing! So my attorney set to work trying to find the back trail. It was tortuous. There is nothing in the world harder to refute than a tissue of lies — there is no structure to attack.

Then my little secretary was tying up a bundle of answered fan letters. She hesitated as though undecided, while she held one letter in her hand before putting it in with the others. She turned and handed the letter to me, saying: 'Here's something I don't quite understand.'

It was an unsigned letter containing clues to the solving of what was one of the most amazing, weird, and astounding cases ever known in this country which, had it not been cleared up, would have been an ever-standing rebuke to the motion picture industry, and would have cost me my life. ''Twas strange, 'twas passing strange.' It was a letter

316

from a mother who had offered her child for adoption. My accuser, Miss ——, took the child, but it died. This was our clue. Following it out, my attorney found that Miss —— had taken a second child for trial adoption. The mother of this child said she had consented to its being taken to California and was overjoyed at her baby's good fortune, but the child was returned ill and with an ugly bruise on his head. ''Twas pitiful, 'twas wondrous pitiful.' Miss ——, confronted with these facts, admitted them. Her reason was that she wanted to influence my career, to prove the strength of mind over matter.

Yet the fact remains that in a situation so absurd as to make the world rock with laughter, I had been helpless, bound, discredited, because a district attorney was gullible, and the unprincipled needed a missile of offense. The evidence gathered and presented to Mr. William Randolph Hearst, a full confession by Miss —— , was printed in his papers.

Then I wanted to get away. . . . There was a band of Arapahoe Indians in camp at Cahuenga Pass — they were appearing in a prologue at a local theater. I went to the friends of my youth, and they took me in. I told them I had been very sad and now the Great Spirit had cleared away the mist. The sun was shining and I was happy. Their pipes were lit for me.

CHAPTER XVIII

'IN THE BEAT OF THE LIVING SUN'

In the early summer of 1923, I yielded to the earnest and almost continuous importunities of Mr. Zukor, Mr. Lasky, and Mr. Kent, and notified Mr. Lasky that I would go to work. The next day my contract was renewed by letter for nine more pictures, the only new clause being that the contract could be cancelled by either party at the conclusion of any one picture. I had the clause inserted, as I wanted to be free to stop work if I should again be attacked.

Mr. Lasky proposed that I make my productions in the Famous Players Lasky Studio. I had made 'The Narrow Trail' there six years previous and I liked to work there, so I readily consented. But when I started work, I found everything so different at the studio that I realized what a great mistake I had made. Where before I had gone ahead and made my picture as any tenant that was renting space should do, the heads of my staff were now constantly receiving orders and instructions as to how they should carry on their work. I was nonplussed, but, outside of telling the heads of my departments to pay no attention to such orders, I did nothing. I thought surely it was all a mistake; that it would all blow over and adjust itself. But it did not do so — it became worse.

Mr. Lasky had gone to New York, so I was forced to have several talks with Charlie Eyton, the studio manager. Mr. Eyton looked over my contract, and then informed all heads of the departments of the Lasky Studio that I was absolutely independent. Charlie Eyton was then and is now a fine man.

318

A GOOD SCENE IN 'WILD BILL HICKOK'

One of the principal sets of 'Wild Bill Hickok' was Dodge City, Kansas. By building two new streets near the depot, we made Victorville, California, into Dodge City, Kansas. At times we had four hundred people on the set, and we got some splendid stuff. It was most amusing to watch the Overland trains pull in and see the startled passengers jump off with a watch in one hand and a time-table in the other. That sign, 'Dodge City, Kansas,' on the depot was surely official. Some of them became quite panic-stricken and acted exactly like a green goods victim when he discovers he has been fleeced. And the train crew, from the fireman to the conductor, enjoyed the joke.

In one of the street fights on this location the action of the story called for me to do some fast 'two-gun' shooting, and it created some talk. It took a private exhibition and a stop-watch to convince some Los Angeles newspapermen that it could be done.

The sales department was clamoring for the picture, so as soon as we stopped photographing, my cutter, my staff, and I devoted all of our time to finishing 'Wild Bill Hickok' before starting another picture. How proud I was when Jesse Lasky, who had just returned from New York, saw our master print. He came to me, both hands outstretched in congratulation, saying, 'Bill, I am simply crazy about it. It is so big that it frightens me. It is a marvelous picture. The best Bill Hart picture so far produced.'

Later in the day I came upon Mr. Lasky and Mr. Kent, who was then the head of the sales organization. Mr. Lasky again congratulated me, and said: 'Bill, I was all tired out. I was in no condition to see the picture, and yet I sat in that projection room an hour and a half and it seemed like ten minutes. I was held spell-bound.'

He then continued: 'Bill, I simply cannot praise you enough. I'm going to send you a wire and state just what I think in writing. I know if I made a picture like that I'd want to keep a record of what people thought of it.'

I was grateful!—grateful!! And said so.

Mr. Kent then spoke up and wanted to know if we couldn't say in a screen title exactly how fast I did my shooting. But Mr. Lasky and I convinced him that it would look like an advertisement and detract from the picture.

The wire Mr. Lasky sent me was even more enthusiastic than his spoken words.

My second picture, 'Singer Jim McKee,' opened with a sort of prologue which wound up with my escape and the death of my horse.

I had been planning the retirement of my little horse, not on account of any physical retrogression, loss of suppleness or activity — the rascal was just as full of pep then as he ever was (and is so to-day)—but it was simply a case of 'the pitcher going to the well.' This being always in my mind and loving the animal as I did, it made me self-conscious, which is harmful. To make dangerous rides and do dangerous stunts in pictures (providing the rider is a horseman), only about thirty per cent caution is necessary.

The rest, or about seventy per cent, must be abandon — and take a chance. If there is any overanxiety or affection for the mount and fear of injuring him, it is bad, very bad, for both horse and rider; for I am positive that a horse senses instantly the slightest uncertainty in the hand that guides him.

It was impossible to double Fritz because of his distinct

markings and individuality. He can be identified as far as he can be seen, either on the screen or off, so he was never doubled but once, and that was when asked to do the impossible.

I had figured out a fall and roll for his last appearance that would outdo anything he ever did, which meant anything ANY horse ever did. In the story, as the escaping bandit — while galloping on the edge of a cliff — my horse was shot and we went rolling and tumbling to the gorge below. There was a location called Sulphur Canyon near the ocean, where in the old days we used to do such falls and rolls, but no one had ever dreamed of going more than halfway up the steep-shaled sides. I planned to do the ride on top of the cliff and take the fall right from the brink of the precipice.

Cliff Smith, my director, and I went to look at the location. The first drop before we struck earth was about twelve feet, and the distance to the bottom which must be rolled was easily one hundred and fifty feet. I knew the little horse could do it, but there was that fear that I knew I had of injuring him. I knew I could not do him justice and help him as I should. I weakened. . . .

We had tried several times to have dummy horses made for the little chap, but outside of using them as a staked down wild horse, or a dead horse, we could never use them. Cliff Smith and I had a talk with two expert mechanics at the Lasky Studio. They took the job. They worked five weeks at a cost of about $2000, and made a horse that was as nearly like Fritz as it would be possible for anything to be. Every measurement was perfect. The mane and tail were real horsehair. We had an artist paint all the markings. Every joint worked on springs. The head swung in the most natural manner, and the weight was within a hundred pounds of what Fritz himself would weigh.

At the conclusion of the picture, we got the scene. It was done in the following manner. I brought Fritz at a gallop and threw him. Then the dummy horse was fixed up with the same outfit we used on Fritz and held in an upright position by piano wires so I could mount. Golly! What a job it was! It took about thirty carpenters and helpers to get the mechanical horse to the top of the precipice and get him set up.

'Are you going to go over with that brute?' asked one of the workmen, a well-set-up young chap.

'Yes,' I said.

'Then from now on I'm satisfied to work at my trade,' he replied.

When the camera started to grind and I swung over my lifeless steed, the wire was cut and down we went.

In assembling, the first part of this scene was cut, and the fall I had made with Fritz was matched into it. The result was such an astounding illusion that I had to go before the board of censors in New York City and tell them my story before they would consent to this scene being shown on the screen. They were positive it was a living horse and a living man that rolled to the bottom of the canyon. The man was alive, but he didn't breathe much. I was shaken up quite a bit; but we never take such scenes until the end of a picture. The censors kept the faith. No one ever knew — this being the second time the story has been told.

We had journeyed again to the undefaced Bret Harte country for many of the exteriors of this picture. I will always associate those scenes, backed by festoons of Nature's foliage, with beautiful Phyllis Haver, who did such splendid work in the leading rôle. It was one of her first opportunities. She had formerly been one of Mack Sennett's bathing-beauty comédiennes along with Gloria Swanson and Mary Thurman. She gave an ideal performance.

When the New York criticisms on 'Wild Bill Hickok' came in, our little company was happy. We knew we had turned out a fine picture, but we also knew that New York was the Mecca of the amusement world. It was wonderful to know we had conquered — that we had won the 'big town's' approval. Tucked away in almost any out-of-the-way corner of the studio was sure to be found some member of the company reading highly laudatory criticisms.

> 'It came — the news like a fire in the night
> That life and its best were done,
> And there never was so dazed a wretch
> In the beat of the living sun.'

Outside of a human life not being involved, these masterly lines of W. E. Henley tell how I felt and how all of my little company felt when a wire, dated New York, came from Mr. Lasky. It was a complete reversal.

Our little band was indeed 'dazed . . . in the beat of the living sun.' My head was throbbing and rocking in wonderment. I could not think coherently or get a grip on myself. Several lengthy letters and wires were exchanged between Mr. Lasky and myself, which covered a period of three or four weeks. Exhibitors' reports were promised to support these strange statements.

Try as I might, I could not pull myself out of the trance-like feeling. Nor did any 'exhibitors' reports' or 'information obtainable,' as promised by Mr. Lasky, ever come to help me.

I had made twenty-five pictures and turned them over to Famous Players for distribution. Those pictures had been the leaders, the mainstay of the Paramount program. And now . . . What was it? I just could not think clearly. I was being told that I did not know how to make Western pictures. Yes, that was it! No other construction could be placed on Mr. Lasky's letter. I could not understand. I took a long walk, but I remained dazed. I could not come out of it. I went home and talked it over with my constant adviser, my sister Mary. I came back to the studio, gathered my staff together, and read the letter to them. They were dumbfounded. We all agreed that the arrow pointed one way — the relinquishment of my independence. Yet I could not believe it!

Mr. Lasky was still in New York. I wrote him that the whole trend of happenings seemed to point to the fact that the Famous Players Lasky Corporation did not take kindly to my making my own productions as I had previously done; that since starting work there seemed to be a desire to control me both in the business and the production end of the game. And if I was correct in this surmisal, let's quit. Because I could not make pictures that way.

I told him both by environment as a boy and by a thorough stage training and by the success of my some hundred Western pictures, I considered that I was qualified to make Western pictures, and I would have to be shown why and where I was wrong before I could intelligently try to change my ways. That the principal criticism he quoted of the Rialto Theater Management was that 'Wild Bill' was very old-fashioned. I explained the frontier West

WAS old-fashioned. How could it be made modern and remain true to nature and history? That the same people who termed 'Wild Bill' old-fashioned probably thought it modern and up-to-date to corral a wagon train in a blind box canyon in a hostile Indian country, or to swim bulls across a river with their neck yokes on, and various other things that would make a Western man refuse to speak to his own brother if he were guilty of such glaring errors. . . .

I then told him what it hurt me to say, that if Famous Players wanted me to start work making and turning over to Famous Players Lasky Corporation for distribution William S. Hart Productions, as per contract, fine. Let's go!

But, if the Famous Players Lasky Corporation wanted to tell me what stories I should do and to dictate how they should be done — let's not go. Let's call it off and save a lot of fuss and worry on both sides.

I asked him to please advise me of his decision.

Mr. Lasky's decision was that they should have something to say about the stories I produced, the continuities of these stories, their treatment while in production, and even the supporting cast; also that, as from the tone of my letters, this would be irksome to me, they elected to accept my suggestion to call it off and that 'Singer Jim McKee' would be the last picture delivered and conclude our contract.

I informed Mr. Grossman, telling him of my split with Famous Players, and asking him to negotiate a new contract for me immediately.

In a couple of days Mr. Grossman wired me that Mr. Schwalbe, of First National, was anxious to do business and for me to see Mr. Rowland, who, fortunately, was in Los Angeles. I called Mr. Rowland at the Ambassador Hotel on the telephone. Mr. Rowland said he would be glad to see me regarding a contract; that he was just going out of town for the week-end and would call me up on his return, Monday, or at the latest, Tuesday. . . . I never heard from Mr. Rowland again.

Mr. Kent stated that he did not like 'Singer Jim McKee,' suggesting that I take the picture to tie in with whatever new contract I might make.

I went to see Mr. Lasky immediately and informed him that our agreement regarding 'Singer Jim McKee' had already been closed. I pointed out to him that it would be suicide for me to try to sell a picture that Famous Players had rejected. Mr. Lasky agreed with me — and so notified Mr. Kent.

Mr. Hays happened to be in Hollywood, and I asked him as a favor to me to look at the picture. He did so. My publicity director, Scoop Conlon, saw it with him. Conlon told me of the ejaculations of delight and words of praise spoken by Mr. Hays all through the running of the picture. He said:

'Mr. Hays did not miss a single point.'

When they came out of the projection room, I saw Mr. Hays.

'Bill Hart,' he said, 'you have nothing to worry about. You not only have a good picture, you have a great picture.'

And, slapping me on the back, repeated again, 'You have nothing to worry about.'

Mr. Grossman wrote me that he was negotiating a contract with Marcus Loew on practically the same terms as my Famous Players contract; that everything was fine and Mr. Loew most enthusiastic.

My position seemed to be so strong, I was winning out so easily, that I became a little sentimental. I always was a bit insane, and I doubt if I ever shall regain my sanity. I had been with Famous Players for four years; they had released twenty-seven of my pictures; the organization was like home to me; they were my people. Perhaps . . . perhaps there was something to their side of the case. Perhaps I was a bit in the wrong.

I went up to my little ranch and walked back into the hills — Fritz, Cactus Kate, Yucca Sal, Lisbeth, and King Valentine all following. They formed a half-circle about me where I sat and looked the wide-eyed sympathy they could not speak. I talked to them for a long time, and they seemed to understand . . . and then the big, round red orb went down over the mountain tops that rippled away in the distance like a wind-blown sea. A soft sheen of golden light came up against the heavens, guided by the hand of the Great Master — God's colors! Yes, maybe I was wrong.

I said good-night to my dumb friends, and I was waiting for my human friend, Jesse Lasky, when he arrived at his office in the morning.

'Jesse,' I cried, 'perhaps I have been wrong; in my zeal for my work, maybe I am overlooking some of your rights. I have decided to give in a whole lot. You all can supervise my stories, providing I have the last word, and I will be glad to consult with you on any reasonable thing concerning my productions.'

Jesse paced the room for some time.

'Bill,' said Jesse, 'you are a producer now. To remain on this lot, or on the Paramount program, you would have to cease to be a producer; you would have to give up that idea entirely and just become an actor the same as our other stars. We would have to produce your pictures, select your stories, select a suitable director to fit that particular story, change your directors whenever necessary, select your cast, and be entirely in control of your productions.'

'Jesse,' I asked, 'if this be true, why in the name of common sense did you ever renew my contract and allow me to go to work?'

'Bill,' he replied, 'the sales organization must be considered; the sales organization must have a voice in the selection of all stories and their treatment.'

'But, Jesse,' I said, 'this is all wrong. Surely you nor any of the Paramount officials can allow such a thing. It is "the tail wagging the dog." A salesman may be the most valuable man in the world as a salesman, but it is ridiculous for a salesman to tell an author how to write a story, or a director how to direct one.'

'Nevertheless, Bill,' Jesse continued, 'the sales organization must have that right; also they have the right to say WHAT STYLE OF STORIES THEY WANT WRITTEN.'

'Jesse,' I replied, 'that simply cannot be. It will stifle all imagination or inspiration. It will stop the creation of all original plays. Everything will be made to order — machine-made.'

We talked for a long time, probably fifteen or twenty minutes. Finally I said, 'Jesse, you have explained the position of Famous Players thoroughly, but it is so hard for me to believe and to understand. Please give me the absolute "low-down" on the whole thing.'

'Bill,' he again said, slowly and deliberately, 'you are a producer now. You know that, don't you?'

328

'Golly! I hope I do, Jesse,' I replied. 'I've made twenty-seven pictures and turned them over to Famous Players for distribution.'

'Well, Bill, you must cease being a producer and become an actor. We will do the producing.'

'All right, Jesse,' I said. 'If that's final, it's good-bye.'

We shook hands and parted. When I came out, I staggered as I walked. . . . All that had been bright now seemed to take on a darkened hue.

CHAPTER XIX
'TUMBLEWEEDS'

Discouraging news came from Mr. Grossman. He and Marcus Loew had been about to sign a contract for me to make four pictures. Mr. Grossman had the contract all prepared when Mr. Loew suddenly left the city and went to Florida.

Scoop Conlon came to me and reported that the most vicious propaganda was being circulated about my pictures; that he had been running into it everywhere.

'Singer Jim McKee' was to be shown at the Metropolitan Theater in Los Angeles. The preliminary advertising, or rather the lack of it, was terrible. The picture was not underlined in any of the newspaper advertising. Even the day before it opened, only about twenty per cent of the usual bill-board advertising was being used — the rest being covered by the advertising for the picture that was to follow 'Singer Jim.'

On Friday, the day before my picture opened, Mr. Kaufman, the manager of the theater, called me on the telephone, saying that he wanted me to come down and help cut two reels out of the picture; that all the employees of the theater who had seen it said it was a bad picture.

I told Mr. Kaufman that, unless he gave me his word then and there that the picture would not be cut, I would see my attorney at once and have him restrained from cutting the picture.

'All right,' he replied. 'I won't touch it, but wait and see what happens Monday.'

330

I had heard a rumor that they would run the picture two days and then take it off the screen. Such an action would, of course, ruin it.

I wired Mr. Grossman, giving him full particulars and asking him to see Mr. Zukor immediately. Mr. Grossman wired back in a few hours:

Just saw Adolph. He knew nothing of reported rumors, denied their truth, and wired Kaufman at length directing suitable advertising and proper presentation.

I saw the picture the opening night. A packed audience received it splendidly, and gave it a big round of applause at the final fade-out.

A little usherette came and whispered to me in the dark:

'Don't believe what you hear, Mr. Hart; all of the girls in the theater just love the picture. It's wonderful.'

Coming out of the theater, the lobbies were packed, the long double lines extended far up and down the street, all waiting for the second show. The crowd that was coming out with me hailed me in congratulation on the picture, calling: 'Atta boy, Bill! Atta boy!' — and other terms of approval that showed their liking. Oh, how grateful I felt!

The picture was a huge, fine success. Nothing could alter that. It thrilled me to know it. It was as though the audience knew, and were upholding me, in my battle. Their faces just beamed with joy.

The critics were unanimous in their praise.

During the week that 'Singer Jim' played, Mary Garden appeared in Los Angeles at the head of her Grand Opera Company. I had the picture run privately for Miss Garden and her friends. My! My! My! How she did enjoy it! I had intended to tell Miss Garden that the officials of

Famous Players did not like the picture, and that the manager of the theater wanted to cut it; but she was so enthusiastic, and the rest of her party were so enthusiastic, that I was ashamed to do so. It would have embarrassed me — she could not have understood.

'Singer Jim' did a tremendous business. The theater was jammed. I had no means of knowing or finding out, but I was told that the week's receipts amounted to nearly thirty thousand dollars.

I felt, oh, so kindly toward Mr. Zukor. He had shown his friendship for me. He had responded at once to my appeal; he had answered when I called. There was no question but what he had stopped some drastic action being taken that would have killed the picture, and the manager's position was unassailable. He had the authority. The theater was not only owned and operated by Famous Players, but the manager also happened to be Mr. Zukor's brother-in-law.

I went to New York.

The first thing on our arrival, Scoop Conlon and I rushed off to a show. Afterwards we went to the Palais Royal. We were not in evening clothes, but the doorman said, 'Hello, California,' and passed us in. The head-waiter knew I was a friend of the band boys, and, while taking us back to seat us near them, I passed Mr. and Mrs. Zukor and their party seated at a table. I was glad to see Mr. Zukor and I believe he was glad to see me.

When the star *danseuse* did her number, there started, from seemingly nowhere, calls of my name that grew and grew until it became quite a chorus. The diners wanted to see me dance. The lady (Florence Walton) stood in the spot-light with outstretched arms. I dare not be a quitter

A New Contract with Mr. Zukor

— I did my best. I imagine my supposed ruggedness, coupled with a business suit attire, gained a bit of sympathy. So, with a whit of dancing skill, the soft glow of indirect lights, an assemblage that liked me, a glorious dancing partner, Paul Whiteman, and the mellow mood of the diners, the dance was a hit. We received an ovation.

Later on, when explaining to Paul Whiteman that my reason for being East was a slight disagreement with Famous Players, 'Good Lord!' Paul busted out. 'It couldn't have been better if it had been staged for you. It's the biggest reception any one ever had in this place, and Mr. Zukor was right here and heard it.'

As I remember, the head of the legal department of Famous Players and Mr. Grossman had a talk, the outcome of which was that Mr. Zukor and Mr. Grossman started negotiations that lasted for nearly two weeks, Mr. Zukor saying at one time, in a joking manner, that he was devoting more time to Bill Hart's contract than to the proposed new Paramount building.

A contract financially satisfactory to both sides was finally worked out. It was also understood that Famous Players and I should mutually agree on all stories, directors, casts, and everything pertaining to the production — with me having the final word. Mr. Zukor turned the matter of preparing the contract over to his legal department and Mr. Grossman, which was merely a matter of routine, as all disputed points had been settled.

I was more than happy — I was jubilant — for while the conferences were being held, I had not been idle. Much had been accomplished. Mr. Block, the head of the scenario department, had called to see me and submitted four stories. I had read them all and accepted three; the fourth was a Zane Grey story, 'The Border Legion.'

I was glad to accept the first three. I liked them immensely and thought them excellent screen material. 'The Border Legion' I considered a powerful story, but the two star rôles were the young lovers, and I judged if I played my rôle — that of a bandit — as I thought I could play it, it would kill the two leading characters and so kill the story.

In rejecting 'The Border Legion,' as an illustration and to make plain the way I saw the story, I suggested to Mr. Block that Antonio Moreno and Agnes Ayers should be cast for the two lover rôles and starred jointly. By a strange coincidence, when the picture was produced by Famous Players, Miss Ayers and Mr. Moreno were the stars and the rôle of the bandit, which was designated for me, was not even featured.

Several days elapsed; I became uneasy, and inquired of Mr. Grossman when the contract was to be signed.

He replied, 'I'm waiting a call at any time.'

'Bill,' I said, 'I'm afraid! Everything looks all right, but I don't like this delay. There seems to be a hold-back, a lack of sincerity.'

Bill Grossman, my friend, looked at me — almost a little sadly. 'Bill,' he said, 'you have been through a whole lot, and you have allowed yourself to become distrustful. You are beginning to doubt everybody's sincerity. I have been for days with Adolph working this thing out, and I know Adolph is sincere.'

I did not reply. Bill Grossman picked up his hat and coat and started out of the door. I could not let my friend get away with it. I was disheartened and a little bit sore. I followed him to the door and called after him, 'Yes, Bill, so was Marcus Loew, but he went to Florida.'

The next morning the telephone rang and a glad voice spoke over it, saying, 'Remain in your room at the hotel, as I may want you to run up to the Famous Players' office, or I may bring the contract down to you to sign.'

I waited, all flushed with the knowledge that it was soon to be ended. I was full of eagerness to shake hands with Mr. Zukor, and start for home. The public wanted me to work, and how I wanted to work!

I was waiting at ten-thirty and watched the hands pass eleven; eleven-thirty, no call; twelve — noon — no call. I was nervous now. Twelve-thirty, still silence. One o'clock. Wouldn't that damned telephone ever ring? One-thirty — I had lost hope. I upbraided myself. I almost cried. I had no confidence — that was it! How could things come my way when I did not believe, when I doubted every one, when, as Bill Grossman said, I had lost faith in every one's sincerity?

About two o'clock came Mr. Grossman. There was a flash of anger in his usually gentle eyes, and I knew it was not for me.

'Bill,' he said, 'I have much to tell you. I promised them I would tell you without comment.'

Every point that had been settled and agreed upon by Mr. Zukor and Mr. Grossman in their many conferences had been cast aside, abrogated, wiped out! ... If I worked for Famous Players, it had to be a complete surrender of all my rights. The director, the supervisor, the story, had all been selected, and the story was 'The Border Legion.'

There was nothing left for me to clutch at. Mr. Grossman went back to his office and I started mechanically to pack my trunk. The telephone rang. It was Will Hays. 'Will you come up to my office right away?'

I could and I did.

Mr. Hays and I went for a long walk and a long talk. We wound up in Central Park. Then his car found us and

335

we drove about the city. But talk and travel and time could not alter facts.

'This is too bad, too bad,' Will Hays said. And then . . . 'Coöperation! My goodness, this isn't coöperation. This means they say it all, and you say nothing.'

I could feel that Will Hays was sad, too! I left for the Coast the next day. Will Rogers was waiting at the train to see me off. I was a little late arriving, and Bill was dashing up and down the platform so fast that his long coattails were standing out behind and those overcoat pockets were weighted, too — and the inside coat pockets were also weighted. After that train pulled out and Bill started home, he must have almost blown away because he no longer had those pocket weights. I know he didn't, because I was lookin' right at them — on the opposite seat.

James Montgomery Flagg came a-honeymooning to my little Hollywood home. Jim had been wanting for years to do an oil painting of my pony and myself, so, planting himself at the wheel of his car and placing his bride beside him, he motored across America.

I was sort of in the dumps, and the few weeks that Jim and Dorothy spent with us did me a lot of good. Jim started his painting up at the ranch; but he hadn't squared things with Fritz. A few days of standing still, with me on his back, and the rest of his family standing around making bright remarks, was too much for the little autocrat. He quit cold. Jim had to continue his work at Hollywood. Fortunately, he had put in all of his time working on Fritz and could finish him from memory. But my end of it was not so easy. Instead of a live horse, I got a saw-horse with a pre-Volstead whiskey barrel on top of it.

Nothing in the humorous line, from A to Izzard, ever

WILLIAM S. HART
Painted from life by James Montgomery Flagg

escaped Jim Flagg . . . and the all too ludicrous sight of the 'bad guy' perched on top of a whiskey barrel kept his keen wit bubbling so much that he was forced to spend his spare moments hiding in a vine-covered pergola where he worked off his mirth on paper; the result being, 'Boulevards all the Way Maybe,' a rich, whimsical description of his journey through Missouri mud and over Nevada deserts, to find for an inspiration, at the end of his rainbow, a bad man — guns an' all — riding a whiskey barrel on a Hollywood lawn. I can understand Jim's book being a laugh-provoker, but I can't understand why he never used the guns when they were always handy.

On the morning of October 2, 1924, I received a letter that caused me to hobble around my little office for fully an hour, stealing an occasional glance at what I clutched in my hand. My amazement amounted to almost a stupor — it was hard for me to think. The letter addressed me as 'Dear Bill' and was signed, 'Thos. H. Ince.'

I answered immediately:

DEAR TOM:

Many thanks for your invitation to attend the first showing of 'Barbara Frietchie.' I know it will prove to be a fine picture.

I would be glad to accept such a personal invitation and would surely be there if it were possible. But one week ago I busted my foot and I'm knee high encased in a cast. But here is hoping that 'Barbara' goes over with a bang.

Since I have become a dad I have often thought of the three fine boys you have growing up. It is a wonderful sensation, isn't it? 'The greatest on earth.'

I saw my wonderful little chap a month ago — and when he put his arms around my neck and kissed me — MY CUP WAS FULL.

I hope Mrs. Ince is enjoying good health. My dear sister Mary has not been well lately, which causes me much worry.

There is no use mentioning your health. I guess it would take more than fire or flood to bung you or me up. We seem to be hard-shelled.

I was glad to hear that John and Ralph are with you.

Best wishes.

Sincerely yours

BILL

'Life's but a walking shadow' . . . Just a little bit later Tom answered the last call. I am glad Tom wrote to me — and I am glad I wrote to Tom.

In April, 1925, the Lambs Club wanted me to appear at the annual gambol in New York. I had been leading such a busy life since going into pictures that I had not been able to do my bit with the rest of the boys, so I made the big jump back to New York and appeared.

The Lambs stand alone in comradery, just as they stand alone in having illustrious talent for their public gambols; but they seemed to have outdone themselves this night. Al Jolson had made a special trip from Florida, his first appearance after an illness that caused him to close his company. Will Rogers was doing a monologue on the Gridiron dinner at Washington, from which he had just returned.

In the dressing-room, where I was squatted on the floor, my heart beating against my ribs, were Tommy Meighan, De Wolf Hopper, John Philip Sousa, Augustus Thomas, John Drew, and General Pershing, our foremost American commander, was doing his bit with the rest of us. The greatest dancers of ages were doing acts that could not be duplicated. It was COLOSSAL!

I was terrified. I had intended for my solo appearance to do some little Western recitations. I now realized, if I made such an appearance amidst probably the greatest assemblage of talent ever gathered, that I would be next door to ridiculous; and then the audience knew I had come such a long way — and for what?

I can draw guns quickly and fire them very rapidly — I WOULD DO IT ON THE STAGE IN FRONT OF THE AUDIENCE! I left the dressing-room and walked among the crowds in the wings, biting my fingers, thinking. I was actually suffering!

During the war the manufacturers of ammunition got in the habit of using very poor metal in their blank cartridges. After the war they somehow forgot to change their ways. A blank cartridge when discharged will sometimes swell, and if it does ... Good night! There is no more shooting — the cylinder will not revolve until the offending shell is removed. It had happened to me many times in pictures — suppose it happened now. Oh, God! It was cruel! I suffered ...

Some one took me by the arm — and led me to the big heavy curtains. They parted — I was facing a seventy-five-thousand-dollar audience. I started to talk — I told a little story I had never told before, nor have I ever told it since ...

How, in 1869, at Abilene, Kansas, there was a marshal, Bill Hickok, a great gun-man; how his enemies, the bad element, imported from Texas a celebrated desperado, named Phil Cole, to kill him; how Cole when he met Hickok knew he was in the presence of his master and became afraid; how he took the coward's course of assassination; how he learned that Wild Bill was fond of animals; how at midnight, knowing Hickok was in the Bull's Head Saloon, he went to a corral and stole a shepherd dog, and took him to the front of the saloon and tied him to the door, then hid behind a post and shot the dog, knowing Hickok would

339

come to succor the poor animal; how the plot worked —
how Hickok did come — a-running — but with a gun in
each hand; how Phil Cole lay stretched staring upwards
with a dying dog trying to lick — the wrong man's hands;
how the bad element, in darkness across the street, were
quickly mustered; how they must get Hickok at once, or
leave town, whipped and beaten, their power gone forever;
how they watched Hickok reënter the saloon — how eight
gun-men, bad men, all followed — there was no back door;
how Hickok stood with his back to them, yet such was the
instinct and courage of this wonderful man that one of the
eight men made the first move ... and then Hickok's two
guns came from nowhere and leaped into life. ... How
when his twelve shots had been fired and the smoke had
cleared away, eight men were dead or dying on the floor of
the Bull's Head Saloon, at Abilene, Kansas, in 1869 ...

The Creator was good to me; my cartridges did not
swell, at the proper moment my guns had 'leaped into life'
— they did not jam. It was one of the proudest moments
of my life. ... I had tried to act as I thought Hickok
would have done.

An hour later, at the little round table in the rear of
Dinty Moore's, Will Rogers grinned at me and said:

'Bill, what in thunder did you do to those folks out in
front to-night — they must 'a' thought you was good!'

'What did you do?' I parried. 'They wasn't so doggoned quiet when you got through.'

'I wore a new suit of clothes, Bill,' he said, and grinned
again.

Before boarding the train for home, two days later, I had
a United Artists contract for two pictures in my pocket.
I called on my bankers. In addition to what money I had,

A United Artists Contract

I needed one hundred thousand dollars to finance the making of my first picture. Would they loan me the money on my note? ... They would. At what rate of interest? Five per cent. ... Was this the usual thing and could I send my friends around? No; it was not the usual thing, and I could not send my friends around!

Later, when I wired them to forward the cash, they informed me that, as money was then cheaper, my interest charge would be four and one half per cent instead of five per cent.

Yes! I am still doing business with the same bank and hoping that they never find out my real character!

One of the most dangerous things in life is to lose your courage. If you can keep your fighting spirit, you always have a chance. The very fact of keeping an undaunted front may cause the other side to weaken. If your courage goes, you are whipped — your enemy and the world soon know it.

'But screw your courage to the sticking-place, and we'll not fail.'

My courage had been hammered down to far below 'the sticking-place' — I had almost 'failed.' The hard facts of exterior circumstance had sadly depleted my fighting spirit. My heart could not much longer answer an appeal to arms. The United Artists contract had come just in time. It had let down the bars. The big iron gate had swung open.

What a joy it was to go to work! King Baggott, my director, told me, half-apologetically, that the first scenes would be taken at 5.30 A.M. I was there, made-up, mounted, and ready to go at five. While we waited for the rising sun, the morning air was like a long, cool drink —

the elixir of happiness. I love acting. I love the art of making motion pictures. It is the breath of life to me!

'Tumbleweeds' was a big story and an expensive picture to make. The many hundreds of vehicles and thousands of people used in the scenes showing the opening of the Cherokee Strip ran into mighty big money. We wanted a big picture and we got one. King Baggott did some splendid directing, and all of the principals made individual hits.

'Tumbleweeds' was scheduled for release December 27th, but it was pre-released December 20th at the Strand Theater, New York City, the week before Christmas — which is the very worst week of the year. However, its success was instantaneous. The night of its first showing, dozens and dozens of wires kept coming all night long. It is hard to find adjectives to describe the joy they gave me.

The 'Los Angeles Times' carried a wired notice by Helen Klumph which was typical of many others:

Down at the Strand it seemed as though all the little boys in town were struggling to get in to see William S. Hart in 'Tumbleweeds.' This was encouraging after the slump of last week when the profits would hardly pay for the handsome decorated Christmas cards which the theater managers were so busily engaged in inscribing. . . .

Of the week's pictures, 'Tumbleweeds' is by all odds the most thrilling. One scene, the mad race of the homesteaders to claim land in the Cherokee Strip, is one of the most exciting I have ever seen. . . .

United Artists and Bill Hart have every reason to be proud of this picture, for it pleases his old fans and lives up to the present demand for something of epic sweep in all but strictly modern pictures. . . .

342

SCENE IN 'TUMBLEWEEDS' JUST BEFORE THE FIRING OF THE SIGNAL GUN

SUCCESS OF TUMBLEWEEDS

But great as was the success of 'Tumbleweeds' with press and public, the astounding factor was the receipts. 'Variety,' the publication that is in the habit of quoting a weekly box office report, gave the receipts at the leading theaters, as follows:

Apollo	— 'Stella Dallas'	$13,500
Astor	— 'The Big Parade'	21,010
Cameo	— 'The Beautiful City'	4,800
Capitol	— 'His Secretary'	64,600
Colony	— 'The Phantom of the Opera'	25,900
Embassy	— 'The Merry Widow'	8,600
Rialto	— 'Siegfried'	16,000
Rivoli	— 'A Kiss for Cinderella' Theater dark until Friday	
Strand	— 'Tumbleweeds'	36,300
Warners	— 'Steel Preferred'	12,000

When I saw that my picture had played to over twice the receipts of one Famous Players Theater and that the other didn't open at all, it was only human for me to feel a bit elated. Human or not, I was, anyhow!

But my elation was short-lived. It soon became apparent that, although the bars had been let down, they had only been lowered far enough for me to fall over them. The big theaters in the big cities, where one must play to get adequate returns for an expensive picture, did not book me. In the few large cities where there were still left a few independent theaters, the contracts were splendid.

The Strand Theater, New York City, gave a guarantee of $5000 with a fifty-fifty split over $30,000; at The Strand, in Brooklyn, the guarantee was $2500, with fifty-fifty split over $20,000; while in the cities where the theaters were under common control I had to take anything I could get — and any price I could get.

At Kansas City, my first run was at Pantages, the rental being $300; St. Paul and Omaha, were the same; and Minneapolis, $400; Baltimore, $800; St. Louis, $750; and so on along the line.

Amidst all the towering syndicate motion picture palaces in Chicago, 'Tumbleweeds' played the little three hundred seating capacity Castle Theater at a guarantee of $500 and fifty per cent over $4000, which netted an added $668.12.

The Chicago critics were responsible for the $668.12. The Castle is recognized as a little second-run house, but, owing to the space and unrestricted praise the reviewers gave 'Tumbleweeds,' the theater was jammed from opening until closing time.

'Tumbleweeds' cost $312,000. Being denied booking in the first-run big city theaters makes it impossible to get the money back. I expect to lose at least $50,000. Had I been able to get time at the first-run, big-money houses, I should have made a profit of probably $100,000.

I owe a deep debt of gratitude to the newspaper men and women in all the large cities. They criticized my picture and gave it the same space as though it were playing at a big syndicate house. I owe a debt of gratitude to all the small out-of-town theaters that took me in and played 'Tumbleweeds,' regardless of the fact that it had been shut out of the big city houses. Had they not done so, I should have been mighty near broke.

It is an awful black eye for a picture to play second-run houses in the large cities, and nothing short of a miracle if you do so and then go out and get first-class prices in the towns and smaller cities throughout the country.

There are about 14,000 theaters in America. As I write this, 'Tumbleweeds' has played in 11,033 of them — that being the number of the last contract. Up to date, 'Tumbleweeds' has played in over eighty per cent of the theaters in America. If there was any way in which it could be determined, I feel quite sure that this would prove to be mighty near a record.

Unfortunately, those first-run theaters in the big cities in which I did not play must be played, or an expensive picture will show a heavy loss. They were mysteriously closed to me.

'Tumbleweeds' was booked for the Mutual Theater, Washington, D.C., the week of May 2d. Shortly before the opening, I wrote to Senator Johnson, Senator Borah, and Senator Ashurst, informing them of the date; these gentlemen, I am proud to say, having always liked my pictures.

The Senators answered me promptly. Their news gave me a sinking feeling. The booking had been changed.

I wrote to Hiram Abrams, president of the United Artists, saying:

I am in receipt of a letter from Senator Johnson which informs me that the booking of 'Tumbleweeds' has been transferred from the Mutual Theater to the Howard [which the Senator deemed to be in an inferior location].

Senator Johnson, Senator Ashurst and Senator Borah have been loyal supporters of my pictures for years and I am highly desirous of extending them the courtesy of seeing 'Tumbleweeds' under favorable auspices. I cannot ask my friends to share my misfortune. So I am writing these gentlemen that I am asking you to allow them to have a film to run individually.

Will you, Mr. Abrams, kindly allow this to be done, and have the Exchange manager in Washington notify Senator Johnson, Senator Ashurst and Senator Borah when he can deliver the film? Of course, I wish to pay any charges made.

345

Mr. Abrams answered that they would immediately comply with my request.

My friends saw the picture and I was glad to know and feel that all the aptitude or capacity for joy had not been knocked out of me; their letters surely helped me to realize that pain had not made it impossible for me to feel happiness. They used adjectives that came from their hearts. They loved the picture. How grateful I was and how grateful I am to these three world-wide famous men. Had it not been for their interest 'Tumbleweeds' would not have been hurriedly played at the Strand, a first-class theater in Washington.

At San Francisco, through some influence or through some demand of which I am not aware, 'Tumbleweeds' was booked at the Warfield, a first-run Marcus Loew theater.

During the week, the city was deluged — six inches of rain falling in three days. Yet the receipts amounted to the enormous sum of $17,621.39. Our contract was a fifty-fifty split over the expenses of the theater and cost of shelving a franchise picture. These expenses were turned in as $14,686.60. The fifty per cent of the balance gave United Artists $1467.39, of which my share, at sixty-five per cent, was $953.80. The cost of shelving that franchise picture must have been terrific!

I do not believe any more eulogistic criticisms of a star or picture were ever written than those signed by George Warren, of 'The Chronicle,' and Idwal Jones, of 'The Examiner.'

CHAPTER XX

A LONG, LONG TRAIL

CHARLIE and Nancy Russell were in town. One could never say Charlie without saying Nancy, too, for they were always together — a real man and a real woman.

I recall this day with Charlie and Nancy, oh, so well! for it was the last time I ever saw my friend Charlie. It seems a bit strange — we seldom talked of the old days — but this day we did. We talked a lot. How Charlie, Nancy, and I, we three, twenty-four years before, had taken strange and unusual trips.

One was to the deserted beach beyond Far Rockaway, on a cold, cloudy January day. The sea was angry, great breakers were smashing their way high up on the shore. It was Charlie's first view of the ocean. Nancy and I were stomping our feet and blowing on our fingers to keep warm, but Charlie — with head uncovered, his tousled blond mane blowing in the wind — was actually wading through the edge of the breakers.

'Come out of there, you doggone sagebrush cow-waddy,' I called. 'You'll get pneumonia.'

'I may never see this crick again, Bill,' his voice trailed back through the wind. He put on his hat, as would a scolded kid complying with a reprimand; his feet were in the water, his boots were soaked, but he kept on walking just the same.

On another day we found a full-rigged sailing ship moored to her wharf on the lower East River. She was getting ready to go to sea. I really believe the captain would have carried us to Australia, us three, as some sort of supercargo.

And then there was the day we went to see the Sunday editor of the 'New York Herald'; J. I. C. Clark was his name. Mr. Clark did not know I was on earth, but I had badgered Wilbur Bates, the publicity director for Klaw and Erlanger, to give me a letter of introduction to him. It was a deep scheme of Nancy's and mine to get Charlie some publicity. Nancy had a couple of little home-made camera shots of Charlie's paintings. We were a pathetic little crowd. Nancy was scared; Charlie wouldn't talk, and what I did not know about art did not need to be told to an art editor. I bruised my knuckles punching Charlie in the ribs trying to get him to speak.

'Is it possible, Mr. Russell, to place a rope around a wild animal in the manner you have it here?' queried Mr. Clark.

The picture was of a cowboy that had tied onto a bear, without consulting the wishes of his pony, and the pony was strong for leaving.

Charlie slowly raised his head. 'Uh-huh,' he said. 'If you kin get the hoss near enough to the bear.'

Our interview was a frost — but the great personality of Charlie wasn't. Mr. Clark gave him a full page in the 'Sunday Herald.' Mr. J. I. C. Clark wasn't so bad, either, for all his many initials!

Charlie painted a picture and Nancy sold it for $300. She couldn't talk for days. She bought herself a fur coat and hung it up where she could see it if she should happen to wake up in the night. Charlie and I celebrated, too! — four fingers!

And then the times when Charlie and Nancy would come to my little home and my dear little mother would

AT THE CUSTER BATTLE-FIELD, JUNE 25, 1926

cook boiled beef and horseradish, Western style. And how she could cook it! Charlie and I would sneak out just before meal-time. Nancy knew what that meant, and Nancy would get mad and sulk just a little bit — but we didn't care — we had ours and we could afford to talk a lot and be happy. And we did — and we were!

Dear old Charlie. He has gone on ahead.

I tried to read some things that Will Rogers wrote for an introduction to a book that Charlie finished, but never saw in print. My eyes got wet and I couldn't see.

June 25, 1926, I was the guest of the State of Montana at the semi-centennial of the Custer battle. I always loved that old Indian country, but this visit left an impression that can never be effaced. The pitiable half-dug breast-works, unchanged, untouched; the hundreds of old warriors in full regalia, many of whom had thrown themselves against these same far too ineffective defenses fifty years agone; the bronzed Seventh Cavalry with their prancing mounts, the volleys fired over the graves of the dead, the soft sound of 'Taps' echoed back by the hills like a benediction, the low, weird death song of the Indian women. . . . All, a never to-be-forgotten picture.

I knew I should be called upon to talk at the evening ceremonies, so I had spent many days and nights, too, preparing a short speech in Sioux, and before making my address to the white folks I asked permission to make a talk to my red brothers.

It is most unusual for a white man who has no Indian blood to speak the Indian language, and it is unheard of for a man to do so with the accent of an Indian. While my talk astonished the people of my own race, the Indians were bewildered — amazed. For the second time in my life I saw the double sign of astonishment used — every single one of those old warriors clapped both hands over his mouth — just as I had seen those young warriors do on the prairies of Dakota when I was a little boy in the long ago.

Hundreds of stories and histories have been written of the Custer battle. Everything that could possibly have taken place seems to have been described; yet 'White Bull,' the oldest surviving chief of the battle, who acted opposite General Godfrey in the ceremonies and presented the blanket to Mrs. Custer, could tell nothing.

The grand old man took quite a fancy to me. It was he that had me named after the immortal Indian chief, Crazy Horse (Ta Sunke-Witko). We talked a great deal through a very dear friend of mine, Chief Standing Bear, who speaks English fluently. Standing Bear and I asked the old gentleman many questions. He was truthful. He could not answer — and he would not attempt to do so.

'There was too much dust,' he said, 'and I could see only when I was close to a soldier.'

'Well, how did you feel in the fight, and what were you thinking of?' I inanely questioned.

The old man answered with dignity, and yet with the naïveté of a child. 'I was thinking of my sweetheart and how bad it was that on account of the thick dust she could not see me fight.'

My auditors had informed me that there were many errors in accounting and deviations from what they considered right under our contract with Famous Players, the result being an accounting investigation of the books of the Famous Players Lasky Corporation that took many months, and which, when completed, showed our claim to be quite a large sum. It was promptly met by Famous Players.

This was no reflection upon the integrity of Famous Players or its governing officials. But an organization that can make financial mistakes over a period of years can have the capacity for making mistakes which involve human beings and their careers. Only in the latter case there are no books kept — and unfortunately there can be no accounting.

I have the clipping of a newspaper article in front of me:

Bill Hart walking alone ... and fast ... wonder if he will ever make another picture — like many other stars, as soon as he reached the peak he thought he could be his own producer — and like most of the others he failed.

Propaganda takes root. The cause of my reaching the peak — if I did reach it — was that I had produced my own pictures.

Of the twenty-seven pictures I PRODUCED and turned over to Famous Players for DISTRIBUTION, the last two, which they claim failed, are, at this writing, fifth and tenth, respectively, in GROSS RECEIPTS.

My mail is just as heavy as the day I finished my last picture. An average of two hundred letters daily come from near-by and distant parts of the world, all asking the same question: 'Bill Hart, why don't you give us some more pictures?' I love those people who like my Western pictures, but I am powerless. I fought cleanly, without rancor or malevolence but as sturdily as I knew how — I was whipped — I salute the victors.

Something just came to my mind. It is strange, but it came in Sioux — the nearly forgotten language of my childhood:

My Life East and West

'Mite oihanple canku ksan ksan, ye yin na i hanke.'
(Trail . . . long . . . winding . . . to land of dreams.)

I see myself as a lad and the little brown boys playing on the bank of a running stream . . . and my trail leads to another day only a few years past — a vast auditorium — thousands of white boys, eager, thronging — and a sweet voice singing:

'There's a long, long trail a-winding,
Into the land of my dreams.'

I SEE MYSELF A LAD

INDEX

355

INDEX

INDEX

357

INDEX

INDEX

INDEX

INDEX

INDEX

INDEX